THE 101st AIRBORNE AT NORMANDY

Mark A. Bando

Publishers & Wholesalers ®

DEDICATION

To the memory of Albert A. Krochka, 501st Regimental and later 101st Divisional Photographer

First published in 1994 by Motorbooks International
Publishers & Wholesalers,
PO Box 2, 729 Prospect Avenue,
Osceola, WI 54020 USA

Library of Congress Cataloging-in-Publication Data

Bando, Mark.
    The 101st Airborne at Normandy / Mark
    Bando.
       p.   cm.
    Includes index.
    ISBN 0-87938-873-0
    1. United States. Army. Airborne Division,
    101st—History. 2. World War, 1939-1945—
    Aerial operations, American. 3. World War,
    1939-1945—Campaigns—France—
    Normandy. 4. Normandy (France)—History,
    Military. I. Title.
    D769.346 1-1st.B36   1994
    940.54'4973—dc20   94-940

On the front cover: The map is from the *Atlas for the Second World War—Europe and the Mediterranean,* West Point Military History Series, edited by Thomas E. Griess and published by Avery Publishing Group, Inc., Garden City Park, New York. Reprinted by permission.

On the back cover: Top, an Albert A. Krochka shot taken when his group paused in a hamlet near St. Marie du Mont on D-day afternoon. *Krochka.* Below, Bruce Cook of HQ/501. *Krochka*

Printed and bound in the United States of America

Contents

Preface..4

Acknowledgments..5

Introduction..7

Chapter 1   **Origins** 9

Chapter 2   **England**..15

Chapter 3   **Landing**..44

Chapter 4   **St. Marcouf**...50

Chapter 5   **Ravenoville**...52

Chapter 6   **Foucarville**..54

Chapter 7   **St. Germaine de Varreville**..................56

Chapter 8   **Haut Fornel—The Legend of Smit's Pond** 57

Chapter 9   **St. Martin de Varreville**.......................59

Chapter 10   **St. Mere Eglise**...................................65

Chapter 11   **Audoville and Le Grand Chemin**.........68

Chapter 12   **St. Marie du Mont**...............................71

Chapter 13   **Pouppeville**...75

Chapter 14   **Bloody Holdy**.......................................77

Chapter 15   **Hiesville and Chateau Colombieres** 79

Chapter 16   **Vierville**...83

Chapter 17   **Angoville au Plein**...............................85

Chapter 18   **Migration**...89

Chapter 19   **Houesville**...92

Chapter 20   **St. Come du Mont**................................94

Chapter 21   **La Barquette**......................................100

Chapter 22   **The Wooden Bridges at Brévands**.......105

Chapter 23   **Catz**...112

Chapter 24   **Cole's Charge at the Carentan Causeway**.......113

Chapter 25   **Carentan**..119

Chapter 26   **Counterattacks on Carentan**...............125

Chapter 27   **This Was the Enemy**...........................133

Chapter 28   **The Far Flung**.....................................137

Chapter 29   **Eagles in Captivity**.............................150

Chapter 30   **The Journey Back**...............................153

Index..160

Preface

Because of a divisional policy banning the use of cameras during the D-day invasion, photos of the 101st Airborne in Normandy seem almost nonexistent. As a result, it has taken me over twenty years to compile the pictures in this work.

A half century has passed since D-day, and the World War II Screaming Eagles become legendary.

Al Krochka in 1944. *Krochka*

As early as the spring of 1945 other paratroopers who followed in the fight were emulating the Screaming Eagles' style and striving to live up to their achievements. One has only to look at photos of the 17th Division airborne troopers wearing scalplock haircuts on the varsity jump to see evidence of the 101st's influence.

It is my wish that this record will serve as a lasting tribute to those individuals who recognized the great historical significance of the invasion and made the great effort to take pictures, despite orders to the contrary. I am especially indebted to those who have shared their works to make this book possible.

I also hope that this work will help to remind the relatives and friends of the World War II troopers of the brave deeds of these "bad boys of the US Army." May they renew their pride in all the World War II Eagles, living and dead, and cherish them as true American folk heroes.

World War II research is a never-ending process, and I have nearly 3,000 wartime photos of the 101st in my personal archive. Any surviving members of the World War II 101st Airborne are requested to contact me with any additional photos or stories of not only the Normandy campaign, but also Holland, Bastogne, Southern Germany, and Berchtesgaden for future histories.

I also welcome maps, gadgets, and other artifacts of those campaigns for my traveling display.

I invite anyone who has corrections or who can amplify the information presented in this work to contact me by mail at the publisher's address. Many thanks.

—*Mark A. Bando*
Detroit, Michigan
1993

Acknowledgments

My research and writing on the WWII 101st Airborne has been blessed by the fortunate circumstance of having so many Screaming Eagle veterans who live in close proximity to me in Michigan.

Donald R. Burgett, author of the firsthand narrative on Normandy entitled *Currahee* (since re-published under the title *As Eagles Screamed*), is a native of Detroit, whose writings helped focus my lifelong fascination with ETO battles onto one elite unit.

Quite by coincidence, Burgett was raised on the west side of Detroit about one mile from where I grew up several decades later. His father Elmer was a patrolman with the Detroit Police Department who retired from the 13th Precinct in 1951. I was later to work at the same precinct in the 1980s. These coincidences aside, Burgett's graphic account of D-Day from a paratroop rifleman's perspective is unsurpassed.

Leo Gillis, who served with F/501, was also a longtime Detroiter, raised in the Fenkell-Dexter area, although he had been born in Canada. I was a novice at 101st research when I met Gillis in 1970, but found him to be a unique source of information, a man who did a lot personally and was willing to tell about it. Sharing his detailed and prolific combat experiences with me on tape, Gillis' brutally frank perspective on killing and surviving give an understanding of what things were really like, as opposed to how they might have been in an ideal world.

George Koskimaki, who served as Gen. Maxwell Taylor's radio operator in WWII, went through the war with an author's eye for what was happening, both from the perspective of the foxhole and the command echelon. The author of an enviable trilogy of books on the 101st in WWII, Koskimaki is a walking encyclopedia of knowledge about the men of the division and their deeds. His generosity in sharing his unsurpassed address rosters made my research possible.

Rare vintage photos taken in Normandy during the invasion battles of June–July, 1994 were shared with me for use in this work by the following:

Fred Bahlau (506), Edward Benecke (A/377), Jack Breier (H/501), Joe Crilley (C/326), Paul Dovholuk (HQ/502), Bill Gammon (A/377), James Haslam (HQ/501), Albert and Caroline Krochka (501), Frank Lillyman (502), George Lage (2/502) via G. Koskimaki, Mike Musura (502), Joseph Pangerl (HQ/502), Joseph Pistone (F/502), Edward Sapinski (F/502), and Jack Schaffer (F/502).

Other 101st veterans who contributed to this work include (sorry for any I missed): Reg Alexander (501), Ambrose Allie (501), Frank Anness (506), Jerry Beam (506), Carl Beck (501), Bruce Beyer (501), Joe Beyrle (506), Frank Choy (502), John Cipola (501), John Cucinotta (502), Gordon Deramus (502), Art DiMarzio (506), Jack Dunwoodie (502), Charlie Eckman (501), G. B. Eldridge (501), Red Flanagan (501), Bill Gammon (377), Bob Greenhawk (501), Ian Hamilton (501), Harold W. Hannah (506), Sammie N. Homan (501), Ray Hood (502), Ed Hughes (501), Clem Jahnigen (501), Ahzez "Jim" Karim (501), Bill Kennedy (506), Bill Knight (506), Rudy Korvas (501), George Koskimaki (Sig), Albert Kouba (C/326), Joe Ludwig (502), Jim Martin (506), Robert Martin (506), Charles Matson (502), Harry Mole (501), Ken Moore (501), Herman Moulliet (506), Vic Nelson (502), Roy Nickrent (502), Bob Niles (501), Frank Palys (506), Art Parker (377), Harry and Connie Plisevich (501), Helen Briggs-Ramsey (ARC/506), Loy Rasmussen (506), Joe Reed (506), Charlie Santasiero (506), Cecil Simmons (502), Mort Smit (502), Bernard Sterno (502), Don Straith (506), Wally Swanson (502), Joe Taylor (501), Clarence Theaker (Div. Arty.), John Urbank (501), Tom Walsh (502), Chet Wetsig (501), David White (502), Dick Winters (506), Jack Womer (506), Robert Wright (501), and Don Zahn (506).

I much regret that the artillery and support units, as well as the 401/327th GIR were not better represented. Neither the 327th nor the 506th had a regimental photographer, but with luck, more photos of those units will hopefully surface in the coming years. No doubt, the support units and assorted 101st artillery battalions had their amateur cameramen and perhaps more photos of them in Normandy will eventually surface.

Relatives and spouses of deceased troopers made invaluable contributions. Alice Larsen contributed photos taken by T. K. "Red" Larsen in Normandy and England (Red had died in 1963, after suffering a stroke). Other relatives who helped include the brother and sister of Stephen Mihok (506), Grace (Luther) Knowlton, Madge (Cecil) Simmons, Hazel (John) Mishler, and sons Rick (Harrison) Summers, and David (Frank) Tiedeman.

Harry T. Mole, a veteran of 2/501 and longtime friend, also collects airborne photos and made most of the copy negatives for the photos in this book. Printing and enlargements were done by the Hoskins Photo Service of Detroit, through the hard work of Mr. and Mrs. Bruce Hoskins, and Charlotte and Chris.

Frank (brother of Louis) DiGaetano, C/326 AEB battalion, has done much research on his Pathfinder brother's unit. (Louis died near Bastogne in the Bulge.) Frank has discovered much rare and useful information and provided the names for the obscure members of Chalk #20.

David Berry, a young historian from the Dayton, Ohio, area, has done superb and unprecedented research on the Normandy Pathfinder operations and also shared his expertise.

A more technical approach to Pathfinder equipment and techniques will be found in a forthcoming book by Michel Detrez of Brussels, Belgium, who is at the vanguard of US Airborne collecting in western Europe.

My numerous French friends have made priceless contributions. The Parey family of La Barquette (especially my pal Christophe) have been most kind. Henri Levaufre of Periers is a lifelong devotee of 90th Infantry Division research. Levaufre has studied that unit for half a century, since they liberated his town in 1944 when he was a teenager. Levaufre also spent a career repairing power lines in the Cotentin Peninsula, enabling him to identify many road junctions and geographic landmarks in vintage photos. He has been most generous and helpful in doing just that.

Philippe Nekrassoff, a French National Police gendarme, is a dedicated historian who is compiling a work on crashed C-47s in the invasion. We have done much mutually beneficial networking on our research.

Thanks also to Mr. and Mrs. Maurice and Fabienne Leonard of Angoville au Plein and Mr. and Mrs. Gerard and Martinique Grandin of the Chateau le Bel Enault, who lodge me during my visits to Normandy.

French-to-English language translations have been done for me by Corinne Minart, a native of Clermont, France, transplanted to Royal Oak, Michigan, and by Sgt. Linda White of the Detroit Police Department, a former French language teacher.

Gary Howard, a British researcher on airborne weapons and equipment, is compiling a work on that subject and has also done networking of info with me.

Steve M. R. made numerous contributions to this work and proved an able and useful travel companion on my first two trips to Europe. Dennis, Bruce, Brooks, and other stateside Airborne enthusiasts have continually stimulated and shared my passion for collecting airborne photos and artifacts.

Last but not least, I thank my angelic wife, Candace Ann, who not only tolerates my WWII activities but provides assistance and companionship in her patient way.

Thanks again to the over 800 WWII Screaming Eagle vets who have shared their stories with me. That a few of these great men call me their friend is one of the proudest facts of my life.

Introduction

The Prohibition Against Cameras, Diaries, and Souvenir Collecting

Shortly before D-day, orders originated at divisional level forbidding the invading troopers from keeping a diary, taking souvenirs, or using a camera. There may be some written evidence of these orders, but they were passed down the ranks verbally, until every private in the division was advised. There were, no doubt, several reasons behind this order, and some are obvious. The diary ban was no doubt an attempt to prevent the enemy from gaining information through captured written record. The ban on souvenirs was obviously to protect any captured trooper from retaliation, should he be found in possession of German items. The ban on cameras was no doubt partially inspired by the same reason as the diary ban—to prevent the enemy from capturing potential intelligence information.

There must have been other reasons as well. Any combat non-com or officer must have feared a diminished battle potential should any of the men in his command have been snapping photos instead of firing their weapons during actual combat. This fear was largely unfounded. As you will see, the troopers who snapped the pictures in this work did it during lulls in the action or immediately after the shooting subsided. The instinct to survive is strong enough to make common sense prevail.

Today, many years later, it is easy to state that the camera ban was unnecessary; but we are looking from a different perspective than the Allied leaders possessed in June 1944. There was still the possibility that the invasion would fail, that the armada would be flung back into the Channel, leaving the survivors abandoned to their fate on the continent. There was even the remote chance of an eventual Axis victory, in which case, the Allied minions would find themselves under scrutiny as possible war criminals. After all, the victorious powers ultimately define and decide what constitutes a war crime and who the guilty parties are.

After interviewing over 700 former World War II Screaming Eagles, I encountered only one who is still vociferously in favor of the rule against cameras in combat. He is former Lt. William J. Russo, commanding officer (CO) of the 2nd Battalion Mortar Platoon, 501st Parachute Infantry Regiment (PIR), in Normandy. Russo said: "Somebody with *damn good reason* made that rule . . . it was-

n't just pulled out of a hat. Everyone knows that a soldier with a camera is going to take pictures of dead enemy soldiers—if he doesn't take pictures of anything else."

As Russo thumbed through my album of Normandy photos, he remarked: "I wouldn't want to be any one of these guys, if we lost the war. . . especially when the Germans start figuring out which units they got tangled-up with. . . ."

"You mean, they might use your photo as evidence that you are a war criminal?" I asked.

"You'd better believe it . . . you bet!"

In his book *The Last Battle*, Cornelious Ryan described an American officer, who, in the last weeks of WWII, had a price on his head. German forces had deemed that this officer was a "war criminal." His crime was that he had killed too many German soldiers in open combat.

The point is that war crimes can be defined in a number of ways, and the vindictiveness of whatever regime reigns victorious at the end of hostilities will determine the question of who is culpable.

Certainly, even beyond the normal carnage of combat, there were acts of brutality by both sides. These episodes are explained, if not justified, by the stress and confusion of the time. Yet, some troopers are haunted to the end by memories of a few spontaneous seconds of action.

We can be grateful now, that a few individuals made the remarkable effort to lug a camera into Normandy, along with all their other equipment, somehow managing to record a small part of what they saw. The camera ban was difficult to enforce, once in the chaos of the invasion, and despite all the factors working against the amateur cameramen, some evidence of their efforts is preserved in this book.

A Letter from Lt. Morton

When World War II ended in 1945, Lt. James Morton of the 506th PIR wrote a letter to his friend Lt. Bill Reed, who had been taken prisoner earlier in the conflict. Part of the letter is a grim recitation of casualties in the Normandy campaign:

Dear Bill:

I am happy to know that you are alive. . . since D-day we have spoken of you and wondered. . . .

We were notified that you had been taken prisoner, but feared you might have been killed later in air raids, or perhaps died in a horror camp. So many of our comrades have been killed. Have you heard the tragic story? Our Third Battalion officers were slaughtered during that fateful night when we invaded Normandy. . . .

Lt. Col. Wolverton was riddled by machine gun fire shortly after he landed. His body was found near St. Come du Mont. Maj. Grant was killed too. "Jeb" Holstun was shot dead as he ran atop the dike along the Douve River, picked off like a duck in a shooting gallery. All our company commanders were killed or missing. Van Antwerp dead in his harness, McKnight, Harwick, and you taken prisoner. Harwick escaped three days later. . . .

Some of our paratroopers descended into a bivouac area of Russian cavalry, mercenaries in the employ of the Nazis. Our men never had a chance. They were butchered by knives, bayonets, and machine pistols as they struggled in their harnesses. Subsequently I saw the scene of this carnage. It was terrible, dead horses, Russians, and paratroopers sprawled everywhere. Several hundred of our troops died in this area. . . .

Headquarters Company Third suffered appalling losses. Littell was killed by a machine pistol on D-day morning, as he tried vainly to hide from a German patrol. "Pop" Machen's body was found. I understand Dilburn was killed while trying to do the Pathfinders' job. Wedeking was shot through the wrist, and Barr got a bad face wound from grenade fragments. . . .

The battalion enlisted staff was virtually wiped out. Sgt. Simmerall, Ross, and others were killed before daybreak. 1st Sgt. Shirley was killed. The company lost 101 of 176 men. Sgt. Robinson and most of the bazooka platoon met an unkind fate. There were only six survivors, two of whom were killed by a direct hit from a 105mm gun several weeks later. . . .

Gerry Howard's plane was shot down, and all were lost. Tom Meehan's plane exploded in midair, and K. A. Beatty was killed when his plane became a flaming torch. . . .

Turner Chambliss was one of the first persons I encountered. I had broken my foot on an antiparachute obstacle and couldn't get around very well. About four o'clock, Chambliss reached our objective. At daylight he peered over the dike. A German sniper shot him through the throat and Chambliss died . . .

During our attack on St. Come du Mont, Lt. Col. Turner studied the terrain from a vantage point atop a Sherman tank. A sniper shot him through the head. Capt. Peters, "Eggie" Knott, Colt, Gross, Gunther, Lavenson, Mr. Hill, were among those killed in Normandy. . . .

'Dixie' Howell had an eye shot out. M. O. Davis was badly hit. Windish was wounded in the ankle. Maj. Foster and Holmes were shot up. . . .

During an attack southwest of Carentan. . . . Christianson's shoulder was shattered by a rifle bullet, and a slug from a machine pistol put Santasiero out of action. We suffered heavy casualties that day, when our precipitous attack collided with an attack by SS troops. They called the scene 'Bloody Gully.' There were dead and wounded on every hand, blood-smeared men staggering and crawling out of the gully to our aid set-up. Raudstein, too, was hit here. . . .

Cox, Ferebee, Rogers, McDowell (and) Tom Kennedy were among the wounded. . . . We were withdrawn from Normandy in July. . . our battalion strength was reduced from 690 to 268 officers and men. I Company could muster only 49 men. . . .

Airborne Photographers
Mike Musura (left) and Albert A. Krochka pose with their Speedgraphic camera in front of a European Eastman Kodak store. Musura started as regimental photographer of the 502nd PIR, and Krochka likewise for the 501st. Unfortunately, the 506th PIR and 327th GIR were without designated regimental photographers. Because of the valuable photos Musura and Krochka took in Normandy, they were elevated to the status of official divisional photographers and transferred to HQ/101 for the duration of the war. The author knew each of these men personally; Musura died in the early 1980s after working as a photographer for the *San Francisco Examiner*. Krochka died in early 1993. Where known, individual photos are credited to one or the other; many others, simply credited to US Army or Signal Corps, were actually shot by the above duo. We are deeply indebted to them both.

The above letter tells only part of the story. As the 506th Scrapbook tells it:

"You fought through Pouppeville, Vierville, Angoville au Plein, St. Come du Mont, and Carentan; and you piled up enemy dead until you gave up trying to figure ratios because an attacking force was supposed to lose more than the defenders, the Book said, yet there were the gray dead stacked like cord wood and only an occasional body dressed in tan."

As Ben "Chief" McIntosh of the 502nd PIR put it: "We went on sort of a rampage." Read on.

Chapter 1

Origins

The 82nd Infantry Division was divided into two separate airborne divisions on 16 August 1942 at Camp Claiborne, Louisiana. Gen. W. C. Lee, the first CO of the 101st Airborne Division, issued an order beginning with these words: "The 101st Airborne Division has no history, but it has a rendezvous with destiny. Like the early American pioneers whose invincible courage was the foundation stone of this nation, we have broken with the past and its traditions in order to establish our claim to the future."

Thus, the new 82nd and 101st briefly shared the premises at Camp Claiborne, before being shipped to Ft. Benning, Georgia, for parachute and glider training. From there they moved on to Ft. Bragg, North Carolina, which would be their assigned station before departure for combat in the European Theatre.

The two new divisions, born of the same parent organization, were to become arch-rivals. Members at the time of the split were given the option of refusing parachute training. But the Army could order a soldier into any vehicle, so the glider troops were coerced into glider training without a refusal option. This was to remain a sore spot with the glider troops as the paratroopers received $50 extra per month as hazardous duty pay; the often-injured glider men did not. Although para and glider troops wore the same shoulder insignia, with the word "airborne" on a tab above, the paratroopers considered themselves a cut above. They jealously guarded their unique status symbols: brown jump boots and qualification "wings."

The 101st Airborne that arrived at Ft. Bragg consisted of the 327th Glider Infantry Regiment (GIR), the 326th Airborne Engineer Battalion (AEB), Division Artillery, and other artillery battalions, including the 81st Airborne Anti-aircraft Anti-tank Battalion (AAATB), 321st Glider Field Artillery Battalion (GFAB), and 377th Parachute Field Artillery Battalion (PFAB), plus headquarters (HQ) personnel, MPs, the 326th Medical Company, and assorted supply and support troops. Shortly thereafter, the 502nd PIR was added as an official Table of Organization and Equipment (TO&E) member of the division. The 502nd, under Col. G. V. H. Moseley, had been activated as a battalion in 1941 and recently expanded into a regi-

"Father of the Airborne"
Gen. William C. Lee, of Dunn, North Carolina, was first commanding general of the 101st Airborne Division and known as the "Father of the Airborne." Lee was forced to relinquish his command when he suffered a heart attack before D-day. *US Army Photo*

ment. In July 1942, the 506th PIR was added (by attachment) at Ft. Bragg, under the leadership of Col. Robert Sink.

Much later, the 501st PIR under Col. Howard R. "Jumpy" Johnson was attached to the division to bring it up to strength for the Normandy invasion. Each attached regiment had an approximate strength of 2,200 men. The 506th was eventually absorbed officially into the 101st Airborne. The 501st PIR was a member by attachment only until its deactivation.

250ft Tower
"C" stage involved a drop from the 250ft free tower; the chute canopy was held open by hoops. *Signal Corps*

The Obstacle Course
Prospective paratroopers of the 506th PIR negotiate an obstacle on the course they designed at Camp Toccoa, Georgia, in 1942. The muddy ditch below was sometimes filled with hog innards through which the troopers were forced to crawl to become accustomed to intimate contact with gore. *Bob Martin*

"Trainasium"
The "trainasium," or "Plumber's nitemare," was copied from a device in the German parachute school. By crawling through a prescribed course, it worked most muscles of the body to the fullest extent. The trainasium was eliminated as a training device before the war ended. *US Army*

It is likely that the members of the 501st and 506th PIRs were in the best physical condition of any US troops because of torturous runs up and down the 3mi Currahee mountain at Camp Toccoa and grueling encounters with its obstacle course. (Currahee is a Native American word that translates to "stands alone." The mountain and its name were adopted as the official insignia and slogan of the 506th.) After basic at Toccoa, the battalions had gone to jump training one at a time at Ft. Benning, Georgia, and most troopers of the 506th marched the 120mi in 72hr.

The 501st PIR followed the 506th in training at Toccoa, under the dynamic leadership of fire-breathing Annapolis dropout Col. Howard R. Johnson, whose mass pep rallies incited his Geronimo troopers into a peak of homicidal enthusiasm. There is no dispute that Johnson was one of the great motivators of all American troop leaders in WWII, even Gen. Patton's "Blood and Guts" speeches were sometimes outdone by those of "Jumpy" Johnson.

The merciless training of the 501st and 506th PIRs continued in North Carolina at Camp Mackall and Ft. Bragg, on sun-scorched sands. The 1943 war games were conducted here and the games

and training forged the survivors into veritable supermen. Morale was high in these units; and men on forced marches carried extra equipment out of team spirit. Many saw black spots in front of their eyes and passed out due to heat prostration.

The 101st Airborne shared Ft. Bragg with the 82nd Airborne until the latter unit set sail for the European Theater of Operations (ETO) in April 1943. The 82nd would be the first US airborne division to see action (participating in the jumps at Sicily and Salerno and the Anzio Beach landing) well before the 101st's combat debut at Normandy. Even before the 82nd saw action, the 509th Parachute Battalion, had made a combat jump into

Mount Currahee

Mount Currahee at Camp Toccoa, Georgia, summer of 1942. This 3mi mountain was the forging ground for the earliest members of the 501st and 506th. Jim "Pee Wee" Martin of the 506th momentarily dropped out from the run to snap this photo of G Company heading back down as another company comes up. The 506th wore blue swimming trunks with a Currahee patch sewn to the front on morning runs. *Jim Martin*

H/506 Troopers

Members of H/506 on a 1943 training problem in the States. Included in the group are Purdy, Lou Vecchi, and Sgt. McCullough. When the 2/506 and 3/506 marched from Toccoa to Atlanta in December 1942, they made it in about 72hr, beating the world's marching record previously held by a Japanese Army battalion. Second battalion covered 118mi, while 3/506 went 132. First Battalion rode a train to Ft. Benning. *Robert Martin*

North Africa. This unit had been redesignated three times.

Ocean Voyage to British Isles, 1943

Most of the 101st Airborne set sail in September 1943 aboard two ships, the SS *Strathnaver*, and the SS *Samaria*. The troops sailed from Camp Shanks, New York. The *Strathnaver* broke down at St. Johns, Newfoundland, and was replaced by the SS *John Erickson*, which finished the job of transporting the 502nd, 377th PFAB, 907th, the 326th AEB, and other miscellaneous units. The

---

Old Abe

An important aspect to the story of the WWII 101st Airborne is its shoulder insignia, a tribute to the Civil War mascot of the 8th Wisconsin Infantry Regiment, a real bald eagle named Old Abe. According to legend, Old Abe was tethered close to the 8th's colors and was carried into battle, during which it would fly forward from its perch, screaming defiance at the enemy and inspiring Union troops. Old Abe was wounded several times, and the Confederate Gen. Price offered a reward for the killing of the bird.

The 101st Airborne now wore a bald eagle upon their shoulder patches and also obtained a new eagle mascot which they named "Young Abe." It is doubtful that any high-ranking member of a rival Airborne organization put a price on Young Abe's head, but the bird was discovered dead of unknown causes at Ft. Bragg on 8 July 1943.

The division was on maneuvers in Tennessee when Young Abe died, and although there were accusations of skullduggery or poisoning by members of rival organizations (the prime suspects would have been members of the 82nd Airborne, but they had sailed for England several months prior to Abe's demise), there may be another explanation for the eagle's untimely passing. Winfield McCraw, a member of the 101st's Division Recon Platoon, sometimes cared for the bird, and thinks that Young Abe may have died due to an allergic reaction to some salt pork he was fed.

---

several weeks spent in Newfoundland qualified these troops for the American Theatre ribbon.

The 501st PIR followed in January and sailed aboard the *George W. Goethals*. They arrived in Glasgow, Scotland, and were attached to the 101st in England, an assignment that would last until after V-E Day.

L. Allen Hurd, of HQ/2 501, wrote a V-Mail letter to his parents during the *Goethals* voyage. Part of it reads:

"My sea voyage is almost over. Man! The waves on this man's ocean are something to see. Huge, rolling mountains of water. We enlisted men are packed like sardines in the hold of the ship. Good place to store cargo. . . if the cargo isn't too fragile. To kill time I'm forced to read 10 year old *National Geographic* magazines, which is just about rock bottom in the sphere of human activities."

Sea sickness and gastrointestinal disorders kept the medics and chaplains busy, dispensing bismuth and paregoric as cures. Craps games flourished and Father Sampson, the 501st's Catholic chaplain, recalls the men often gambled while waiting in line to go to confession.

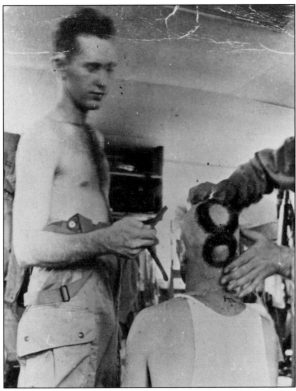

Airborne Haircuts
What began as a form of punishment for misconduct in the States, continued overseas as a form of pride. Left, the "8 Ball" haircut. This chronic offender had his hair styled by

Claude Langston of D/501. *Ritzler*. Right, a trooper was given a Native American scalplock haircut as punishment for going AWOL, Camp Mackall, 1943. *Author's collection*

"Look Out Hitler! Here We Come!"
A gruesome looking member of G/501 menaces an effigy of Der Fuhrer on the streets of Schicklegruberburgh in

1943. This training camp was a mock German city built near Camp Mackall, North Carolina, for combat maneuver exercises. *Urbank*

Playful Fellows
Members of the 501st PIR at Camp Mackall, North Carolina, practice knife fighting with the trusty M-3 trench knife, commonly worn on the ankle by paratroopers. *Krochka*

Left
Strongman
In an impressive strongman feat, Pvt. James McHugh, B/501 (from Pennsylvania) hoists an unidentified buddy overhead at Camp Mackall in 1943. McHugh was noted as the strongest member of B Company and later proved to be one of the best combat men in the outfit as well. *Rich Harper*

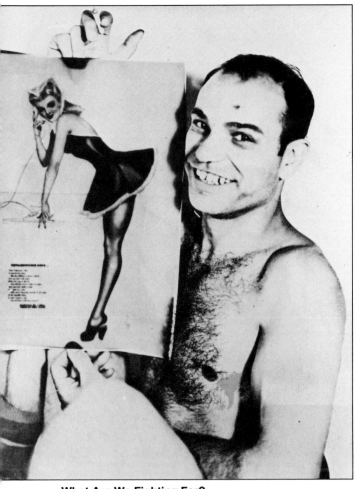

What Are We Fighting For?
Sgt. Frank Anness of D/506 offers his answer to the famous question in this 1944 photo. Publications like the 506th's *Para Dice* magazine followed this theme by printing photos of the sweethearts and wives of Currahee troopers. Frank's example is less specific, but the general idea is the same. *Anness*

Col. Howard R. "Jumpy" Johnson
The hard-bitten CO of the 501st PIR embodied and personified the very soul and spirit of his regiment. At unit assemblies he would shout: "Who's the BEST?" "*We* are!" the troops would scream in reply. *Krochka*

Chapter 2

England

Despite complications on the ocean voyage, most of the division arrived in England in the fall of 1943. The 502nd PIR was stationed in assorted types of tents and buildings, including Quonset huts, stables, and M34 pyramidal tents. Officers usually acquired manor houses or similar billets. Most of the 502nd was situated in and around Hungerford, at Chilton Foliat and Denford.

The 509th Battalion had been stationed in the Chilton Foliat area before the 101st Airborne arrived and had established good relations with the locals. The 101st's Rigger Sections moved into the area and remained there until after the Battle of the Bulge.

Most of the 506th PIR was stationed close by. The 2nd Battalion with HQ/1, A and B companies, were some distance away, at Aldbourne, with some troops living in horse stables. The HQ was at Littlecote, C Company at Manor Park, and Service Company at Chilton Foliat. The 3rd Battalion was close by at Ramsbury. The billets overlapped into Wiltshire and Berkshire, two British counties.

Most of the other assorted divisional units were scattered around Berkshire county. The 907th GFAB with their 105mm howitzers were at Benham-Valence Park. The 326th Airborne Medical Company was at Donnington. The 101st Airborne HQ was located at Greenham Common. The 377th PFAB was at Wickham. The 327th's glider troops were near Reading. The 81st AAATB was at Basildon Park, as was the 326th AEB.

In January 1944, the 501st PIR landed in Glasgow, Scotland, and traveled by train south to Newbury. Arriving in the middle of the night, they were assigned one squad per tent to M34 pyramidal tents, which the Corps of Engineers had set up before they arrived. Thick mud was everywhere and large concrete slabs had been laid as floors for each tent. The troops later devised a method of digging secret compartments for hiding swiped food, live ammo, and contraband under certain slabs.

The HQ/501 and 2/501 were at Newbury. The 1/501 and 3/501 were stationed many miles away at Lambourne. Some of the troops lived in Nissen Huts. Other lived in brick stables.

There were a number of brawls and other mischief, mainly with the Air Corps, and many fines were assessed for poaching deer and blowing up of

Louis Frey of New Orleans, Louisiana
Frey, a member of the 2/501's S-2 Section, studies a map during training exercises in pre D-day England. *Frey*

Picadilly Circus, London, England
A group of 101st Airborne Division paratroopers visit Picadilly Circus in London before D-day. Picadilly Circus became the most popular spot to visit in London, and was noted for an abundance of female entertainment. Prostitutes who worked the area were known as "Picadilly Commandos" and the more predatory ones were dubbed "Picadilly Snipers." *Krochka*

15

Demonstration Jump, 23 March 1944
The 506th PIR, minus 1st Battalion, makes a demonstration jump for Churchill. He had reviewed 1st Battalion in a ground inspection that day.

VIP Visit
British Prime Minister Winston Churchill with Maj. Gen. Maxwell Taylor pass the colors of the 327th GIR.

326th AEB Pathfinders
These three men were the only members of the 326th AEB to serve as Pathfinders in Normandy. They are (from left to right) Pfc. Louis DiGaetano (KIA, Bastogne), Pvt. Albert Kouba, and Cpl. Calvin Jackson. All belonged to C/326. *Kouba*

English trout with hand grenades in the local streams.

Machismo in England

In a letter to the author dated 19 January 1991, Ray Hood HQ/2 502 wrote:

We stood in line for meals, for movies, and for everything else. We had a sergeant whose pet hate was people who bucked the line, got in ahead of others. On one occasion on a weekend, the battalion was standing in line waiting to see a show, and a corporal from one of the other companies got in ahead of the sergeant. He didn't say a word. He suddenly punched the guy, floored him then went to work with his boots. Nobody really blamed him for knocking the man on his ass, because bucking the line wasn't popular. But kicking the guy was too strong, and the sergeant was pulled off.

He was berserk, raving and literally frothing at the mouth and he challenged the whole battalion. He meant it too—he wasn't blowing smoke.

Another corporal, a friend of the man the sergeant had kicked, stepped out of the crowd, and I still remember what he said: "I think I'll try you out sergeant, and see how you do against somebody who's ready for you." The sergeant started toward the corporal. The corporal raised his hand and he said, "Get your breath back before you start—believe me, you don't want to start from behind."

As it was everybody wanted to see the sergeant lose, but we were all disappointed when the O.D. [officer of the day] showed up and stopped it before it started.

Just Another Jump

Capt. Cecil Simmons wrote the following short story, describing a late-afternoon practice jump in England. Due to typical adverse circumstances, including a pilot flying too fast and high winds on the drop zone, the jump became a hazardous event.

British Paras
Two British paras from the 6th Airborne Division in front of a brick stable, visiting B/501. During February and March 1944, an exchange program sent several hundred American paras to trade places for two weeks with British paras. There was an exchange of ideas and training with weapons, jump equipment, and tactics. *Mishler*

Swiped Tommy Gun
Sgt. Ed Benecke took many of the photos in this book. Here he displays a Tommy gun swiped from a troop carrier plane. "We needed them more than they did," he said. *Benecke*

"Should I Have Shot Him?"

On a practice jump before D-day, two battalions of the 506th landed and assembled to impress a delegation of VIPs including Prime Minister Winston Churchill, Supreme Commander Dwight D. Eisenhower, and Maj. Gen. Maxwell D. Taylor.

Among those jumping was Jack Womer, a member of the 506th Demolitions Platoon. "I hated that jump," Womer later said, "because . . . what the hell are we jumping for?"

At the pre-jump briefing, the troops were instructed to camouflage themselves on the drop zone immediately after landing. The officers wanted a first class job to impress the Brass.

Womer landed in a large field, devoid of any possible cover, except for the large haystack at the edge of a road. He and another trooper decided to get in the hay to take shelter from a light rain that had started to fall.

The duo completely covered themselves with hay and could not be seen and could barely see out. Not long afterwards, a staff car came up the road and stopped alongside them. In the staff car are Churchill, Eisenhower, and Taylor. As Womer recalls:

"Churchill gets out, walks over to the hay pile, and starts pissin' all over my boots. That's why I ask, do you think I should have shot him? I don't care if he's a prime minister or not, I don't want him pissin' on me! Well, I figured I can't drown, cause they only come up to my ankles, but they never did find out we were in that hay pile. Because with two generals behind him . . . you don't interfere with the Brass. And I tell everyone who hears this story, I was so close that I know Churchill needed to be circumcised . . . only me and his wife knew that."

Many have hailed British Prime Minister Winston S. Churchill as "The Man of the Century," although many revisionist historians disagree. Jack Womer of the Filthy 13 might be inclined to agree with them. *Krochka*

"Go."

With that command, the captain jumped out into the darkening cold of the prop wash. He knew when he jumped that the plane was going at least 20mph too fast. He had the green light. He had his orders, jump on the green light. During the first three seconds all of the ugly cuss words he could think of were hurled at the pilot of the ship that he had just left. There was a fierce blast of cold air tearing at his clothes. It almost threw his feet up over his head. Just as he began to wonder whether he better count, he got a jerk that nearly cut him in two. Almost at the same time something hit him in the back of the head that made a "bong" on his helmet. Suddenly he saw all of the prettiest

Maj. Gen. Maxwell Davenport Taylor
Gen. Bill Lee, who had commanded the 101st Airborne from the start, suffered a heart attack in England on 5 February 1944. For a brief time, Gen. Don Pratt, Lee's assistant, took command. Lee was retired after being sent back to the States on 9 April 1944. On 14 March, Gen. Max Taylor, former artillery commander of the 82nd Airborne, took command of the 101st. A West Pointer, Taylor had already become legendary for his exploits in Italy, most notably a daring mission behind the lines in Rome. There, Taylor met with Marshal Badoglio to arrange the Italian capitulation. Before D-day, Taylor addressed his 101st troopers and told them to shout "Bill Lee!" instead of Geronimo, in honor of their former commander, on their first combat jump. *US Army*

stars whirling around each other and he thought, "How nice it would be to get some sleep, I'm sooo tired. Fight. Fight What? You're jumping. Oh, God yes, open your eyes you damn fool."

He opened his eyes and shook his head as much as he could with a heavy helmet down over his face, pushed the helmet back on his head and looked up. Yes, there it was. . . outlined against the sky was the heavy silk that was holding him up. All in one piece too. . . good deal. He had a headache, but knew that because of a poor body position, the connector links had hit him in the back of the head on the opening shock. He checked the ground and saw that he was drifting like the devil. Looking back and up, he saw the rest of his stick drifting father apart. He checked the ground again and saw that he was going to hit pretty hard. He made a body turn so that he would come in frontwards, and saw that he was headed right for a cement crossroads. To hell with that. He let go of the risers and snapped himself back to his original position. He grabbed the two front risers that would slip him into the wind and tend to make him slow up his drift towards the crossroads. But, at the same time, it would increase his rate of descent because of the partially collapsed canopy. Between the devil and the deep blue sea,

and only a matter of split seconds to decide . . . he took the rapid descent.

The ground came up and hit him with a crash and, with a grunt, he gave a backward tumble. The wind, which had increased to 22mph, caught his chute and started to drag the skipper to the barbed wire fence which surrounded the field and bordered the road. He got to his feet and ran around to the windward side of the chute to find the fence between him and the top of the chute. He cleared the fence in a leap, and slid into the ditch between it and the road. Part of the suspension lines were fouled on the barbed wire, and despite the wind, they kept the chute from dragging the officer any farther. He got up and collapsed the chute and was taking his harness off when he heard a shout from above. He saw one of his men, who had jumped in one of the planes following his, headed for the same spot on the crossroads.

"Slip, boy, slip," he shouted. But the man was coming in so fast that he either didn't hear the skipper or was too occupied trying to rock his chute to prevent a ground oscillation, that he hit almost the exact center of the crossroads. He hit with a dull thud and the wind started to take him off up the road. The Skipper ran over and collapsed the chute and took a look at the man who

Training Jump, 1944
Members of 3/502 on a training problem in England, 1944. The trooper in the center wears a parachutist's first aid kit, which consisted of a cloth bag with tie strings containing sulfa powder, compress bandage, cloth tourniquet, and disposable one-shot morphine syrette. *Musura*

Officers of the 502nd PIR
England, Spring 1944. The training time before the great invasion is becoming short. (Left to right) Capt. Cecil L. Simmons, H/502; Lt. Col. Robert Cole, CO 3/502; Capt. Carl Trimble, D/502; Maj. John P. Stopka, executive officer, 3/502; and Capt. Cleveland R. Fitzgerald, B/502. Fitzgerald survived a bullet wound to the chest at Foucarville on D-day, only to die in a car crash in Germany after V-E Day. *Simmons*

501st PIR Regimental S-2 Platoon
S/Sgt. John F. Tiller, S-2/501, reads the mission before a practice jump, England, 1944. Also visible are Gerald Beckerman (far left), Waldo Brown (fourth from left), Ken Collier, Jimmy Ganter, and Irby H. Palmer. Col. Howard Johnson considered his hand-picked S-2 platoon as the elite of his regiment. *Krochka*

had not even tried to get up from the ground. He could see from the crazy angle of the man's left leg that it was broken. . . evidently a compound fracture, from the way the trousers tried to stick out in the wrong place.

He removed the harness from the man, handed him his own weapon and ammunition and told

him he would send the first aid man as soon as he saw one. "Meanwhile, take care of yourself." With that, the Skipper got his own gun out of the holster (an M-1 carbine in leg scabbard), adjusted his musette bag and harness, and took off for the assembly area where he would meet his men and

Healy and Spear
F/502 members in the plane before a practice jump in England. Front, Healy and George Spear (KIA, Holland). Rear (left to right), Beszouska, Chiccoine, Floerchinger (KIA), Sgt. Manuel (standing), Tiedeman, Bennett, Sapinski. *D. Tiedeman*

prepare for the night attack. En route to the assembly area, he met a medic and told him where to find the man with the broken leg. When he arrived in his unit area, he was reminded of the crack on the back of his head by a headache . One of his officers asked how his jump was. "I landed just like a sad sack, as usual, but oh that opening shock," he said, as he felt for the first time where the connector links had hit him. There was a large lump on the back of his head and he knew that the skin had been broken a little by the streak of blood on his fingers as he drew his hand across the wound.

As he received the reports from the jump casualties, he was surprised that there were not more men hurt in the high wind they had jumped in. The men were really getting rugged and they showed that, despite the difficulties they encountered, they could cope with the situation.

As they gathered in the assembly area, the captain gave the word that every man was to have his face blackened with cork, mud, or anything that would prevent his being seen. It had started to rain right after the jump, and now it was dark. The officers who commanded the platoons were with the Skipper when he issued the order, and promptly began to smear mud on their faces.

It was getting colder and darker by the minute, and every minute that passed, it seemed like the rain beat down that much faster.

"Ah, I found a good place," said one of his officers as he continued putting mud all over his face. . . he reached into a small place that looked like a particularly juicy puddle and began to smear it on his face.

"Judas! This stuff stinks!" he snorted.

"Why, you damn fool, don't you know that even in England there are cows?" as he went a little closer to the place to get mud for his own face.

"So help me if it ain't so," he said as he started to spit and snort. "What a Hell of a life."

Unrepentant Patriot

The following are excerpts from a V-Mail letter written by Capt. Cecil L. Simmons to his parents, 23 February 1944. Simmons commanded H/502.

Dear Folks,

Sorry I haven't had the time to write you . . . but then we never have all the time we would like to have for ourselves. . . . I have been quite busy out in the field.

I have had a hundred wild experiences that I would like to tell you about, but can't on account of the censorship. I got a letter telling of the work that Madge is doing, and although I don't approve of it, I guess there is nothing I can do about it from this distance. By rights I guess I should be there like a good husband instead of some of the dizzy things I am doing here in a foreign country, with so many men depending on me for their lives . . . to tell you the truth I am not so repentant as I should be, for when I get back to my home I will know that I have every right to it because I have fought for it . . . if I don't get back, I will go down

Soft Landing
A soft landing for a change. Pictured is William Baird of Waco, Texas. The green nylon camouflaged chute canopy is the type used in combat in Normandy and Holland. *Musura*

Unrepentant Patriot
Capt. Cecil L. Simmons scales a tall hill of baled hay, England, 1944.

Sand Table
Louis Frey, Louisiana; Fred Baynes, New York; and Sgt. Alfred "Pop" Dornick, Indiana, of the 2/501 S-2 Section, admire the work they did in constructing sand tables for briefing the battalion on its objectives.

Using maps and aerial photos as references, the features of terrain such as hills, roads, and rivers were reconstructed to scale. Sand, small sticks, pieces of carved soap, and coloring were used to create the dioramas. Reference grids were laid over the top using pieces of string. Officers were briefed, followed by each platoon of each company. The purpose was to acquaint the troops not only with the location of their objective but also to familiarize them with the general vicinity they were to land in. This proved valuable for those fortunate enough to drop in the correct area. Pfc. Donald Zahn of H/506 later said that as he floated down on DZ D, "I felt like I was looking down on a giant sand table of the DZ—everything looked just as I had expected from the briefing."

knowing that I have made it safe for my kids to grow up to be free people. . . . When the history of this war is written, those of us in the Paratroops will have our place in it . . . I believe we will go down as fearless and competent fighters who don't know when to give up and who, after fighting a good fight have accomplished our mission—what more can a man ask of life? I enjoy your letters so write when you all get the chance.

Love,
CEC

Pathfinders

Specially-trained teams of parachutist Pathfinders would jump about one hour ahead of the main serials to land on each of the designated drop zones. These men would set up special Halifane lights and Eureka radar sets, using the British GEE system and 717-C screen. The BUPS beacon was also used, with signals sent from the Rebecca device in each plane triggering the Eureka set on the ground. The whole program's accuracy could be rendered useless if the ground teams

501st PIR Demolitions Platoon
Part of the Regimental Demolitions Platoon, 501st PIR, just prior to going to the marshaling area. (Standing left to right) Sgt. Leon "Pappy" Brown, California; Pfc. Edward Case, Arizona; Pfc. King J. Bogie, Minnesota; Cpl. Thomas Arrey, New Mexico; Pfc. Lafayette Hillman, Pennsylvania; Pvt. Marvin Johnson, Minnesota; Pvt. Clement Henwood, California; Lt. Jess Tidwell, Tennessee. (Bottom row left to right) Pfc. Irvin Lloyd, Virginia; Pvt. Howard Finch, California; Pfc. Richard Wisniewski, New York; Pvt. Louis Sorace, New York; Pfc. Nae Paugh, Michigan; and Pvt. John Kildare, Nebraska.

It is evident in this photo that most of the troopers have shaved their heads. In his book, *Look Out Below!*, Father Francis Sampson wrote: In addition to head shaving, men allowed their whiskers to grow out before a jump. "We always wore them [beards] into combat—supposed to make you look tough, I guess."

Some troopers cut Indian scalplocks on their domes, but simple cropping had a practical purpose. It would be much easier to keep short hair clean under field conditions. Most troopers wouldn't enjoy a shower for the first two weeks in Normandy.

were dropped in the wrong place to begin with, or neutralized by enemy fire, as happened in some instances. Pathfinder teams were comprised of nine to fourteen signaling specialists with two Eureka sets and nine Halifane lights, plus a five-man security detachment to protect them while they performed their signaling functions.

Early in 1944, a handful of volunteers from each company in the division left their parent units to train at the new Pathfinder School in Nottingham, England. There was no TO&E or precedent for such training, but over 350 American and British signaling technicians were trained as Pathfinders here before D-day. In requesting volunteers, preference was given to those with communications school training as they were familiar with radio equipment and the Morse code.

As the first men to land in enemy occupied France, the Pathfinders were viewed as a potential "suicide squad," and in the years since the war, a definite mystique has attached itself to the men who served in that capacity. It is interesting to see how the actual selection was done.

Joseph Haller's company commander requested that he volunteer. "We'd like to have you in the Pathfinders because you can speak German," Capt. Simmons told him.

"If it's my time to die, I'm going to die no matter where I am," Haller said. "If you want me in the Pathfinders, I'll join the Pathfinders." There was more to it, however. Haller often talked Pro-German around his buddies to entertain himself and to provoke them. "Today Germany—Tomorrow the World. . . . then *I* shall rule in this district!" Haller would loudly proclaim.

Joe's best buddies were Joe Dejanovich, a Serbian trooper, and David Hadley. "The Three Kings," Haller called them. All were from the communications platoon and worked together as a team through training. But Capt. Simmons suspected that Dejanovich was a Communist—he had been heard threatening to go over the hill once he landed on the continent so he could join Tito and fight with the partisans.

Lt. Albert Watson, known as "The Gremlin," was the battalion mess officer and not popular with the top officers in 1/501. Somehow, he wound

Last Minute Preparation
Albert A. Krochka of HQ/501 sews an eagle patch to his M42 jump jacket shortly before D-day. *Krochka*

1/327 GIR, Dartmouth-Brixham, England
Members of the 1/327 Glider Infantry were transported to Normandy by ship, rather than by air, due to a limited number of gliders and tow craft. This photo was taken in the Dartmouth-Brixham area near Slapton Sands. US Army

OFFICE OF THE REGIMENTAL COMMANDER

Soldiers of the Regiment: D-Day

     Today, and as you read this, you are enroute to that great adventure for which you have trained for over two years.

     Tonight is the night of nights.

     Tomorrow throughout the whole of our homeland and the Allied world the bells will ring out the tidings that you have arrived, and the invasion for liberation has begun.

     The hopes and prayers of your near ones accompany you, the confidence of your high commanders goes with you. The fears of the Germans are about to become a reality.

     Let us strike hard. When the going is tough, let us go harder. Inbued with faith in the rightness of our cause, and the power of our might, let us annihilate the enemy where found.

     May God be with each of you fine soldiers. By your actions let us justify His faith in us.

Knight
June 5, 1944

Colonel

Sink's Message
Most history buffs have seen Eisenhower's Great Crusade invasion message, but the above memo from Col. Robert Sink to all his 506th troopers is much more obscure. This specimen was preserved by Sgt. William Knight, C/506. *Knight*

Invasion Currency
Capt. William G. Burd, CO of HQ/501, distributed invasion currency. Invasion currency was used by the troopers to pay French civilians for food and other necessities. Burd was killed at Heeswijk, Holland, during Operation Market-Garden. *Krochka*

Capt. Frank Lillyman, 1943
Lillyman in a photo taken at Ft. Bragg, North Carolina. He commanded I/502 before forming the division's Pathfinder School. *Koskimaki*

up volunteering for the Pathfinders, along with "The Three Kings."

Many members of the division were never given the opportunity to volunteer for Pathfinder duty as the slots were filled before they even heard about the outfit.

Around February 1944, Leonard Newcomb of F/501 was in his tent at Hamstead Marshall, minding his own business, when Lt. Hugh Hendrickson, the executive officer of his company, walked in and stated that volunteers were needed for a special outfit to jump in ahead of everyone else in the invasion to signal the other planes. In a letter to the author dated 16 April 1973 Newcomb wrote:

> I asked him if he was going in it and he said yes—so Joe Bass and I both said okay. Red Larsen

who had the first bed in the tent said he wanted to be in it, so Lt. Hendrickson said yes. Harold Sellers came in the tent to get mail at this time, and he said he wanted to join—for we were all in the same squad.

Thus were all the available slots for F/501 filled. Only one other slot was available and Ralph "Pinky" Newton of F/501's 2nd Platoon got it. No one in the 3rd Platoon even had a chance to volunteer before the slots were filled. Also, as Leo Gillis of that company points out, certain non-coms who were considered essential to the functioning of a company wouldn't have been allowed to go, either.

The 2/501 group of volunteers had little idea at the time that they would land on Drop Zone D, the hottest of all on D-day. Sellers was killed upon

Off To Pathfinder School
Pathfinder Volunteers of 2/501 posed at Newbury, England, before going to Lillyman's school at Nottingham. Russ Waller, top left, was KIA in Holland. To his right are Bob Sechrist of E/501 and Bob Howard of D/501. At bottom left

is T. K. "Red" Larsen of F/501. To Larsen's right is Harold "Gene" Sellers of F/501. Laying down, with pipe and hatchet is Leonard Newcomb of F/501. Sellers was KIA on landing in Normandy. Newcomb was captured. *Alice Larsen*

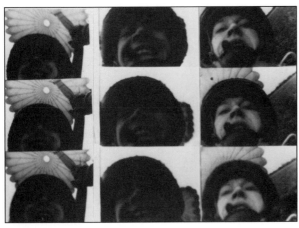

Lillyman's Landing
These 16mm movie sequences filmed by a camera attached to Lillyman's chest shows his chute blossoming; Lillyman's face with a cigar clenched in his teeth; and his landing on the ground. *US Army*

landing, becoming the first fatality of F/501 in the war. Newcomb was captured on D-day afternoon and spent the duration as a prisoner of war (POW).

Lt. Hendrickson was struck by a laundry truck while crossing the street in Nottingham. His leg was badly broken before D-day and he never got into combat until the Korean War.

Capt. Frank Lillyman, who had previously commanded I/502 in training, organized and ran the Pathfinder School. Lillyman was a flamboyant, publicity conscious and controversial officer. He was a diminutive man, filled with determination,

Pathfinder Wing
An original British-made Pathfinder sleeve wing, worn by Hilary McKenna of E/501 who served on the security detail of the 501st's Base Stick on DZ D. Security personnel who had served in that capacity on an actual combat mission were also eligible to wear the wing.

who wanted to be sure his Pathfinders received their due recognition for being the first to land in enemy territory. Lillyman's ego must have rubbed someone the wrong way as he was a captain going into Normandy and was still a captain when the war ended in 1945. He was then given command of the divisional MP platoon, an additional slap in the face. Members of that platoon at the time were forbidden to wear the Airborne tab above their eagle shoulder patch.

One of Lillyman's passions was photography, and not being satisfied with still photos, he carried a 16mm movie camera with which he recorded most every aspect of training. His most famous stunt in pre D-day England was a jump he made with his movie camera attached to his chest and aimed at his own face as he jumped from a plane. This camera recorded his facial expressions (he had a cigar clenched in his teeth), and showed the blossoming open of his canopy and landing on the ground.

As S.L.A. Marshall pointed out in *Night Drop* (Battery Press, Nashville, Tennessee, 1962), Frank Lillyman was a pioneering soul, who was born years before his time. He would have been more at home in the era of space exploration.

Certain pilots and crews from the Ninth Air Force's Troop Carrier Command worked in cooperation with the parachutists and were also considered part of the Pathfinder teams. A special insignia was designed before D-day, but in most cases not issued until after the Normandy campaign, to indicate Pathfinder training. It could be worn on the lower left sleeve above hash marks and overseas bars by any parachutist who had completed Pathfinder training and by Air Corps personnel who had completed the corresponding training. The patch depicts a flaming golden torch and the earliest examples are of typical British construction, with the design sewn in cotton thread on a blue flannel base.

The photos of Pathfinder sticks were taken by Air Corps personnel and appear thanks to the Pathfinder Association. A few sticks are missing, but ironically, there are more photos of Pathfinder sticks available than there are of regular rifle company sticks.

On D-day, Pathfinders jumped carrying their lights and radar sets. Other than that, their equipment was similar to that used by regular paratroopers. Notably in the 101st, the Pathfinders' helmets were devoid of the regimental playing card symbols used by the regular troops. Although they would rejoin their original companies on the ground in France after performing their initial signaling missions, they had left their parent units before the stencils were applied. Unlike the regular troopers, the Pathfinders were not issued crickets for ground recognition. (Some of the security personnel received them, according to Larry McKenna of the 501st PIR.) Instead they had a password and countersign: "Boise" and "Idaho." Other troopers of the division were to use "Flash" and "Thunder" as an alternative to cricket challenges.

Unlike the regular serials, the planes carrying the Pathfinders would fly a constant speed of 150mph for the entire course, instead of slowing down during the drop. As a result, many of the jumpers had their weapons and equipment torn off by especially violent opening shocks.

On the approach to the Cotentin across the Channel, the planes bearing Pathfinders flew at extremely low altitudes to avoid German radar de-

tection. Some of the Pathfinders recall the tops of the waves on the Channel splashing into the open door of their plane.

Joe Haller had consumed a lot of coffee at the North Witham Airfield before taking off on D-day night. As a result, he had to urinate during the flight across. He stood in the open door of the C-47, unzipped, and let go. The wind from the propellers blew the urine back into the plane, spraying his mortified buddies. Naturally, there was a lot of cursing and protesting.

"You guys are gonna have a lot more to worry about than a little *pee!*" Haller told them. Like many of the others aboard, Haller was smoking a cigarette. He began to sing a song he had heard in

Base Stick, 502nd PIR, 5 June 1944
Most of the personnel in this photo, taken at North Witham Airfield, have been identified as follows. (Standing left to right) 1st Lt. Samuel McCarter (KIA), Lt. Robert "Buck" Dickson (S-2), Pvt. John McFarlen, Pvt. August Mangoni, Pvt. Bluford Williams, Pvt. John S. Zamanakos, T/5 Owen R. Council, unknown, T/5 Thomas G. Walton, Pfc. Delbert Jones. (Kneeling left to right) 2nd Lt. Reed Pelfrey, Pvt. Francis Rocca, Pvt. Raymond Smith (medic), Pfc. Fred A. Wilhelm, Pvt. John G. Ott (S-2), Pvt. Jarris C. Clark (S-2), unknown.

Also listed on the manifest for this stick were Pvt.

James Bement, Pvt. Paul O. Davis, and Pvt. John H. Funk (KIA), all of whom were security personnel. Two of these three men are probably the unknowns in the photo. Although Capt. Frank Lillyman himself jumped with this stick, he is not pictured. Dickson, Ott, and Clark of S-2 were along to recon a route to the 502nd's primary objective, the 122mm guns near St. Martin de Varreville.

Lt. Col. Joel Crouch, CO of the 9th Troop Carrier Pathfinder Group, piloted Lillyman's lead plane. Incidentally, Air Corps troop carrier personnel who flew Pathfinders also wore the Pathfinder wing.

a western movie:

> I'm smokin' my last cig-a-rette,
> sing that cowboy song
> I ne-ver will for-get. . .
> I'm smokin' my last cig-a-rette.

"Shut up, you bastard!" the men shouted; they didn't want to hear that.

Joe wasn't too scared, even when violent flak began to rock the plane. Over DZ D, the plane banked and the first three jumpers fell out the door; they didn't even have to jump. Haller was one of them. As he fell, his Tommy gun flew down in front of his chest but he caught it. Shrapnel burst open his chest reserve chute and he grasped that desperately in his arms. He soon hit the ground and could see tracer bullets passing over him as he struggled to get out of his harness.

"The Germans must have been scared too," he later said. "They weren't far away—they could have rushed me."

Haller began to walk, went through a gap in the hedgerow and crossed a dark road.

A German voice yelled, "Halte!"

Haller answered in fluent German, "There's more of them over here—be careful!"

Haller could hear a commotion as the Germans were capturing another member of his stick. He was able to escape and rejoin his regiment after signaling in concert with Russell Waller, of the 2nd Battalion stick, whom he encountered in a large ditch. This was near St. Come du Mont.

Capt. Lillyman's Team A was the first to land in the DZ A area. The team was scheduled to land at 1220, but the plane arrived over the area 10min early. The pilot passed the DZ, circled back, and dropped the stick flying from northeast to southwest. The last three members of the stick were members of the 502nd's S-2 Section. Lt. Buck Dickson, Jack Ott, and Jim Clark. They were supposed to recon a route to the St. Martin de Varreville coastal gun battery, but landed so far west

377th PFAB and 326th AEB

This plane included stick 2, 377th Lt. L. J. Hensley jumpmaster and part of Team E for DZ E. Team E was supposed to drop on DZ C at 0027, northeast of Hiesville. Instead, they landed west of Angoville, about 3,000 yards off target. Paratroopers aboard included: Pfc. John J. Hosta, Pvt. Saul Sancedo, Pfc. Louis DiGaetano, Pvt. Arthur L. Brooks, Pvt. Albert Kouba, T/5 Donald N. Green, Pvt. Norman D. Gannon, T/5 Jerold J. Quinn, Cpl. Vincent L. Cart, and 1st Lt. Lawrence Hensley.

The last five troopers to exit, including DiGaetano and Kouba, landed in the flooded wastelands east of Angoville and were missing for the first two days. The Air Corps crew was 1st Lt. Paul Egan (pilot), 1st Lt. Richard Young (co-pilot), 1st Lt. Fern \Murphy (navigator), S/Sgt. Marvin Rosenblatt (radio operator), and Sgt. Jack Buchanan (crew chief). (Information on this stick was researched and provided by Frank DiGaetano, Louis' brother.)

(near Beuzeville au Plain), that they never got to that objective on D-day. A last minute delay in the plane had caused the jumping order of the stick to change slightly, and although Lillyman claimed credit for being the first American to land in France after midnight on D-day, he was actually the second or third. Pfc. John G. McFarlen had switched places with Lillyman and actually left the plane first. As he points out: "Unless Capt. Lillyman found a way to beat me to the ground, I was the first to land."

Each 6 June, the local media in Odessa, Texas, celebrates John McFarlen as the *real* first American to land in France on D-day.

After assembling near the church at St. Germaine de Varreville, Lillyman set up a Eureka set and signaled the large flock of planes that came over some time later. But the fog and cloud bank encountered over the west coast of the Cotentin had already badly dispersed the formations. As a result, many of the sticks intended for DZ A where Lillyman was, dropped troopers as far north as St. Marcouf and as far south as St. Marie du Mont. Conversely, many planes of 2/506 intended for DZ C, dropped their men on Lillyman's signal far to the north of the intended landing area. Like an omen of the fouled-up misdrops to come, the Pathfinder stick of Lt. Rothwell (506th PIR) was shot down and ditched in the Channel.

Departure Airfields
Aldermaston Airfield

The Chicago Mission was to land important surgeons, medical supplies, and anti-tank guns a few hours after the paratroopers were on the ground. They flew the same route as the para-

501st Pathfinders, D-1
There only seems to be one Air Corps photo in existence of 501st Pathfinders on the eve of D-day and this is it, taken at North Witham Airfield. Like the other regiments, the 501st used three sticks of Pathfinders, and it seems that men of all three battalions mingled together to make this photo. Of course, most are missing, but there seems to also be a mixture of trained Pathfinders and security people. The man bending forward at far left may be Mileski, of E Company, who went along as part of the security detachment. It is only via the diamond stencil on his helmet that we can even speculate that this group is of the 501. Trained Pathfinders didn't have regimental unit stencils on their helmet as they were a divisional organization and had

left their parent units to train in isolation in Nottingham some time before the stencils were applied. The security people were assigned less than two weeks before the invasion and thus brought stenciled helmets with them.

In any case, it is possible that Red Larsen is at upper left, standing beside Joe Dejanovich (HQ/1; POW), Michael Rofar (I/501; KIA) stands right in the center. The trooper beside him is possibly Lary McKenna (E/501 security). Of the three sticks, the Base stick (2/501 men) and Primary Stick (1/501), landed on DZ D and took the highest casualties of any of the Pathfinder sticks killed and missing. The alternate (3/501) stick landed closer to Hiesville to light the DZ C area.

Cherbourg Choo-Choo
A C-47 of the 74th TCS. *Krochka*

chutists, as opposed to the evening Keokuk Mission of British-made Horsa gliders, which came in across Utah Beach at 2130.

The anticipated Panzer thrust of German tanks never materialized until a week later, and then in the form of the 17th SS Panzer-Grenadier Division. This unit was understrength and arrived too late to push the invaders back into the Channel. The only armor the Germans had behind Utah Beach were a handful of Renault tankettes of the 100th Panzer Battalion. Nevertheless, elements of the 81st AAATB with 57mm guns were brought in to repel tanks in the morning, and the anti-tank platoon of the 327th GIR landed with their 37mm pieces in the evening lift.

The Chicago Mission departed Aldermaston airfield at 0221 with gliders arriving between 0400

Queenie
This C-47 belonged to the 73rd TCS and towed a glider to LZ E on D-day. *Krochka*

and 0600 in France. The mission was flown by 434th Troop Carrier Group (TCG), which consisted of the 71st Troop Carrier Squadron (TCS; planes marked CJ), 72nd TCS (CU markings), 73rd TCS (CN markings), and 74th TCS (ID markings).

A similar Detroit Mission took off and landed around the same time to resupply the 82nd Airborne.

Many of the gliders struck Rommel's Asparagus poles or collided with hedgerows in fields that were too small.

It is well known that Col. Mike Murphy of the 434th Troop Carrier Group (TCG) piloted a CG-4A named *Fighting Falcon* into Normandy with Brig. Gen. Don Pratt aboard. Gen. Pratt became the first American general to die in the invasion when *Fighting Falcon* collided with a hedgerow outside Hiesville. The general had a parachute underneath him while seated in a jeep inside the glider. The parachute raised Pratt's head just high enough to cause it to strike an overhead beam, breaking his neck upon impact.

Few people know that there were two *Fighting Falcons*—Pratt died in *Fighting Falcon No. 2*. The original *Fighting Falcon* was replaced by a newer model at the last minute. This newer ship became Glider No. 1 in Murphy's 72nd Troop Carrier Squadron (TCS). The newer model was equipped with a "Griswold Nose," to help insulate against frontal impacts, a feature that the original Falcon didn't have. The original *Fighting Falcon* reverted to glider No. 45 in the 52 glider serial and was piloted to Normandy by Robert Butler and Everard Hohmann. Lt. Lawrence Hensley's Pathfinders had set up a green lighted *T* on LZ E, but the second glider to land smashed into the string of lights as it slid over the grass, forcing the rest of the serial to land by moonlight.

Glider pilots and co-pilots were to fight as infantry and make their way to HQ/101. A number of pilots and co-pilots were lost on landing or en route to the assembly area. These included Jack Willoughby, pilot of Glider No. 3; Thomas Ahmad, co-pilot of Glider No. 42, who landed 7mi south of Carentan; and Clinton Griffin, co-pilot of glider No. 40, listed as killed in action (KIA). Four other pilots were listed as missing in action (MIA). (A special thanks to George "Pete" Buckley and Martin Wolfe for information on glider pilots and Troop Carrier markings.)

Greenham Common Airfield

Serial 1 consisted of thirty-six planes, carrying troops of 2/502 and 3/502. Serial 2 consisted of forty-five planes, carrying half of the 377th PFAB. The two serials combined were supposed to land a total of 1,430 troops on the amber colored *T* of lights on DZ A. The Air Corps claims an accuracy of 80 percent on the drop.

CG-4A Waco Glider
Typical shot of a C-47 towing the US-made CG-4A Waco glider. The towplane would cut the glider loose over the LZ and the glider pilot would glide the engineless craft to the ground. The CG-4A could carry a 3,750lb payload; that is, thirteen infantrymen, a jeep with trailer, or a 57mm gun and crew. *Musura*

British Horsa Glider
The unique profile of the larger British-made Horsa Glider, used in the evening Keokuk Mission. The 327th PIR's anti-tank platoon with 37mm guns landed in Horsas. The British Horsa could carry a 6,700lb payload; it could carry thirty-two infantrymen or a jeep with attached howitzer. *Musura*

In reality, many jumpers in Serial 1 landed far south near DZ C, outside St. Marie du Mont. Others landed west of the DZ near St. Mere Eglise and much of the 377th PFAB was scattered far north, near Montebourg, Valognes, St. Vaast la Hocque, etc.

These serials departed England from Greenham Common before 2330. The mission was flown by the 438th TCG, which included the 87th TCS (3X markings), 88th TCS (M2 markings), 89th TCS (4U markings), and 90th TCS (Q7markings). Those planes from Serial 1 that found the DZ dropped troopers between 0048 and 0050 on 6 June. These earlier serials received less ground fire from the surprised Germans.

A sizable group under Lt. Col. Robert Cole 3/502 joined forces with a group from 2/506 (intended for DZ C), which had also landed near St. Mere Eglise.

Near dusk on 5 June, Gen. Dwight Eisenhower, the supreme commander of Overlord, personally visited troops of the 101st Airborne at two departure fields. We have photographic evidence that he saw the 2/502 at Greenham and the 3/501 at Welford. The car trip from Portsmouth to the Newbury area took 90min of winding through troop convoys and checkpoints. Eisenhower arrived unannounced to avoid disrupting the loading schedule.

Greenham Common Airfield, D-1
Lt. Col. Robert Cole, CO of 3/502, stands at upper left, posing with the Air Corps crew of *Snooty*, his C-47. We cannot see the nose markings of the plane but knowing that it belonged to the 89th TCS, 438th TCG, we can surmise that the markings were 4U. The tall man standing next to Cole is Wright Bryan, a journalist from the *Atlanta Journal*, who flew over with the troops in a round-trip flight. When he returned to England, he filed the first story of the parachute invasion. Bryan's daring in trying to get the hazardous stories eventually resulted in his capture by the Germans in the fall of 1944, as he was observing the front lines near Chaumont, France. He spent the duration as a POW.

After landing in a tree and experiencing great difficulty getting free of his chute harness, Cole headed in the wrong direction and realized it when he arrived on the eastern fringe of St. Mere Eglise. He reversed his group and eventually deployed them near exits 3 and 4. He was destined to become the first Medal of Honor winner in the 101st Airborne. *Maxwell*

"Don't worry General . . . "

The troopers quickly put Eisenhower at ease with wise-cracks: "Don't worry General, we've got it under control!" Note that a censor has obliterated the eagle patches, and the troopers have switched their musette bags to their backs for this impromptu inspection. On the jump, they would wear them in front of their bodies, just below the reserve parachute chest packs. The trooper with his back to the camera is Tom Beszouska, of F/502. Eisenhower's aide de camp, Navy Commander Harry C. Butcher, is highly visible at Eisenhower's rear in the blue uniform. Butcher was a close friend and nearly constant companion to Eisenhower. The trooper at far left clearly has a gas detection brassard on his right shoulder, and the paratrooper second from left is Lt. Col. Mike Michaelis, who assumed command of the entire 502nd PIR after Col. Moseley broke his leg on the D-day jump. *Sapinski*

He was a popular figure and was quickly recognized, despite the covered stars on his staff car. Ike was troubled by the predictions of British Air Chief Marshal Sir Trafford Leigh-Mallory, who had estimated 80 percent casualties among the paratroopers of the 82nd and 101st Airborne Divisions, some 13,000 of which would make the initial landings.

Eisenhower continued through the admiring ranks, asking some individuals what state they were from, what their job was in the Army, and what they had done in civilian life. The visit seemed to do more to lift the general's morale than it did to bolster the paratroopers' morale; they were ready.

Membury Airfield (Serials 3 and 4)

Planes of the 436th TCG—which consisted of the 79th TCS (S6 markings), 80th TCS (7D markings), 81st TCS (U5 markings), and 82nd TCS (3D markings)—departed from Membury Airfield, which was situated north of Greenham Common, for DZ A (marked by amber lights). One serial of the 436th TCG flew 1/502 (Lt. Col. Cassidy's troops) in thirty-six planes, delivering them to the vicinity of DZ A, where they jumped between 0055 and 0102 on 6 June. Another serial of the 436th TCG carried elements of the 377th PFAB, including twelve 75mm pack howitzers, broken down into drop bundles. Most of the artillerymen and their weapons landed too far west or north of the intended DZ, and only one of the howitzers was retrieved by Charlie Battery.

The artillerymen dropped between 0055 and 0108 on 6 June. Misdrops among them were the rule rather than the exception, with many landing in the Montebourg-Valognes area and others between St. Marcouf-Ravenoville (see Chapter 28). In the two above serials, a total of 1,084 paratroopers were dropped into France.

All DZ A units were to concentrate on the St. Martin de Varreville area and the four 122mm guns situated southwest of town.

Lt. Col. Cassidy's 1/502 was to eradicate the German artillerymen stationed in the XYZ complex at Mesieres. The 2/502 (Chappuis) was to team up with the 377th's howitzers to knock out the actual emplacements, using combined artillery support and demolitions.

Lt. Jim Keane of HQ/502 was assigned to investigate why parts of two A/502 sticks were misdropped in the Channel, resulting in numerous drownings. During the course of his probe, he learned that the serial carrying 1/502 was the only one of those carrying 101st Airborne troops that suffered no losses.

It is fortunate that Sgt. Edward Benecke, of A Battery, 377th PFAB, was at Membury with his camera. Thanks to his photos, some 436th TCG's nose art has been preserved for posterity. Few paratroopers remember the name of the plane they rode in, and even a few pilots no longer recall the name of their own plane after all these years.

Uppottery Airfield (Serials 5 and 6)

The 439th TCG—which consisted of the 91st TCS (L4 markings), 92nd TCS (J8 markings), 93rd TCS (3B markings), and 94th TCS (D8 markings)—flew from Uppottery with 1/506, 2/506, and HQ/506 to attack DZ C (marked by green lights). These troops had numerous missions, including the capture of exits 1 and 2 at Pouppeville and St. Marie du Mont. The 1st Battalion, as well as the majority of regimental HQ, had a fairly concentrated drop near Holdy, although many troops from A and C companies landed way up near Ravenoville. We know that Capt. Brown's HQ/506 stick also landed near Montebourg, far to the northwest.

Most of Lt. Col. Strayer's 2/506 landed in a concentrated area near DZ A at Foucarville and headed south after assembling. Some 2/506 sticks landed in or near St. Mere Eglise, nearly an hour before elements of the 82nd Airborne arrived. It is small wonder that the 505th dropped into an aroused hornet's nest around 0200.

Serial 5 departed Uppottery around 2350 on 5 June, dropping its paratroopers over France at 0114 on 6 June. Serial 6 departed Uppottery around 2356 on 5 June, dropped its paratroopers over France between 0114 and 0120 on 6 June. A total of some 1,357 troops of the 506th PIR, minus 3rd Battalion were carried in these two serials.

Col. Robert Sink's regimental command group

A Week Later
Tom Beszouska in France. Beszouska was misdropped near St. Mere Eglise and fought for a week with the 82nd Airborne. Note that he is wearing German paratrooper gloves—a favorite souvenir with the 101st troopers. *Sapinski*

Load Up
This photo snapped by Eddie Sapinski's camera at Greenham Common shows his F/502 stick preparing to load. The C-47 belonged to the 438th TCG. The trooper with coiled jump rope, second from the left is Eddie Sapinski. *Sapinski*

33

"Total Victory—Nothing Less!"
Press captions for this photo throughout the Western World claimed that Eisenhower was demanding, "Total Victory—nothing less!" as he talked to Lt. Wallace Stroebel of Saginaw, Michigan. Stroebel says that when Eisenhower learned he was from Michigan, he said, "I've been there and liked it . . . good fishing there!"

This is probably the most famous invasion photo from D-day and certainly ranks as one of the great photos of WWII. There has always been a great debate over the names of the troopers pictured. Without engaging in that controversy, it can be stated that Schuyler "Sky" Jackson is closest to Eisenhower's nose. Jackson was a member of regimental demolitions, assigned to 2/502 for his D-day mission. Most of the other troopers belonged to D/502 and E/502. Enough said.

We can state with some certainty that the lieutenant facing Eisenhower is Wallace Stroebel of Saginaw, Michigan. Stroebel, a Hungarian-American, belonged to E Company. For those who follow astrology, this is a classic pairing of two compatibles, Eisenhower (Libra) and Stroebel (Gemini). In fact, the photo was taken on Stroebel's birthday, 5 June. As of this writing, Stroebel still lives in Saginaw; Sky Jackson, one of the most popular members of the 101st Airborne Association, passed away in early 1993. *US Army*

established a command post at a cluster of farmhouses known as Culloville; Maj. Kent, the surgeon, set up an aid station just down the road.

Welford Airfield (Serial 7)

Serial 7 of the 435th TCG—which consisted of aircraft from the 75th TCS (SH markings), 76th TCS (CW markings), 77th TCS (1B markings), and 78th TCS (CM markings)—carried the jump element, mainly medical and communications personnel from HQ/101 under Gen. Maxwell Taylor, as well as Lt. Col. Julian Ewell's 3/501, which was considered in "reserve." Third Battalion's mission was to provide security for divisional HQ at Hiesville. The 677 troopers dropped from 45 planes in the vicinity of DZ C (marked by green lights) between 0120 and 0126 on 6 June 1944. Much of this serial landed reasonably close to Hiesville, but some planes bearing troops from HQ/101 and 3/501 strayed far south, dropping men west of Carentan, near Baupte, and also far south of Carentan.

Merryfield Airfield (Serials 8 and 9)

One serial of forty-five planes of the 441st TCG—which consisted of the 99th TCS (3J markings), 100th TCS (8C markings), 301st TCS (Z4 markings), and 302nd TCS (2L markings)—from Merryfield Airfield carried HQ/501, Service Company, and 1/501 to DZ D, where they landed between 0126 and 0131. Another serial of forty-five

Shack Rabbit
This aircraft carried one of at least three nose art designs all having the same flying woman, but with varying names, including *Shoo-Shoo Baby* and *Dark Beauty*. All were painted by glider pilot Adelore Chevalier, of Urbana, Illinois. *Benecke*

Ma Petite Jeanne
This C-47 was another member of the 80th TCS departing Membury. *Benecke*

A Message From Col. Sink
1st Lt. Carl McDowell reads Col. Robert Sink's invasion message to his stick. (Left to right) Don Emelander, Tom Alley, McDowell; trooper at right is possibly Bill Green. All of these men belonged to Company HQ, F/506. The white scarves worn at their necks are cloth maps of France from the escape and evasion kits. *Young*

planes carried 2/501 and elements of C/326 AEB to DZ D (marked by red lights), where they jumped between 0134 and 0137. These combined serials dropped a total of 1,475 paratroopers in the area east of St. Come du Mont.

The objectives of the 501st PIR were to capture St. Come du Mont, the Douve River Bridge on the Carentan Causeway (N-13), and the LaBarquette lock. The 1/501, which landed farther south than 2/501, dropped close to the lock, in the same area as 3/506. The casualties of 1/501 were very high. Lt. Col. Robert A. Ballard was one of the few field grade officers in the night drop to recognize where he was from terrain features, immediately upon landing. His 2/501 troops came down in and near the flooded area southeast of Angoville au

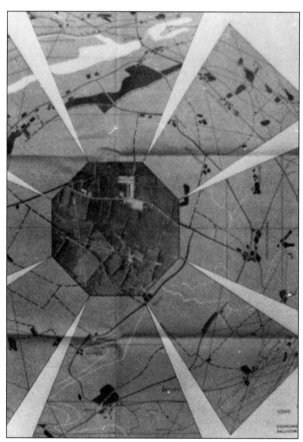

Drop Zone Maps
DZ maps like this were issued to some of the troopers who landed on DZ C and a similar map exists for DZ A near St. Martin de Varreville. The maps are about 20in square and printed in black and white. Although the center section is a reproduced-to-scale aerial photo of the DZ, it is done with tiny dots similar to newsprint photos in a newspaper. This map shows the St. Marie du Mont zone C, which was the intended target of the troops who departed from Uppottery and Welford airfields. *Hood*

Col. Howard Johnson's Stick
The pilot of the C-47 that carried the stick was Col. Kershaw. Among others, the passengers included Pfc. Leo Runge (center front, with eyes closed), who distinguished himself at Hell's Corner. Beside him is Maj. Francis Carrell, the regimental surgeon of the 501st PIR, wearing a Red Cross brassard. *US Army*

Plein, concentrated in a reasonably small area.

Exeter Airfield (Serial 10)

The ill-fated 3/506 had as its mission the capture of the two wooden bridges near Brévands.

Johnson's "Knife Speech"

It was at Merryfield that Col. Howard R. Johnson, the fire-breathing CO of the 501st PIR, made his famous blood-thirsty "knife speech" to his troops before boarding the planes. Johnson exhorted his men to give their all in the invasion. Standing before them he yelled: "We've worked together, sweated together, trained together . . . but what we do tonight will be written in history!" The carefully calculated climax to the colonel's speech called for him to raise a trench knife over his head for the dramatic final line. He stooped to release the weapon from his ankle, but for a few embarrassing moments, the knife would not yield from the scabbard. Turning red-faced at this unseemly interruption, Johnson removed his trusty Randall Bowie knife from his waist and raised it on high.

"Ere another dawn . . . I hope this knife is buried in the back of the foulest, black-hearted Nazi bastard in France! Are you with me?"

His faithful minions replied with a bloodcurdling roar.

"Then let's go get 'em! Good hunting!"

Only 130 men managed to find and assemble at that objective the following afternoon. Many had been killed, captured, or were wandering around lost.

This serial departed Exeter at 0020 dropping its 723 troopers between 0140 and 0143 on 6 June. Demolition saboteurs from the Filthy 13 were also along, in case the bridges needed to be blown.

The 3/506 was flown from Exeter to DZ D (marked by red lights) by the 440th TCG—which consisted of the 95th TCS (9X markings), 96th TCS (6Z markings), 97th TCS (W6 markings), and 98th TCS (8Y markings).

This serial had a fairly accurate drop south and east of St. Come du Mont, but this was not necessarily fortunate. The Germans had anticipated that this was an ideal area for an airborne landing and had prepared a hot reception. A barn at the edge of the landing fields had been doused with gas and set alight, making many of the troopers clay pigeons as they floated down. Add to this the fact that all the other 101st serials had already landed, giving the Germans more time to react and prepare for this one. Many of these men were hit before they reached the ground, or pounced upon and killed or captured while still in their harnesses. Some landed on a bivouac area of Ost volunteers from Russia and a wholesale slaughter ensued. Other groups were ambushed while en route to the bridges. The survivors of Serial 10 were in-

Final Inspection
Lt. Alex Bobuck of HQ/3 506 performs final parachute inspection before his men board the plane. *US Army*

deed fortunate.

The Filthy 13

Jake McNiece, a Native American from Ponca City, Oklahoma, conceived this group of demolitions saboteurs from HQ/506. The group, which always seemed to number more than a dozen men, changed members from time to time. Their basic premise was to take solemn Indian vows not to wash or shave until they had returned from battle. This vow was taken around December 1943, and the men were pretty ripe by D-day, living apart from the others in their company by mutual agreement.

Frank Palys, a one-time member of the 13, suggests that nobody stationed in the area took many baths, as water was not readily available. He says the group first started in Camp Toccoa in 1942 as "The Warsaw Seven," a group of Polish boys that included himself, Martin Majewski, Eddie Malas, Joe Oleskiewicz, and others, including Jake McNiece, who was made an "Honorary Po-

The Dirty 13
The group known as the Dirty 13 started out as the Dirty Dozen. It was comprised of men from Company HQ and 1st Platoon, F/501. The first twelve members had the identical tattoo of a skull, bones, and 13 on their left forearm. The thirteenth member, John Zeilmeier, had his on the right arm. Glen Haley and Rudy Korvas reveal their matching tattoos at a 501st reunion in Columbus, Georgia, 1990. After the war, Haley became fire chief in Seymour, Indiana. Korvas drove a delivery truck in Chicago. The preoccupation of many paratroopers with fate, chance, and good versus bad luck helps explain their choice of the number 13 in a number of situations. By embracing that unlucky number, they were thumbing their noses at fate. *SMR and Author's Collection*

War Paint
A war-painted trooper poses in the door of a transport on the eve of D-day. This may have been one of the Filthy 13, although this is unverified. Also, the location may have been Exeter, although this is also unverified. *US Army*

"I Let the Order Stand"

When asked at a High School Press Club meeting in Chicago, 1947, what was his toughest decision of WWII, Dwight Eisenhower told about the decision to send paratroopers ahead of the seaborne landings on D-day. He explained about the four causeways, elevated roads leading inland from Utah Beach across otherwise impassable salt marshes. He told how crucial to the landings it was for the causeways to be secured and the German defenders to be neutralized. Eisenhower also told of Air Chief Marshal Leigh-Mallory's prediction that 80 percent of the paratroopers would be killed and wounded and that 90 percent of the gliders would be casualties before reaching the ground.

Eisenhower admitted he had agonized many hours over the decision but realized that the plan had been scrutinized by other top leaders and approved. He also thought about what the beach landings would be like without the prior air drop.

After a dramatic pause, with voice low, Eisenhower spoke these five words: "I let the order stand."

The next edition of the Chicago Daily News carried the story "Ike's Greatest War Decision." This Keen Teen Press Club meeting was the first time Eisenhower had publicly revealed that decision and it made headlines across the country.

A high school teacher in Illinois told writer Val Lauder that she had been a Red Cross worker in England, passing out coffee and doughnuts to paratroopers at the airfield on the eve of D-day. When Eisenhower drove up, she handed him a cup of coffee, but noticed his hand was shaking so badly the hot coffee was in danger of splashing out and burning him. She gently eased the cup from his hand, and understood the incident better when she learned what he said after the war.

At Welford, General Eisenhower arrived as it was getting dark, and some troopers there saw him peek in the door of their plane and wave just before takeoff.

From Al Krochka's album: "General Eisenhower spent several hours circulating among us. As usual, his visit was well-received by all. This time, his visit was particularly welcome. His cheerfulness and ever-ready wit, his display of confidence in our ability in choosing us, to strike the first blow at the enemy . . . all of this was very heartening. He displayed all this cheerfulness even though his own problems were many. His heart was heavy because he was very down to earth and very human in his dealings with troops under his command. As he waved at the troops who were boarding the planes, it must have hurt him to know many of his sky fighters would be dead before morning. For tears were rolling down his face, yet he made no attempt to wipe them away. He just kept smiling through the tears and waving, until the last transport cleared the field."

Cricket
Toy Cricket noisemaking device (British made). This was the standard design for the infamous signaling device, made of brass with a spring-steel snapping plate attached to the bottom. As was common practice, a nail hole has been punched through this specimen to affix it to a cord and prevent loss. This one was carried by Sgt. Bill Knight, C/506, who landed near Ravenoville.

Contrary to what they told us in *The Longest Day*, few if any 82nd Airborne troopers were issued crickets. Gen. James Gavin of the 82nd later wrote: "There was a lot of gadgetry around, and a lot of it didn't make any sense. In Normandy, we used an oral password. That was enough." *Author's Collection*

Airborne Switchblade, M2
These spring-activated switchblade knives were carried in special dual zippered pockets below the front collar of M42 coats (jump jackets), and many troopers used them to cut their way out of overly-tight T-5 harnesses. This specimen was carried in Normandy by S/Sgt. Jerry Beam, I/506, who fought at Brévands. *Author's Collection*

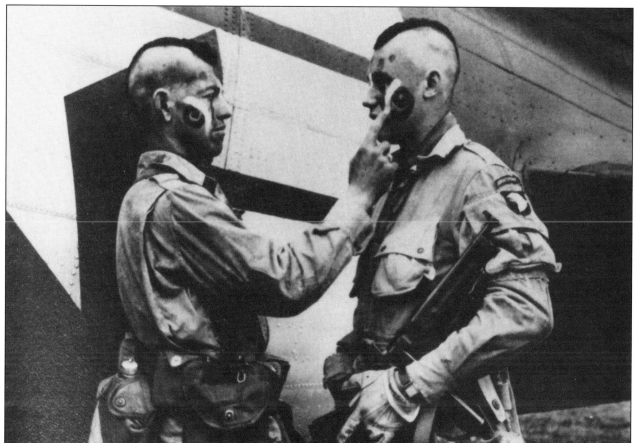

The Filthy 13

A famous photo taken at Exeter that came to symbolize not only the Filthy 13 but also the entire 101st Airborne Division in Normandy. Two demolition-saboteurs of the Filthy 13 ap-

ply war paint before boarding for D-day. Clarence C. Ware (left) was from San Pedro, California, while Charles R. Plaudo was from Minneapolis, Minnesota. *US Army*

lack" at the time.

Later in England, McNiece started his own group and there were Poles and many other ethnic groups represented in it, contrary to articles in the *Stars n Stripes*, which stated the group was composed entirely of Native Americans, with a Caucasian lieutenant who could whip them all in command.

"No reflection on Lt. Mellen," says McNiece, "but any one of our group could have whipped him without working up a sweat." Mellen was found dead in Normandy, with his arm and leg bandaged. "The first bullets didn't stop him."

Largely due to highly sensationalized articles in *Stars n Stripes* and also a famous photo showing two members of the group wearing Indian scalplocks and war paint, the Filthy 13 gained great notoriety. They were certainly the real life inspiration for the later novel and movie *The Dirty Dozen*, although none of them were criminals.

Although the roster of Filthy 13 members changed from time to time, the basic original group consisted of: Jake McNiece, Jack Womer,

John Agnew, Lt. Charles Mellen, Joseph Oleskiewicz, John Hale, James T. Green, George Radeka, Clarence Ware, Robert S. Cone, Roland R. Baribeau, James E. Leach, and Andrew Rassmussen. Others, including Frank Palys and Chuck Plaudo, were sometimes members of the group.

All Aboard For France

Shortly before Lt. Col. Robert Wolverton's men of 3/506 boarded their planes at Exeter, he led them in a prayer. As they knelt, he told them to look not down, but up at God, as he asked, "That if die we must, that we die as men would die, without complaining, without pleading, and safe in the feeling that we have done our best for what we believed was right." His request proved to be tragically appropriate because of the many casualties his battalion suffered on DZ D.

The men had spent the last hours being briefed at sand tables and there were plenty of dice and poker games day and night. A great variety of last minute haircuts had proliferated, and Ed Benecke of the HQ Battery of the 377th PFAB recalls seeing a group of 502nd PIR troopers at Membury, who stood in a row, bowed their heads, and displayed the word V-I-C-T-O-R-Y. Each trooper had one large letter of the word cut from the hair on the dome of his head.

Joe Taylor of A/501 was at Merryfield and heard Col. Howard Johnson's famous knife speech. He also recalls Johnson raising a clenched fist and shouting: "Blood!" His men screamed "Guts!" in reply.

Taylor and another friend were concerned about the depressed and haunted look of one of their fellow jumpers. They discussed his look and demeanor and agreed that they didn't think he would survive the mission. Their guess later proved to be correct.

Many men who survived Normandy to jump again into Holland have stated that they really didn't realize how terrible combat was going to be, and approached the Normandy drop with a far more casual attitude than they did future missions.

Harry T. Mole, a radioman with HQ/2 501, later wrote of the pre-jump period:

> You want to know how I felt before the invasion? Just as apprehensive as before any other jump. I think paratroops have an advantage over

other types of troops because we are as concerned with our equipment as we are with the coming battles. In other words, our thoughts are projected into so many different directions that we cannot allow ourselves to overly worry about being killed. I never gave the enemy a thought. I always felt I could handle that situation when it arose. My concern was if the plane should crash, if I should break a leg on the jump. . . . I worried about landing in water and drowning. I became airsick and worried about smelling of vomit.

Sgt. Leo Gillis of F/501 says "We felt very powerful as a group," and his lieutenant, Clair Hess later wrote, "The feeling was like we were going to play in the Super Bowl, and we would win."

Not all the troopers were so upbeat, and David Webster of E/506 wrote of his buddies as they marched toward the planes: "Nobody sang, nobody cheered—it was like a death march."

The ominous significance of what they were about to undertake was sinking in, and Joe Taylor wrote:

> When the planes started taking off we flew over England for almost two hours; it took this much time for the hundreds of planes to form the planned formation. A thousand different thoughts went through my mind during the o-so-short 21 mile Channel crossing. Everyone was unusually quiet. Absent was the usual bantering, shouting, and kidding that had always taken place before the many Stateside and England training jumps.

The Flight Across

The photos in this section were snapped in the blacked-out interior of one plane by Albert Krochka of HQ/501. Krochka was probably the only man in the airborne invasion to take photos in the plane while actually en route to Normandy. Most of the shots are candid, in that the men were not posing or prepared when Krochka's flashbulbs popped in the darkness. Thus, the men are shown napping, meditating, and simply enjoying the ride. In addition to identifying some of the faces, Krochka's original written narrative, which he penned in his personal album, accompany the shots.

These unique photos give a rare peek at the men and their equipment as they prepared to open the greatest invasion of modern history.

Krochka wrote:

> The eagle soldiers were thoughtful in that two-hour ride and some perhaps lived a lifetime in those two hours. All of us were a little tired because of the heavy equipment which was strapped very tightly to our bodies. Some of us attempted to snooze. Others just closed their eyes and relaxed as well as possible. Long, hard days lay ahead, and strength would be needed. It would be difficult to even guess what went through each man's

M/Sgt. Peter Frank
The trooper in the foreground is M/Sgt. Peter Frank, a native of Belgium, who served as interpreter. Frank later distinguished himself on the famous "Incredible Patrol" in Holland, winning the Silver Star. At right is Norman Blanchette, who died in an ambush near Neffe, Belgium, in December 1944 during the siege of Bastogne. Peter Frank reportedly returned to Belgium after the war. *Krochka*

The Flight to France
Men on both sides of the aisle; (left) Sgt. Frank and Blanchette. Standing at the end of the aisle is Lt. Beams-ley, then Tiller and Dick Thorne, facing camera. Beamsley appears to have a large map case hung under his musette bag. *Krochka*

mind as the transports roared over the country-side and out to the English Channel. On this and the following pages I attempted to catch various men's expressions while they were not aware of my actions, since the interior of the plane was dark. My own mind was occupied with cameras, flashbulbs, exposures, etc., trying to keep on my feet and at the same time hold the camera. . . .

My own mission upon reaching the ground gave me cause for concern, for I memorized both it, and a course of action. As all the rest, I had too much time, since the ride was so long, to dwell on what was in store for us. And I wondered how in the hell I ever got mixed-up in this novel way of ending an interesting life. I kept wishing that the fellas back home could see me then . . . back home!

Prayer

Last minute prayers, murmured or thought on the flight across the Channel, were a highly per-sonal matter, indulged not only by the religious and thoughtful, but even by some who didn't usu-ally talk to God.

However, many of the callow youths were oblivious to the gravity of the situation. This, com-bined with the paratroopers' necessary ability to blot out negative thoughts, gave some individuals a sense of well being. Many troopers fell asleep on the flight across. Others prayed continually, throughout the operation.

In his book, *Currahee*, Pfc. Don Burgett of A/506 wrote:

We had so much equipment on and were so un-comfortable that the best way to ride was to kneel on the floor and rest the weight of the gear and chutes on the seat itself. Later I read an account by a reporter who didn't jump but who did make the round trip in one of our planes. He wrote that we were knelt in prayer. Actually, it was just a comfortable way to ride.

Although Burgett later stated that he never attended church in his life and didn't know *how* to pray, his serene attitude indicates that he probably wouldn't have prayed anyway. He fur-ther wrote: "After taking the [airsickness] pills I felt a happy glow on and at peace with the world and even managed to sleep a little during the flight."

Art "Jumbo" DiMarzio of D/506 later recalled:

I remember it was almost like daylight in our plane, because the moon was out real bright. Lip-inski got over and got on his knees. He was pray-ing, but not out loud. He was my age, and what he was thinking about or what he thought he knew about combat was beyond me. I couldn't realize or fathom what was ahead of us. It was a . . . nothing to me . . . like a *ball* game or something . . . really not understanding it. Yet, being so naive, coming out of high school not a year earlier, going into a situation like that . . . *awesome* experience . . . *dev-astating* experience. . .

Frank Sayers
Sayers was known as "Chief," like hundreds of other Native Americans in the service. Sayers was from Ballpark, Minnesota, and worked as a hunting guide. Note his gas detection arm brassard, Griswold Bag, jump rope, Mae West, reserve chute, and other equipment. *Krochka*

A Prayer
This 506th PIR trooper, with blackened face and helmet removed, appears to be kneeling in prayer. Visible on his ankle is an M3 knife in an M8 plastic scabbard.

The 506th Parachute Infantry Prayer
(Written by Lt. James G. Morton)

Almighty God, we kneel to Thee and ask to be the instrument of Thy fury in smiting the evil forces that have visited death, misery and debasement on the people of the earth. We humbly face Thee with true penitence for all our sins for which we do most earnestly seek Thy forgiveness. Help us to dedicate ourselves completely to Thee. Be with us, God, when we leap from our planes into the dread abyss and descend in parachutes into the midst of enemy fire. Give us iron will and stark courage as we spring from the harnesses of our parachutes to seize arms for battle. The legions of evil are many, Father. Grace our arms to meet and defeat them in Thy name and in the name of freedom and dignity of man. Keep us firm in our faith and resolution, and guide us that we may not dishonor our high mission or fail in our sacred duties. Let our enemies who have lived by the sword turn from their violence lest they perish by the sword. Help us to serve Thee gallantly and to be humble in victory. Amen.

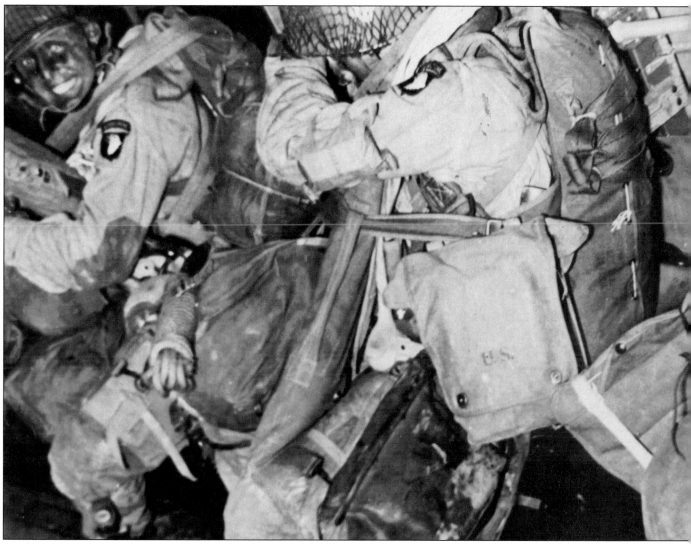

A Famous Smile
This famous shot has found its way into several publications. Flak hasn't started to greet them yet and Thorne gives a confident smile. As of this writing, Thorne lives in Arlington, Texas, while Sayers passed away in the early 1980s. *Krochka*

Chapter 3

Landing

The Troop Carrier pilots were supposed to hold their course and formation and avoid evasive action, speeding up, sudden altitude changes, and so on. But the neat formations suddenly went into dense fog and cloud banks when crossing the west coast of the Cotentin Peninsula. The pilots spread out to avoid bumping other planes in the zero visibility. By the time they emerged into clear moonlight again, they had dispersed like the spokes of a bicycle wheel. Some began trying to readjust their course but the flight over the peninsula took only about 10min. Lots of 20mm cannon fire and flak began to come up at the planes, and many pilots did take evasive action. Often, the lighted Ts of the Pathfinder teams were not visible on the ground, so pilots sometimes forgot to turn on the green light to signal the start of the jump.

On an HQ/3 501 plane, the pilot suddenly did a sharp climb, pointing the nose of the plane straight up. This caused men in the plane to slide to the tail and a few, slipping in vomit, were unable to make the jump.

Several planes went over the Channel with paratroopers still aboard—they had crossed the entire peninsula without getting a green light from the pilot. Two pilots in the DZ A serial turned the green light on anyway, resulting in the drowning of one entire stick of A/502 and most of the men in another stick of the same company. These troops drowned off the coast of Ravenoville Plage and the dead included Capt. Richard L. Davidson, the A/502 commander.

A few para officers were successful in talking their pilot into making a U-turn and taking them back over land.

Sgt. Roy Berger of HQ/3 506 was on such a plane and went up to converse with the pilot about going back over land. The pilot initially refused, and battalion legend has it that Roy had to show him his .45 automatic to persuade him. Roy denies this but admits he "convinced" the pilot to make another run over France.

The pilots were supposed to slow down as the jumpers exited their plane. At least some of them did. Sgt. Joe Kenney of E/501 noticed that his pilot slowed down and lifted the tail of the plane in textbook fashion as he and his men jumped out. Other troopers, such as Sgt. Arthur Parker and his group of the 377th PFAB, were forced to jump from aircraft that were flying too low, too fast, and were taking violent evasive action. Said Parker:

> As we came out of the fog and clouds from the west, we were supposed to be flying at 1500 feet, but we could see that we were much lower than that. Anti-aircraft fire, every color in the rainbow, started to come up and the pilots began to take evasive action. My pilot dove down, banked to the left, and picked up speed. I didn't think a C-47 could move that fast. Our plane did suffer a few hits as we could feel the old bird shudder and hear bullets and shrapnel like stones on a tin roof find the plane. No one was hit in the cabin and the red light came on. The men stood and hooked up.
>
> We moved three heavy equipment bundles to the door and hooked their static lines under difficult conditions. We were being bounced around by the evasive action of the pilot and the shell bursts rocking the plane. We managed a quick equipment check—I was third man in the stick. Our plane never did slow down to the proper jump speed. As we waited, it seemed that the sky was full of planes going in all directions at different heights, and I just knew there was going to be a midair collision or if we did jump now, we would be chewed up by the planes around us.
>
> The green light came on and out went the

Map courtesy of Ivan Worrell & 101st ABD Association

equipment bundles and away we went, ass over elbows. Everything we had tied to us was blown off by the prop blast. My chute opened with such a jerk that I thought I broke my neck and cut my balls off at the same time. All the planes that were around us a minute ago were gone and I was hanging in the sky, all alone. Just before I hit the ground, I looked around and didn't see one parachute in the sky or on the ground. I landed with a bounce and laid there for a few seconds, listening. The straps had tightened up and the long struggle to get out of my chute seemed like half an hour. I got my folding stock carbine out of its holster, loaded it, and laid it beside me. All this time, planes were crossing the sky in all directions, but no jumpers were leaving the planes . . . gave my trusty cricket a few chirps and waited for an answer. No luck.

Lt. Bill Sefton of HQ/2 501 was convinced that he was about to jump over the Channel. He could look down and see moonlight glinting on the shallows of the flooded fields east of Angoville. He knew that returning to England with the plane was out of the question. He did not exit dramatically, shouting "Bill Lee!" as prescribed. Instead, Sefton said, "Oh shit!" then "tumbled out the door like a drunk falling off a ledge."

Upon landing, he was pleasantly surprised to hit solid ground, and he had a long hike to reach the 2/501 assembly area.

Sgt. Howard Colley of 3/502 came down through the branches of an apple tree. The crashing impact dazed him to unconsciousness. He later told his friend Gordon Deramus, "The moon was shining; I heard nightingales singing like mockingbirds. . . . I awoke smelling blossoms and hearing birds singing. I thought I'd died and gone to heaven."

An unknown paratrooper who landed in and hung up in a tree near Boutteville was aided by a French teenager, Paul Mauger, who came into his backyard and found the trooper struggling to get out of his harness. Mauger stood below the trooper, who handed him a knife and asked him to help. Mauger took the knife and cut the trooper's harness straps. Before the grateful trooper vanished into the night, he gave Mauger the knife as a present. At this writing Mauger, who lives on the N-13 near Dead Man's Corner, still has it.

Many troopers, especially in the 506th PIR, dropped heavy equipment attached to their leg in a British leg bag. After their chute opened, they were supposed to lower the bag on a 20ft rope to dangle below them so the weight of the equipment therein would hit the ground before they did. A number of planes in the DZ D area flew over so fast that the opening shock ripped the bags and even some other equipment clean off each jumper. Pee Wee Martin of G/506 managed to retain his, but couldn't release it on the way down, so he had

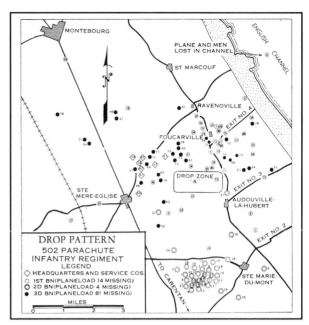

Map courtesy of Ivan Worrell and 101st ABD Association

Paul Mauger
French civilian Paul Mauger lived at Boutteville, France, in 1944. In this 1989 photo, he displays the sheath knife given to him as a present on D-day by a grateful American paratrooper who Mauger cut down from a tree. *Author's Collection*

to land with it attached to his leg. Miraculously, his leg wasn't broken.

Various colored lanterns, bells, whistles, bugles, and other signaling devices were brought to Normandy to aid in night assembly on the ground, but few troopers saw or heard them. The typical troopers landed in isolation in a dark field, with nobody in sight, except perhaps some cows or horses. But on DZ D, the Germans had ignited a large barn doused with benzine. This gave an eerie brightness to the scene and the first troopers to land there could see following men actually coming out the door of their transports, clearly visible from the ground. It was a dramatic scene as some of the planes were on fire and losing altitude as the paras bailed out.

Most feared of all were water landings. The shock of hitting cold water after a brief descent in darkness had a terrible effect. With many pounds of deadweight equipment strapped on, a number of troopers drowned in even the shallow water created by the flooding from the LaBarquette Lock. The fields south of Angoville were inundated and symmetrical deep ditches (some as deep as 8ft) crossed

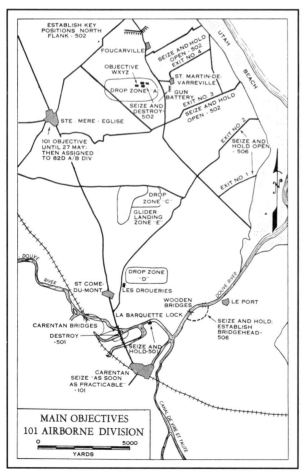

Map courtesy of Ivan Worrell and 101st ABD Association

at intervals. Many troopers far west in the 82nd Airborne's area also drowned in floods from the Merderet River.

The flooded ditches and fields became a trying obstacle for the survivors as well. In navigating across the shallow floods of the fields, they had to wade across the ditches, some of which had barbed wire on the bottom, under the water.

The Air Corps pilots in many cases also dropped their sticks at a low altitude, allowing barely enough time for the chute to pop open before landing. T-5 Hugh Pritchard of D/506 landed in chest deep water with a heavy radio strapped to his leg. He had only about eight seconds to prepare for landing after his chute opened. He wrenched his back from the opening shock and could not release the bag from his leg before landing. The wind caught his canopy and dragged him, repeatedly. His account in George Koskimaki's book *D-day With the Screaming Eagles* (Vantage Press, 1970) says:

. . . just as I started to unhook my harness, the chute jerked me down and I was dragged face down in the water. Fortunately, when I thought I could hold my breath no longer, the chute stopped and I scrambled to my feet and was able to gulp a few breaths before being jerked down again. This was repeated several times before the canopy collapsed in the water. I know I am not the bravest man in the world, nor do I think of myself as a coward. But the stark terror I saw and lived through in the Normandy campaign, and especially the first night, remains so vivid even today, that sometimes I wake up in a cold sweat and nearly jump out of bed.

Father Francis L. Sampson, the Catholic chaplain of the 501st PIR, landed in a flooded area east of DZ D. He lost his government-issued Mass (Communion) Kit in waist deep water then was dragged some distance away from it by his chute. When he returned to the approximate spot where he had dropped the kit, he retrieved it by diving under the murky water a number of times. He got it on the sixth try. This incident was depicted in the movie *The Longest Day*, but for some reason a British "Padre" was shown performing the dives instead of Father Sam.

A number of daring troopers jumped with a fully assembled bazooka in addition to a rifle or submachine gun and all the other usual equipment. These landings were tricky to say the least. Dick Knudson of F/506 did it and broke his pelvis on landing. His days in the paratroops were over and he laid in no-man's land outside St. Mere Eglise for several days before being evacuated.

Gus Liapes of HQ/1 506 belonged to a special squad of bazookamen known as the "Ha-Ha Squad" or the "8-Ball Squad." This group was under command of Lt. Wayne "Bull" Winans (KIA in

Holland). Liapes landed with a fully assembled bazooka in the V of land formed by the roads north of Dead Man's Corner. He succeeded in landing without breaking any bones, and killed a German who rushed him before he could get out of his harness. Gus had been in the 29th Division Rangers before transferring to the paratroops.

Some troopers landed on barbed wire fences and got hung up. Joe "Pappy" Walkowski, of G/502, landed on such a fence and got twisted around in it. He was injured and trapped and unable to get loose for two days, whereupon he was evacuated to England. A member of F/502 was killed by his own M-1 rifle when he leaned it against another barbed wire fence with the safety off and climbed over. A twig caught the trigger and fired the weapon as he was going over.

One of the most memorable stories about D-day night comes from Capt. Cecil Simmons, who commanded H/502. When he was growing up, Simmons and his twin brother took many belt thrashings from their father, a hard-nosed disciplinarian. He would take the boys in the bathroom, bend them over the toilet, and lash away with a belt. Simmons' brother would cry and yell, but Cecil practiced being silent, despite the pain. He later told his wife, Madge, that this training proved useful on D-day.

Simmons had barely gotten out of his chute when he became aware of many German troops running in his direction. He jumped off the road and concealed himself in the gorse in the ditch near the shoulder. But Simmons left one hand out, lying flat on the shoulder. A German soldier ran up, stood right on Simmons' hand with his hobnailed boot, and spun around, looking for American parachutists. Seeing no one, he darted off to continue searching. Germans were running everywhere in this area, but Big Cecil stayed quiet, which saved his life.

Not far from there, Sgt. Gordon Little, of S-2/502, was moving along a ditch east of St. Mere Eglise with a medic named Rogge. They spotted a road sign and Rogge walked up to try and read it. As he stood there in the moonlight, a German dispatch rider pulled up on a motorcycle. Little was only a few yards away in the ditch—he blew the startled German right out of his seat with a burst from his Tommy gun.

The men soon learned there were many, many Germans in the area and they began moving quickly eastward, evading large enemy groups for most of the night. A slug went through the crown of Little's helmet before dawn.

This may be an apocryphal story, but Glen Bartlett of HQ/3 501 swears it's true. Moving in the area east of St. Marie du Mont in the morning darkness, Bartlett's group encountered an American MP who was soaking wet. The man said he

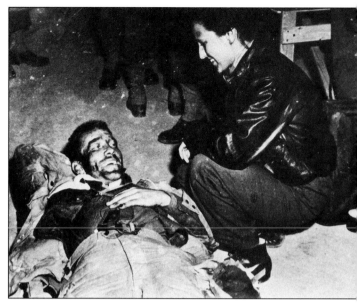

Wounded Trooper
Back in England, a trooper who was seriously hurt by flak in his plane tried to jump anyway, but the Air Corps crew restrained him. Helen Briggs-Ramsey suggests this might be John P. Androsky of G/506, who was killed several months later in Holland. *US Army Air Corps*

had joined the army to fight and had jumped into the Channel from a boat in the invasion fleet several miles off shore. He had swam to shore and was allowed to join the 101st in fighting behind Utah Beach.

Capt. Frank L. Brown of the Pathfinders reported on experiences of his men upon landing. One of the best ones reads:

The Pathfinders, having accomplished their mission, were attempting to infiltrate through the German defenses and reach the 101st Division Command Post. A group of one officer and five men were moving away from the DZ. A sergeant requested permission to return to the DZ and attempt to locate more of the men and lead them to the CP. Permission was granted and en route the NCO saw a group of seven men moving along a road. A low wall separated him from the group. Taking cover behind the wall, he challenged the group, thinking possibly that they were friendly. One of the group came forward and at a distance of about four feet, answered the challenge in German. The sergeant immediately opened fire and emptied a thirty-round clip into the nearest of the enemy. Dropping behind the wall, he threw two fragmentation grenades over the wall and reloaded his weapon. Rising, he again opened fire. Two of the group escaped. In relating the incident, the sergeant cursed fervently and blamed the escape to poor light and lack of guts on the part of the Germans. Although the American was fired upon, he apparently so surprised the enemy that their fire was inaccurate and he was unhurt.

"Rommel's Asparagus"

"Rommel's Asparagus" were simply tree trunks transplanted into open fields by the Germans and were intended to smash gliders upon landing or impale descending paratroopers. Some had barbed wire running from the top to the ground like Maypoles. Others had wire from top to top. Most were not completed by D-day. Many French civilians had been pressed into work gangs to help install these poles. At first light on D-day, many US paras were dismayed to see French civilians busily installing them as usual. The area near St. Marie du Mont was heavily planted with such poles, and some were reported on DZ D. Due to the shortage of wood in Normandy, the French used all of them for other purposes after the war.

Prior to being briefly captured, Lt. Jim Haslam, a 501st officer who had landed on DZ D with the Pathfinders, hid for almost a whole day in a large hole that had been dug for one of the poles. Jim and several others were captured by a small squad of Germans who used them as point men, forcing them to walk in the vanguard each time they moved. While double-timing past a church with an aid station inside, the Germans pointed at the entrance and kept running as the POWs trotted right into the entrance. Haslam and his companions were free and continued to serve in future battles.

Evidence that the Germans had plans to make the pole obstacles even more deadly was presented by former 101st Division Chief of Staff Col. Gerald Higgins. Writing in George Koskimaki's consummate history, *D-day With the Screaming Eagles,* Higgins recalled: "One

"Rommel's Asparagus" in a Norman field. *Krochka*

captured German officer, who had been in charge of planting the poles in the fields, told us that the Germans calculated the earliest date the Allies could make the drop and the invasion proper, would be the 21st of June. Accordingly, they had their sights set on finishing the job by 15 June, with the real pressure to be put on in the last ten days. In fact, in order to keep the mines which were attached to the barbed wire strung from pole to pole from being detonated by grazing cows, the mines were not to be activated until the 18th of June. After that, the French were to keep their cattle out of those fields, under penalty of their cows being shot. As you know, this never came to pass as the invasion took place some two weeks earlier than their calculations."

Lt. Col. Robert Cole, commanding 3/502, landed in a huge rosebush and struggled helplessly to get out for 15min, the thorns tormenting his face and hands. He was finally able to reach his trench knife and cut his way out. In the process, he lost his cricket and the first man he encountered was

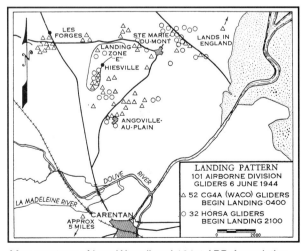

Map courtesy of Ivan Worrell and 101st ABD Association

Capt. George Buker, the regimental S-2 officer. Buker recalls clicking his cricket at a silhouetted trooper in the darkness. He heard a voice say "Who is that?" in an irritated tone. It turned out to be Cole, who explained he had lost his cricket. (This contradicts the account in the book *Night Drop,* based on what Cole told S.L.A. Marshall.)

Cole moved west for some time, gathering more men, until they knocked at a door and a French-speaking 82nd trooper determined that they were on the edge of St. Mere Eglise. Cole reversed directions and met a group under Lt. Richard Winters, of E/506. They marched east for some time, ambushing a convoy of German soldiers and horse-drawn wagons. The Germans were decimated by combined fire from both sides of the road, but Maj. J. W. Vaughn of the 502nd was killed while attacking a three-man German machine gun crew. He fired into them as he fell dead from their fire.

When the force reached the D-14, Winters struck off to the south with his men, and Cole dispersed the 502nd personnel to cover exits 3 and 4, where they were able to ambush retreating Germans later in the morning.

We shall never hear the stories of troopers who were killed before they could get out of their harnesses, but some, like Cecil Hutt of G/506, went down shooting and survived to tell about it. Hutt found himself in a sizable group on D-day night, but they didn't want to move. Impatient to get on to his objective at Brévands, Hutt found a kindred spirit in Cpl. Stanley Zebrosky of I/506. They set off down the road together and were ambushed en route to the bridges. A fusillade of bullets came from Germans concealed in bushes. Zebrosky fell dead and Hutt heaved a grenade and sprayed the bushes with his weapon before going down with multiple wounds. He managed to kill one German and wound two others before being captured. Hutt spent the duration as a POW.

Some troopers actually experienced a peaceful landing—Maj. Hank Hannah, S-3/506, had jumped without a long gun, armed only with his rechambered .38cal Colt Peacemaker and a trench knife. He set off to find Culloville with a grenade in one hand, a pistol in the other, and his trench knife in his teeth. He wrote in his journal:

> The night was clear and cool, the air was fragrant, the grass long and green, the fields small. There were many dairy cattle and horses roaming in the fields like shadows. Nearly all fence rows and roadsides had high banks and trees. I was thrilled beyond words.

Cpl. Stan Zebrosky
Zebrosky (left) of I/506 teamed up with Cecil Hutt (not shown) of G/506 on D-day night. A German ambush killed Zebrosky and made Hutt a POW. In this 1943 photo, Jerry Beam of I/506 stands at right. *Beam*

Chappuis and Vaughn
Lt. Col. Steve Chappuis (left) and Maj. J. W. Vaughn were photographed at Ft. Bragg in 1943. Chappuis' 2nd Battalion was to take the guns at St. Martin d. V. de Varreville. Vaughn was killed when Cole's group ambushed a German convoy on D-day night. *Buker*

Chapter 4

St. Marcouf

The northern boundary of the consolidated 101st Airborne drop was in the Crisbec-St. Marcouf area. Most of the troopers who landed north of there were either killed or captured. Dozens of troopers landed in the northern areas of Montebourg, Valognes, Quinéville, and St. Vaast la Hocque. Most of the men who landed south of Crisbec managed to fight their way south to rejoin their units, although too late to arrive at their objectives on D-day.

Troops who landed in the St. Marcouf area were about 10mi north of their assigned DZs near St. Martin de Varreville and St. Marie du Mont. The Crisbec gun battery area was the scene of some early encounters between American parachutists and German Marines on D-day night. Troopers who came down in the area southwest of St. Marcouf found a number of coastal gun emplacements in concrete casements. Several hundred over-aged German Naval reservists under command of a Lt. Ohmsen manned them. The average age of Ohmsen's troops was thirty-eight, but

the canny older men would fight with distinction. At the position were four 210mm guns, one 150mm gun, and six 75mm anti-aircraft guns. In the months before D-day, Allied bombers had dumped some 600 tons of bombs on the concrete fortifications, but failed to destroy them. Indeed, half a century later, they are still a major tourist attraction, although the guns have been removed for salvage.

German historian Paul Carrell, in his book *Invasion—They're Coming* (Bantam Books and E.P. Dutton), described early encounters between members of the 502nd PIR, misdropped near Crisbec, with some of Ohmsen's garrison. Around 0100 on 6 June 1944, Ohmsen's men were alerted to Allied parachutists landing in their area. Some of the German Marines went on patrol in the darkness and heard strange clicking sounds coming from the bushes. They butt-stroked a paratrooper who tried to signal them with his cricket device. As they continued walking in the area, more soldiers challenged them with the clicking device. According to Carrell, Ohmsen's men soon realized that the cricket was a recognition signal and proceeded to equip themselves with more and more captured crickets, with which they were able to capture or kill a number of other troopers.

Some of the troopers who were taken prisoner in this manner were later liberated and told media reporters that an intelligence leak before D-day had given the Germans information on the crickets. They were under the impression that the German Army had supplied its troops in Normandy with crickets of their own.

The cricket signaling device got mixed reviews. Pfc. Charles O'Neill of F/501 says "The first thing I did was throw mine away." But Maj. Allen W. "Pinky" Ginder of the 502nd felt the person who conceived the cricket idea deserved a medal. If Carrell's story is true, we can realize in retrospect what actually occurred.

Ohmsen, who later became an admiral in the West German Navy, had quite a saga of his own. His reservists would wage a private war of their own with the US fleet sitting off the coast near Utah Beach. For seven days, the battered garrison held out, claiming one US destroyer sunk (the US Navy claims the destroyer hit a mine in the Channel) and repulsing numerous infantry attacks from

Guns of Crisbec
One of the huge guns at Crisbec was photographed by Lt. Jim Haslam, a Mormon from Utah, who jumped as Pathfinder security on D-day. Haslam spent a brief period as a POW then mistakenly headed north in search of his regiment. He got as far as St. Marcouf before changing directions. *Haslam*

the 4th Infantry Division, as well as heavy counterbattery fire from the US Navy. In one assault, US engineers actually succeeded in surmounting the casements to plant demolitions charges but were killed by artillery shells before they could set them. Ohmsen had called for artillery on his position from neighboring German guns at Azeville. When an assault group from the 9th Division was brought in, they were relieved to find that Ohmsen's garrison had withdrawn to the north. He had received orders to fall back to Cherbourg with his survivors.

Ravenoville and St. Marcouf
On D-day morning, Sgt. Benecke and his group from A Battery, 377th PFAB were on the loose between Ravenoville and St. Marcouf, as this photo proves. *Benecke*

St. Marcouf
One of the most famous invasion photos was taken near the wall of the church in St. Marcouf. The US government's official history, *Utah Beach to Cherbourg*, gives the information that the men pictured are from the 4th Infantry Division. But blackened faces, bloused trousers, gauze arm-

flags, and trench knives on ankles all point to them being paratroopers. Men of the 508th PIR were in the area and wore the gauze flags, as did troopers of the 506th PIR. The stairway is blown down to rubble by one of the 8in guns of the cruiser USS *Quincy*. *US Army*

Chapter 5

Ravenoville

So many troopers of the 101st Airborne and even the 82nd Airborne landed in the vicinity of Ravenoville that it became a hub of activity on D-day. Men of the 502nd PIR, 506th PIR, and 377th PFAB assembled on the outskirts and eventually wrested the town from a strong German garrison of at least a company in strength. The photos that appear in this section suggest the confusion that reigned as troopers came into the town from the north and east, but departed headed east or south.

To add to the confusion, there is another group of dwellings known as Ravenoville Plage (Beach), situated on the coast. The actual town of Raven-

oville proper is several kilometers inland from the Channel. Don Burgett's A/506 stick landed near Ravenoville Plage and worked their way west, eventually attacking the German garrison in Ravenoville proper in a spontaneous attack led by Lt. William Muir, a former policeman from Bay City, Michigan. Although Burgett credits Muir with leading the attack, an enlisted man of the same company was decorated with the Silver Star for leading the attack that resulted in the capture of Ravenoville. Pvt. (soon to be sergeant) Donald Brinninstool, of Jackson, Michigan, was credited with aggressive leadership in orders for his Silver Star. According to the write up, Brinninstool's ag-

French Family at Ravenoville, D-day
This remarkable photo was taken on D-day morning outside Ravenoville. Sgt. Benecke of the 377th PFAB encountered this French family sheltering from the naval and aerial bombardment of their and other coastal villages. It is possible that they heard the BBC radio broadcast on 6 June after midnight, warning French coast dwellers to move inland and take cover. *Benecke*

gressiveness resulted in ten enemy dead, thirty captured, and the capture of an ammo dump, two recon cars, and a staff car.

It is unknown if Burgett and Brinninstool fought in the same group on D-day, but in any case, the German garrison was driven from the heavy stone houses in Ravenoville by a relatively small force of troopers. There was some fighting in and near the town church, and a Renault tankette was captured in the area.

Charles "Red" Knight, an A/506 man from Speedway, Indiana, was in a small band of troopers who were captured early on D-day. When the Germans searched him, they found a canned chicken which had been sent by Brinninstool's mother before the invasion. Not wanting the Germans to enjoy the chicken, Knight lied and told them the can contained explosives. The Germans made him dig a hole and bury it. "We would have liked to mark that grave," he said later. The troopers never did get back to dig up that chicken. Shortly afterward, Knight and his group escaped and went on to fight through the war with the 506th. Contrary to previous reports, Brinninstool says he was not in the captured group and was at no time ever a POW.

Being captured and then escaping was to become a common experience within the 101st Airborne. Many troopers were captured while in the midst of the enemy only to be liberated a matter of minutes or hours later when the circumstances changed.

Sgt. Bill Knight of C/506 met a small group from his company and they hid out for the first two days in the yard of an ancient farmstead near Ravenoville. Lts. Albert Hassenzahl and Bill Pyne, also of C/506, led a group of their men east out of Ravenoville to the coast, then followed the coast road south toward their original objectives in the DZ C area.

Most of the troops who left Ravenoville headed directly south on the D-14, toward Foucarville. Burgett's group did so early on 7 June, after spending the night in Ravenoville. The A Company group of the 506th repulsed a German counterattack that night, during which a concussion grenade landed in Lt. Muir's foxhole, exploding between the dirt wall of the hole and the gas mask in the rubberized invasion bag attached to Muir's leg. The concussion of the blast broke Muir's femur. He tried to walk south with the group that departed the next morning, but couldn't keep up. He stayed behind and was evacuated to England.

Paratroopers Advance
This photo of paratroopers warily advancing past their own dead is usually attributed to the Carentan area, but Don Burgett of A/506 claims he saw the photographer take the picture at Ravenoville on 7 June. *US Army*

En route to Foucarville early on 7 June, Burgett's group walked through an area along the D-14 that had been totally desolated by naval or aerial bombardment. The area was spooky looking as Burgett reported in his book, *Currahee*:

On the march we passed through a section that had been blasted to rubble. I don't know whether it was from bombing or shelling from one of the large battleships. The trees were shredded stumps with wisps of smoke or ground fog laced through them. The ground was plowed into loose dirt with large craters scattered all over. The whole scene reminded me of some oil paintings I had seen that were reputed to have been done by some demented artist. Not a single bird flew in the area nor did I see an insect on the ground. A deadly silence hung over the area like a suffocating blanket.

The shuffling of our boots, along with an occasional pebble being kicked across the hard surface of the blacktop sounded loud. I thought to myself that this must be the home of death itself.

We kept walking and soon left the desolate place behind. The fields on either side of the road became greener and more peaceful as we moved along.

On a lighter note, as Sgt. Ed Benecke of the 377th PFAB was walking out of Ravenoville with other stray troops, he noticed that snipers seemed to be singling him out. More enemy fire seemed to come in Benecke's direction. He eventually figured out it was caused by the squirrel's tail he had attached to the back of his helmet, so he took it off.

Chapter 6

Foucarville

Pre-invasion planners had decided that Foucarville was to be the far north flank of their airborne bridgehead. A known strong point on a fortified hill near the north edge of the town had been identified. A barrage from the 377th PFAB was to eradicate it; and the 1/502 was to establish roadblocks to prevent German reinforcements from driving to Utah Beach from the north or west.

Shortly after 0100 on D-day, a small group under Capt. Cleveland Fitzgerald, CO of B/502, assembled and "attacked" the town. S.L.A. Marshall wrote in *Night Drop* that this was the first French

1/502 Company Commanders
Shown before D-day are Richard L. Davidson (top left), Cleveland Fitzgerald (top right), Warner Broughman (bottom left), and Fred Hancock (bottom right). *Smit*

town to be brought under attack by American forces on D-day.

In the courtyard of one house, Fitzgerald killed a German at point-blank range, but received a bullet through his chest in return. He told his men he was dying and wanted them to leave him. He was saved, however, but died a year later in a car crash in Reims, France, after V-E Day.

A number of 502nd PIR troopers dropped almost on top of the fortified strong point and were immediately captured. Lt. Joseph Smith was one of them. He was shot and captured after giving the Germans quite a battle. Other POWs on the fortified hill included Sgt. Charlie Ryan, and Hewitt Tippins, both of A/502.

Throughout D-day, Ryan and his buddies plotted a way to escape. They acted apprehensive and told their captors that the planned artillery barrage was going to wipe the hill off the map in the evening. The Germans became restless and unsure of their situation. In the evening, part of the German force broke and ran from the position, leaving others behind who wished to surrender. Troops outside opened fire on the fleeing Germans and they were killed. Ryan killed the German major who had commanded the strong point, and acquired his pistol.

There was shooting in all parts of the town throughout D-day, with persistent sniping from the church steeple. Pvt. John T. Lyell was among those killed, and A/502 characters like Asay, Zweibel, and Nicolai kept the Germans busy.

A stray trooper from the 82nd Airborne had stayed in the bushes near the church all day because he didn't feel like fighting. Late in the day, he saw several Germans coming out the church door a few feet away and shot them all.

Capt. Jim Hatch was in town late in the evening and was too tired to guard his prisoners. He placed them in a wooden farm shed, told them to throw their boots outside, sprinkled thumbtacks outside the door, and slept soundly.

502nd Machine Gunners
Troopers of the 502nd PIR pose with their M-1919A4 light machine gun in Normandy. *Musura*

Left
Lt. Wallace Swanson
Swanson assumed command of A/502 after the company CO, Capt. Richard Davidson, drowned in the Channel. Swanson set up a road block west of Foucarville that was instrumental in preventing German reinforcements from reaching the coast. This Stateside photo shows Swanson wearing his prized leather A-2 flight jacket with chest insignia of the 502nd PIR. *Swanson*

Survivors
Surviving officers of 1/502 posed in France near the end of the campaign. (Standing, left to right) Hancock, Choy, Hatch, Michaelis, Schmidt, Smit, Cassidy, Sutliffe, Dr. William Best. (Below, left) Emzy W. Gaydon. (Below, right) Sid Clary and Wally Swanson. *Choy*

Chapter 7

St. Germaine de Varreville

Although Capt. Frank Lillyman's Pathfinder team had rendezvoused at the small church in St. Germaine, that village continued to be a passing point for troops moving north as well as south on D-day. Lt. Col. Pat Cassidy, the CO of 1/502, landed right on the main crossroads of the D-14 and came under machine gun fire immediately. Like Lillyman, Cassidy moved south, toward the gun batteries of St. Martin de Varreville. Cassidy's main focus was to set up a battalion CP at Objective W (see Chapter 9).

Lt. Col. Strayer's 2/506 passed through St. Germaine as well in the early morning darkness.

St. Germaine de Varreville, 1990s
Part of the small village of St. Germaine de Varreville as seen looking south on the D-14, in the early 1990s. Lt. Col. Patrick Cassidy's parachute landing put him down in the crossroads at left. He came under immediate machine gun fire, but escaped to make his way to Objective W.

This group had landed and assembled near Foucarville, far north of their intended DZ and were moving south toward their objectives.

Lt. Col. Cassidy was a man of many roles on D-day and figured in the events at a number of locations. He made important decisions during the XYZ fight, and in the afternoon was personally reconning a route toward C Company's fight near Haut Fornel.

Cassidy's battalion was hailed by S.L.A. Marshall as the unit that did the one best job for America on D-day. But Cassidy had his human foibles as well.

In a letter dated 1991 from C. E. "Jack" Applegate of 2/502 to his wartime buddy Ray Hood, Applegate recalled spending the first five days in Normandy with Cassidy's group. In the brief story that follows, Applegate recalls Cassidy with typically rough GI humor:

> Me and my buddy had been through Demolitions School; I was skinny then, so I carried a lot of explosives. Every time we got near Cassidy, he yelled at us to get the Hell away from him! He seemed to have a spring in him. Every time anyone saluted him, he'd scream "You son of a bitch" and hit the ground!!! You suppose he was afraid of snipers???? I guess he'd heard they like to shoot at officers.

Lt. Wally Swanson, who assumed command of A/502, had landed in the salt marshes near the coast, close to Exit 4. He led his assembled group to the gun batteries, then north through St. Germaine to establish roadblocks near Foucarville.

Of course, the usual hedgerow hide-and-seek and defense against German probes went on in the area throughout D-day.

Chapter 8

Haut Fornel—The Legend of Smit's Pond

D-day afternoon saw elements of C/502 probing toward Beuzeville in the confusing maze of hamlets west of Foucarville. Lt. Morton J. Smit and Pvt. Harold Boone found themselves on point, entering the courtyard of a sizable chateau in Haut Fornel. This chateau had been used as a German barracks (in a 1992 correspondence to the author, Smit felt that the chateau was more likely used as a CP rather than a barracks). The compound was filled with enemy equipment, although it was presently devoid of troops. When a truckful of Germans pulled up in front of the stone gate, Smit and Boone sprayed the debarking soldiers with their weapons, inflicting about ten casualties.

Like hornets from an aroused nest, the surviving Germans began swarming into the courtyard in search of the Americans. Smit and Boone ran through the chateau then out the back door (in that same later correspondence, Smit also indicated he ran around the back of the building after firing at the Germans, rather than through the inside). The two Americans found the back wall too high to surmount with their weapons and equipment. Encountering an algae-covered pond in one corner of the courtyard, they slid into the water and submerged until hidden from view of the searching Germans.

In *Night Drop*, S.L.A. Marshall has a carbine-equipped Smit breathing with just his lips and nose protruding through the algae. Smit's own account in Koskimaki's *D-day* says he disassembled his M-3 Grease Gun, and breathed through the barrel, while submerged. Smit says the idea was derived from watching a Western movie shortly before the invasion.

The troopers succeeded in hiding this way for nearly an hour, until attacking Americans drove the Germans out. A trooper named Lesinski saw Smit emerging from the water and nearly ran him through with his bayonet. He couldn't recognize the muck-covered officer until Smit shouted to identify himself, just in time.

As the story goes, the Germans counterattacked at that moment, causing all three troopers to enter the pond for another extended period of hiding.

Lt. Morton J. Smit, C/502
Smit and Pvt. Harold Boone were trapped in a walled courtyard and saved themselves by submerging themselves in a pond.

Sgt. Charles Tinsley was also in the area and is credited in Smit's written account as being the man who almost ran him through with the bayonet. But Tinsley himself, interviewed in 1992, did not recall the incident.

The chateau had remained mostly unchanged until the present owners bought it in the early 1980s. Much work has been done to repair the roof, heighten and expand the wall, renovate the pond, and terrace the yard.

Capt. Fred Hancock
Hancock commanded C/502. He and his men sprung an ambush east of Haut Fornel that stopped German reinforcements from reaching the coast. *Smit*

Lt. Col. Patrick Cassidy
A fine study of Cassidy, CO of 1/502. S.L.A. Marshall wrote of the battalion saying it "did the one best job for America on D-day." *Buker*

Mystery Solved
Lt. Bernard Bucior (far left) of C/502 was seriously wounded at Haut Fornel, and staggered back toward the beach for evacuation. En route, he met Lt. Col. Cassidy, but reportedly vanished between there and the beach. S.L.A. Marshall called his disappearance "one of the haunting mysteries of the Normandy campaign." In 1969, a C/502 enlisted man named Phillip Shofner, read Marshall's book *Night Drop* and wrote to the *502 Newsletter* saying he had also been wounded and saw Lt. Bucior at Utah Beach. The boat evacuating Bucior hit a mine in the Channel and all aboard were lost. Also pictured are Lt. Thomas Cahill and Lt. Jack A. Borcherdt, also of C Company. *Smit*

Chapter 9

St. Martin de Varreville

Allied planners considered the St. Martin de Varreville area of high military importance because of the four concrete-emplaced 122mm guns situated in a field southwest of the village and the series of stone houses west of the village (at Mesiéres), which housed their crews. The large guns were reportedly captured on the Russian Front and brought to Normandy to help protect the "Westwall."

Because of the trajectory of these large caliber guns, they were sited some 2–3mi behind the coast, to cover Exits 3 and 4. The guns were manned by the 1st Battalion of the 1261st Army Coastal Artillery Regiment.

The RAF had bombed the field where the guns were situated on 29 May. The field was bombed again on the night of 5 June, just before the paratroopers dropped. It developed that on 29 May, one bunker had caved in (possibly from the sheer weight of 500lb bombs landing on the roof, as the other three bunkers were undamaged), and the 122mm gun at this collapsed bunker was trapped out in front of it. The Germans, realizing that the position had been pinpointed, hastily moved the other three guns away from that site to an unknown location.

The final bombing had torn up the field and tossed crates full of German munitions and equipment all over the field. A small Renault tankette had been flipped over by the bombing. When Capt. Lillyman's small group scouted the location near dawn on D-day, they located the field and found it was deserted, with the guns removed. Leaving part of his force behind, Lillyman went back up the D-14, where he met Lt. Col. Cassidy and reported what he had found. The absence of the guns was a major relief as they had been considered a serious threat to the D-day beach landings. Lt. Col. Steve Chappuis, CO of 2/502 arrived and stayed at the bombed field to intercept his troops as they arrived and to reorganize them for another assignment.

It is interesting to note that at least one trooper landed right in the field where the gun battery was situated. He was Lt. Gordon Deramus, of HQ/3 502.

Capt. LeGrand "Legs" Johnson commanded F/502. He later recalled that F Company had won a competition during training in England and was

Objective W, 1990s
In June 1944, this house was known as Objective W. It actually lies west of the town of St. Martin de Varreville northwest of the intersection of the D-14 with the Mesiéres Road. Pre-invasion planners had earmarked it for Lt. Col. Pat Cassidy's 1/502 CP. When Col. George Moseley broke his leg on the drop and failed to show up at the designated regimental CP at Loutres, France, Lt. Col. Mike Michaelis assumed command of the 502nd PIR, moving his assembled group into the house at Objective W and establishing it as the new regimental CP. From here S/Sgt. Harrison Summers of B/502 jumped off on his epic assault on the group of houses along the Mesiéres road, known as Objective XYZ.

During D-day afternoon, Lt. Joseph Pangerl, the IPOW officer of the 502nd, began interrogating German prisoners in the kitchen of Objective W. As he spoke to a prisoner, two fully armed and equipped German soldiers emerged from the root cellar of the house, acting surprised that there were Americans in the house. They surrendered to Pangerl without incident.

About 1km east of Objective W lies the small village of St. Martin de Varreville. Not much fighting took place there, although a patrol drove some Germans out of the church and captured a radio transmitter and an arms cache. These items were placed in the street and blown up with explosives. *Author's Photo*

POWs Digging Trenches, D-day
This photo has appeared in print before, with the erroneous information that the German POWs are digging graves near Hiesville. It was actually taken D-day afternoon, behind Objective W. The POWs are digging trenches to repulse the anticipated German counterattacks from the west, which might threaten the CP. Shortly after the photo was taken, the guard with the Tommy gun shot a German who walked over to the bushes at the side of the field without permission. Hearing the shots, Lt. Pangerl and Sgt. Patheiger rushed out and talked to the wounded POW. He stated he wasn't trying to escape but only wanted to urinate, and was too shy to ask permission. Another photo, which does show POWs digging graves, was taken by Sgt. Benecke of the 377th PFAB (see Chapter 15). *Musura*

designated as the assault company of 2/502. They had envisioned storming the de Varreville battery bunkers with artillery support from the 377th PFAB. The plan, if all else failed, was to use ropes and grappling hooks to surmount the bunkers in-

dividually and plant explosive charges. Legs recalls scouring English hardware stores before D-day to find the ropes and grappling hooks, which were dropped in an equipment bundle but never recovered by his men. He later said, "No doubt some French farmer found that bundle and wondered how we hoped to defeat the enemy with grappling hooks."

In the years since WWII, the field housing the gun bunkers has not been a tourist attraction because of its obscure location. Accessible only via a two track cart path, even many history-minded residents of the Cotentin Peninsula don't know the location. Add to this the fact that the farmer who owns the field doesn't want tourists tramping around it (he has even covered the bunkers with rose and raspberry bushes). Three of the four bunkers are intact, with subterranean tunnels connecting them. The fact that two heavy bombing raids, concentrated on four bunkers in an area about the size of a football field, failed to destroy three of the four bunkers is interesting. Like the bunkers at Crisbec, it is evidence of the ineffectiveness of aerial bombardment on concrete fortifications.

S/Sgt. Harrison Summers at the XYZ Complex

Although this section is being included with the St. Martin de Varreville chapter, the series of stone houses that housed the German artillerymen were actually in the hamlet of Mesiéres, just west of St. Martin. Starting from Cassidy's CP at Objective W near the D-14/Mesiéres crossroads, S/Sgt. Harrison Summers led the attack on the complex.

After visiting the area, one realizes that the

Gun Battery Site, D-day
Upon arriving at the gun battery site on D-day morning, Capt. Frank Lillyman took this photo showing the field plowed up and a Renault tankette flipped over from the bombing. *Lillyman*

The Bunkers, 1990s
One of the bunkers photographed in the 1990s—the farmer has disguised them with rose and raspberry bushes. *Author's Photo*

502nd Troopers Guard Prisoners
On 7 June 1944, Sgt. Benecke of the 377th PFAB passed through the St. Martin de Varreville area and snapped this photo of 502nd troopers guarding German prisoners. *Benecke*

term "barracks complex," which has been applied to the area in previous writing, is misleading. The term "barracks" conjures up rectangular buildings all of a relatively uniform shape, size, and type of construction. This XYZ complex is nothing but a series of stone constructed old French farmhouses of varying shapes and sizes, which straddle both sides of the Mesiéres road west of the D-14. The 122mm gun battery that was situated several hundred yards away, across the D-14, was manned by troops who had simply commandeered this group of houses to billet troops in.

When Summers started out on D-day morning to drive German troops from the series of houses, he had an understrength platoon to work with, most of whom were strays from other companies and didn't know him or each other. This made them reluctant to follow orders and reticent about joining the fight. Many were no doubt preoccupied with thoughts of their own assigned objectives.

As a result, Summers became a one-man army, attacking each house in the complex single-handedly, although he was joined from time to time by other individuals. By the time he had reached Building 11 in mid-afternoon, Summers had personally killed several dozen enemy soldiers and routed a company or battery sized unit of over 100 men.

After taking Building 11, Summers sat down for a smoke. When asked about his behavior that day, he later said: "I have no idea why I did what I did that day. I know now that it was a crazy thing to do and I wouldn't do it again under the same

Destroyed by a Bangalore Torpedo
Capt. LeGrand Johnson, CO of F/502, says that T-4 Frank Clay of his company found a bangalore torpedo in an equipment bundle and used it to spike the barrel of the only remaining gun at the St. Martin de Varreville battery. *Musura*

circumstances. The other men were hanging back—they didn't seem to want to fight."

If the 101st ever had a "Sgt. York" in WWII, it was Summers, a mild-mannered and soft-spoken man who became a coal mine inspector after leaving the Army. S.L.A. Marshall called him "laughing boy in uniform." He campaigned to get Summers the Medal of Honor for his feats on D-day, but as mentioned elsewhere, higher powers seemed to feel that one per campaign for the division would suffice. Col. Cole won the honor for Normandy, but Summers survived until the 1980s to bask in his accomplishment, if not fame.

The name of Harrison Summers and others like him should be known to students in all American schools. But this has not come to pass, and his D-day triumphs have only been recognized with the Distinguished Service Cross (DSC). Half a century later, a walk through the XYZ complex reveals that the houses themselves have changed little, except for the addition of TV antennas on the roofs. Some houses had firing ports cut in the stone walls but the French people closed them after reclaiming their homes.

Eyes of a Hero
S/Sgt. Harrison Summers of B/502 with a Hawaiian girl taken before WWII while he was stationed at Schofield Barracks. Summers was a veritable one-man army at the XYZ complex. *via Rick Summers*

A Well-Earned Meal, D+1
A group of 502nd officers make a meal in front of a house in les Mesiéres. (Left to right) Capt. Ivan Phillips (regimental communications officer), Lt. Gordon Johnson (platoon leader), Lt. Jim Kean, Lt. Joe Pangerl (IPOW officer), Lt. Bill Geddes (assistant communications officer), and an unknown platoon leader.

Phillips had assembled a large force in the area north of St. Martin and just behind the coast on D-day morning. He found the camouflaged Ford in the photo in his travels en route to the Objective W area. It was marked "Assembled in England." Lt. Kean was sent by Gen. Anthony McAuliffe to investigate what happened to Capt. R. L. Davidson and his men who had been misdropped in the Channel on D-day night. He learned that the Navy had recovered their bodies from the waters off the coast and that every plane of the serial that dropped them had made it back to England—the only serial carrying 101st men that could make that claim. *Pangerl*

Buildings 2, 3, and 4, Summers' Charge
Sgt. Harrison Summers, armed with a Tommy gun, attacked Building 1 alone. He kicked in the door, shot four Germans and others escaped, running west on the Mesiéres road toward the next buildings. These three buildings are clustered in a group. In Building 2, Summers found only a sick child. In approaching Building 3, Summers got covering machine gun fire from Pvt. William Burt. Summers burst in and shot six more Germans. Building 4 was empty.

Building 8, Summers' Charge
In attacking Buildings 6, 7, and 8, Summers was joined by Pvt. John Camien, who had a carbine. They took turns on these three houses, trading weapons. One would kick the door and cover with the carbine, as the other jumped inside and sprayed with the Thompson. Together, they killed another fifteen Germans combined in these three houses.

Building 5, Summers' Charge
Crossing to the north side of the road, Summers attacked building 5, which sat back some distance from the road. On the approach, Summers was joined by an unidentified captain from the 82nd Airborne. They attacked the house together but the captain fell dead from a rifle bullet. This is a large house, which required a room to room search. Summers entered alone and gunned down six more Germans in the various rooms.

Left

Building 9, Summers' Charge
From Building 8, it is about a quarter-mile walk down the road to the driveway north of the road, which gave access to the last three buildings of the complex. Building 9 is a large, impressive chateau that the German artillerymen used as their mess-hall. Summers entered and found fifteen Germans seated at a long table, eating. They were either oblivious to the fight outside or, as Summers put it: "The biggest chowhounds in the German Army." At any rate, as they rose to get weapons, Summers swept the lot of them with his Tommy gun.

Building 11, Summers' Charge
Building 10, a sizable wooden shed that contained munitions, once stood beside this building. It was set afire by tracers from William Burt's machine gun and the ammo started exploding. Thirty Germans were flushed from the building and shot by Summers and others who had joined the fight. Lt. Col. Cassidy had sent more troops up to join the fight and now Summers had help, although seven of the others were killed and four wounded in taking the last two buildings.

Building 11 was a large, two-story farm building that was used as a barracks to house a company of German troops. They were firing out of the windows at two different levels. S/Sgt. Roy Nickrent, the HQ/1 502 operations sergeant arrived, kicked one foot into the dirt embankment of the road, and fired a number of bazooka rounds at the roof of building 11. This finally started the building on fire. More than eighty Germans came pouring out of the building, some running north across the open field at the rear. They were caught in a crossfire from three sides, including fire from Michaelis' group and a group in the vanguard of the 4th Infantry division. About fifty Germans were killed and the rest surrendered.

Chapter 10

St. Mere Eglise

St. Mere Eglise is one of the few sizable cities on the N-13 between Carentan and Cherbourg and lies somewhat in the center of the Cotentin Peninsula. It was originally to be the drop area for the 101st Airborne, but their DZs were moved east when the German 91st Air Landing/Infantry Division moved into the region less than a month before D-day.

The 82nd Airborne, which was originally slated to land near St. Saveur le Vicomte, shifted its area east, putting St. Mere in the center of its activities. Because John Steele of F/505 landed atop the town church and dangled from the steeple, feigning death, the town has been closely identified with the legend of the 82nd Airborne. Yet it also has a place in the annals of the 101st. Stray sticks from the 506th and 502nd PIRs landed in or near the town by mistake as much as 45min before 505th PIR troopers began to arrive, inciting the defending garrison into a frenzy of activity. In the town were some headquarters elements of the 91st Division, and, according to German historian Paul Carrell, a Luftwaffe flak battalion. The 82nd finished the job of taking the town by 0300 or 0400 and Carrell blames the flak battalion's hasty withdrawal for yielding-up a crucial objective early in the invasion.

Lt. Turner Turnbull of the 505th PIR led his platoon in a fierce battle on D-day afternoon, stopping a battalion-sized German attack that was driving toward St. Mere Eglise from the north. Turnbull, who was killed shortly thereafter, has become a legend of the 82nd Airborne.

The 91st Division was an anomaly in the German Army—its members had started as Luftwaffe ground troops but in 1943 were converted to a regular army unit. A former member of their headquarters element returns to the town from Germany each year in June. Sgt. Rudi Escher was one of those who removed John Steele from the roof of the church. Steele was soon liberated when the town was captured and Rudi Escher went into American captivity.

The legends of St. Mere have been repeated many times over, so here are a couple of lesser known stories you probably haven't heard.

Glenn Dempsey, E/502, landed on the tiled rooftop of a house in St. Mere Eglise. He could hear Germans inside, talking. Still in his chute, he feared they might have heard some of the tiles that dislodged, so he tossed a grenade in the window and blew them up. He squirmed out of his harness and got to relative safety outside the town. He was seriously wounded near Carentan 11 June.

Para-Cavalry, D+4
Two paratroopers patrol the town on horses captured from the 795th Ost Battalion (Georgian), which had been stationed in nearby Turqueville. The entrance to the town square and approaches to the famous church (Eglise), can be seen at the upper right rear. *US Army*

Fifty Years Later
The same spot in the early 1990s. The store fronts have changed, but the location is still recognizable. Phil Juttras, curator of the Airborne Museum, chats with a citizen in the doorway. *Author's Photo*

A young French girl who had a German soldier for a lover lived in an upper story apartment in town. When the alarm came of Allied parachutists landing, the German soldier grabbed his helmet and ran outside to help in the fighting. A 505th trooper came under sniper fire from an upstairs window. He ran up the stairs and shot the French girl, who had picked up her boyfriend's rifle and fired it at the invaders. Today, she is listed among the names on the town honor roll as one of those who died in the 1944 liberation of her community. Many people in the town know this, but no one speaks about it.

Combat Condom
Two 82nd Airborne troopers dug in at the base of a hedgerow. One has fitted a condom over the muzzle of his folding stock carbine to keep rain out. *Sapinski*

German Sgt. Rudi Escher
Portrait of Sgt. Rudi Escher in the early 1940s—before the 91st Air Landing Division was converted to a regular army division. He wears a Luftwaffe non-com's uniform. Herr Escher survived the fighting and still makes annual pilgrimages to St. Mere Eglise. *Escher*

Wounded Paratrooper
Who is he? Eddie Sapinski and a handful of others from F/502 were misdropped west of St. Mere Eglise and fought with a group from the 82nd for the first six days. Sapinski took this photo of a wounded paratrooper in that area. John Cucinotta, also of F Company, claims this man was a 508th Pathfinder and that he died of wounds about two days after this photo was made. Howard Matthews of F Company claims the man is Willard L. Davis, an F Company man from Texas. Sapinski can no longer remember, but we are indebted to him for a most dramatic photo. *Sapinski*

Left
Foxhole Living
Sapinski recorded these two 82nd Airborne Division troopers (note small mesh helmet nets), in their hole west of St. Mere Eglise. *Sapinski*

Chapter 11

Audoville and Le Grand Chemin

Shaub's charge at Audoville certainly ranks with the actions at Holdy and le Grand Chemin for valor, yet little is known about it. To set the stage for the action, it must be explained that Joe Pistone of F/502 was the man with the camera. Pistone was supposed to land on DZ A to attack the St. Martin 122mm gun battery. He was mis-dropped miles south of there on the DZ C area near St. Marie du Mont. He saw Col. Robert Sink of the 506th PIR on D-day, which means he was even farther south, near Culloville. After getting his bearings, Pistone set off to the north to try to reach his objective. Others he met from his company joined him en route. (see Chapter 12).

Rendezvous With Destiny, the Divisional history of the 101st Airborne, written by Leonard Rapport and Arthur Norwood (Infantry Journal Press, Washington, D.C, 1947), has mentioned that twelve 105mm guns of the German 191st Artillery Regiment were stationed in the area behind Utah Beach. We know that the four covering Exit 1 at Pouppeville were destroyed at Holdy. Another four, covering Exit 2 at St. Marie du Mont, were destroyed by Lt. Richard Winters and company at

the Brécourt Farm near le Grand Chemin. It has been suggested by the official US government history, *Utah Beach to Cherbourg*, that the remaining guns and their crews escaped from the invasion area. It is possible that the battery shown wiped out in this series of Pistone's photos depicts the missing battery. Since Pistone and friends were making their way north toward de Varreville, it is logical that they would have passed through the Audoville area en route. It also seems logical that the Germans would have had an artillery battery somewhere in that vicinity to cover Exit 3. Exit 4 was presumably covered by the 122mm guns at St. Martin de Varreville until they were removed between 29 May and 5 June.

No better way of pinpointing the location has yet become available, unless some local French people recognize the locale from the photos. Joe Pistone cannot tell us where he took the photos because he didn't know where he was at the time.

When a small group of F/502 strays—including Pistone, Benjamin Shaub, Floyd Baker, Mike Milenczenko, and William Carberry—came upon the German artillery battery, quite by chance, Shaub challenged them with walking fire, shooting his M-1 from the hip. Steadily advancing and firing, Shaub broke into a run and jumped into a long ditch where the Germans had taken cover. Stopping only once to insert a new clip in his rifle, Shaub ran along the ditch, spraying the occupants with his fire. When he was finished, the Germans were all dead. Shaub's companions had given him covering fire, but it was basically a one-man feat and all over in less than a minute.

A strange silence and isolation hung over the area as the men paused to rest and posed for Pistone's photos. In a field in front of the German position were some dead paratroopers who had landed there on D-day.

Ben Shaub, the intrepid hero of the incident, lost his life in the fighting in Holland in October 1944. Shaub stepped on a land mine, which blew off his foot. As his buddy, Silfies, was dragging the wounded man out, he stepped on another mine, which inflicted mortal wounds to Shaub's head and upper body.

The Silver Star was awarded to Shaub, thanks to the witnesses to this one-man charge, but he didn't live long enough to wear it. Mike Mi-

Shaub's Charge, D+1
Somewhere in the vicinity of Audoville la Hubert. (Left to right) Joe Pistone, Floyd Baker (medic), and Sgt. Mike Milenczenko, a.k.a. "Mike the Cat," with German artillerymen killed in Benjamin Shaub's one-man charge. *Pistone*

Pistone and Shaub
Joe Pistone (left) poses with Benjamin Shaub, the hero of the action, and one of the German cannons captured in the solitary charge. Shaub refused to pose over the men he had killed. *Pistone*

Spoils for the Victors
Mike Milenczenko and Bill Carberry (facing camera) examine the living quarters of the late German artillerymen. Looting and pilfering of enemy equipment and possessions was a favorite pastime of the troopers. Carberry died in the fierce fighting at Bastogne, Belgium.

lenczenko, who changed his name to Mike Miller after the war, died in the 1970s. Floyd Baker had his nose shot off in subsequent fighting and his current whereabouts, if living, are unknown. William Carberry, the other witness to this incident, was killed at Bastogne.

Le Grand Chemin:
The Battery at the Brécourt Farm

The small group led by Lt. Richard Winters hit the D-14 on D-day morning and joined the bulk of Lt. Col. Strayer's 2/506, moving south from Audoville. Winters was soon to inherit E/506, as the unit's CO was MIA.

To this day, the spot where the D-14 joins the D-913 seems inconspicuous, but it was a pivotal turn for 101st troops headed south on D-day and D+1. On the morning of 6 June, some German paratroops and a four-gun battery of 105s were dug in at each corner of a large farm field, just south of the D-14, across from the Brécourt family farm at le Grand Chemin. All the 105s were zeroed

in on Utah Beach, Exit 2 and taking them quickly would save the lives of many men landing on that beach.

This was no easy task for Easy Company, so Lt. Winters led his intrepid band personally. They had to approach the guns one at a time, which was difficult because of the skilled German paras who defended the approach and sniped at the attackers persistently.

With Winters in the lead, his dozen brave men mopped up the gun positions one by one. Guanere, Malarkey, Toye, Lorraine, Wynn, Ranney, Lipton, and Lt. Compton of E/506 were instrumental in the action. Pvt. John D. Hall of A/506 also joined them. After taking the first three guns, the exhausted group paused to rest. At that time, Lt. Ronald Speirs, that deadly killing machine from D/506, came up with Jumbo DiMarzio, Ray Taylor, Rusty Houch, and a handful of others from Dog Company.

As soon as the final gun emplacement was pointed out to Speirs, he made a spontaneous one-

Brécourt Farm
The entrance of the Brécourt family's farm on the south edge of le Grand Chemin. The action of Lt. Richard Winters' group took place in a large field across the road to the left of this photo. Michel DeVallavielle, the future mayor of St. Marie du Mont, was shot here on D-day in a case of mistaken identity. He was the first French civilian to be evacuated to England for medical treatment. *Author's Photo*

man charge across a long open area, spraying the German gun pit with his Tommy gun as he ran. Ray Taylor heard the men comment, "Look at that crazy mother—go!!"

The German artillerymen were scarcely a match for the unmitigated fury of a warrior like Speirs and knew it. They jumped out of their emplacement and ran, just as Speirs came sailing in feet first. He sprayed them in the back as they ran, and narrowly survived the blast of a concussion grenade the Germans left behind before vacating their position.

During this action, Winter's company lost four men killed, two wounded. Houch from D/506 was also killed. The troops counted fifteen German dead, many wounded, and twelve prisoners.

After the action was over, four Sherman tanks that had come up from the beach on Exit 2 joined with Winters and his men. It has been a continual source of irritation to Winters that ever since *Night Drop* appeared, these tanks have wrongly been credited with knocking out the German artillery positions just described. This myth was repeated as late as 1993 in one of the latest Airborne histories.

ETO historian S.L.A. Marshall had also written that E/506 had 195 men of 2nd Battalion available to take the battery. "With that many E Company men, I could have taken Berlin," Winters says (see *Band of Brothers*, by Stephen Ambrose, Simon & Schuster, 1993, for a complete history of E/506).

A final incident, which took place after the action, should be mentioned. Michel, a teen-aged boy who was a member of the DeVallavielle family at Brécourt, was shot in the courtyard numerous times by two American paratroopers, but he survived. He later became mayor of St. Marie du Mont. The French were not happy about the inci-

Battlefield Promotion
Dick Winters of E/506 was a lieutenant on D-day but was soon to become a captain. He posed for this photo in his A-2 jacket with 506th pocket patch in place before leaving the States in 1943. *Winters*

dent and claimed that the men who shot him were laughing when they did it. Michel himself never held a grudge and became great friends with US veterans of D-day in the years following WWII. Stephen Ambrose writes that Michel was mixed in with a group of Germans when shot. This has been a touchy subject with the French locals until quite recently.

With Exit 2 cleared, 4th Division troops as well as armor began pouring inland, and paratroopers who landed between St. Marcouf and Audoville were able to move south to the D-913, make a sharp right, and proceed to St. Marie du Mont, or other points south.

Richard Winters was among those considered for the Medal of Honor, but the award was reduced to a DSC. After the war, he became an executive with the Hershey Chocolate Company and developed a system for utilizing the waste products of candy making in a mixture for cattle feed.

Chapter 12

St. Marie du Mont

St. Marie du Mont on D-day was definitely 101st country. It was near the center of the 101's area and a hub of activity. The village with the domed church steeple is to the 101st what St. Mere Eglise is to the 82nd Airborne. The round steeple enabled Gen. Maxwell Taylor, the 101st CO, to figure out where he was at first light. In reading the town's rich D-day history, one detects a feeling of tragedy and regret. The French observers had sympathy for the fate of those lost on both sides.

The Legend of Ambrose Allie

A humble private from Two Rivers, Wisconsin, Ambrose Allie of 3/501 will long be a folk hero in St. Marie du Mont. Ambrose had come to earth in a field north of there and near first light walked into town with another trooper.

As they entered the town square at the north bend of the D-913, the duo was cut down by German machine gun bullets. Ambrose was wounded in the arm, and his companion severely hit in the head. German troops immediately pounced on, disarmed, and searched them. The wounded captives were dragged into the nearest house in a hurry. The town was being hotly contested and the outcome was still in question. For an hour or two, the frantic Germans rushed their wounded prisoners from house to house, glancing out windows and occasionally firing their weapons.

St Marie du Mont Steeple, D+1
Ed Benecke's 7 June photo shows clearly where the bore-sighted shell from Holdy went through the steeple. *Benecke*

St. Marie du Mont, D+1
American troops march past the front of the church on 7 June 1944. *Musura*

Pfc. Ambrose Allie, 1943
Ambrose Allie's German captors were about to execute him and a gravely wounded companion when they were rescued by American paratroopers.

3/502 Troopers, D+2
Elements of 3/502 move south from their D-day positions near Exit 3 and head west toward les Forges at the N-13. After regrouping, they defended the Blosville-Houesville area against German counterattacks, then advanced along the N-13 causeway towards Carentan. Among those identified are Pvt. William Reed (far left),T/5 Robert Marois (third from left), and Fox, Boddie, and Urbanczyk (in the center foreground), all of Company H. *US Army via Ludwig*

Eventually, the Germans became too concerned about their precarious situation and became tired of dragging their prisoners around. They marched Ambrose and friend into a nearby yard, stood them against the wall of a house, then backed up to shoot them, firing squad style. But a fusillade of bullets struck them down, fired by American paratroopers who had come upon the scene in the nick of time.

The Hunter in the Town Pump

This story comes from the town's history records.

At first light on D-day morning, an American paratrooper was seen to hide in the recess of the

A Hero Among Heroes
7 June 1944 in a field near St. Marie du Mont. Sgt. Joe Pistone and Pfc. Ben Shaub pose for this photo, taken with Pistone's camera, soon after they joined forces on D+1. Shaub, from Pennsylvania, almost single-handedly wiped out a four-gun German 105mm artillery battery, for which he received the Silver Star. In this fine study, note that Shaub wears the Air Corps issue ammo pouches and, for some reason, has discarded his jump trousers, wearing OD trousers instead. He wears his M3 Trench knife on his waist. Pistone's paper gas detection brassard shows the wear resulting from crawling through hedgerows under fire and will soon be discarded. His gas impregnated, reinforced M42 trousers are complete with rigger applied leg tie-downs. *Pistone*

town pump. He was "stocky, obviously older than his fellows, his face wrinkled with fine furrows, pale eyes without expression, and bow-legged, like a rider." Holding his rifle in the bend of his elbow like a hunter, he looked out from the recess and began to fire on the German garrison, who were "stricken by fear." He is credited with ten kills, of whom two were shot at a range of less than 50m.

Western Style Shoot-Out With an Ironic Outcome

Also in the morning, the town saddler witnessed a duel that happened a short distance from the pump, in front of the town's WWI monument. An American and a German suddenly met in front of the monument and simultaneously raised their weapons to shoot. Each man fell wounded by the other's fire. The American died of his wound. The German, seriously wounded, was carried to the boucherie where an American doctor saved his life.

Three Troopers, Twenty-Eight German Casualties

The missing commander of the 502nd PIR, Col. George Van Horn Moseley had never showed up at the planned CP in Loutres. His leg was badly broken on the night drop and he had landed far south of the intended area on DZ C. Found in the afternoon by several troopers, including Fascinella, Sky Jackson, Vic Nelson, and all of Moseley's regimental Headquarters Company, Moseley was eventually hauled to the Division CP at Hiesville in a wheelbarrow.

About 1600 on D-day, Sky Jackson chased two Germans behind a hedgerow and fired into it. This story has appeared in print in at least four different books and magazine articles—each account contradicts the other in details.

Sky himself wrote a short story called "My Part in The Invasion of France." His comments on this action:

Meeting the Mademoiselles
This famous invasion photo shows paratroopers trying to fraternize with French girls near the town pump in St. Marie du Mont. They are believed to be from 1/506. The girl at far left is Andree Desselier, who later married Frank Polosky, a 101st trooper from Chicago. Her wedding gown was sewn from the reserve parachute worn by Polosky on the night drop. Polosky has since passed away; he belonged to HQ/1 506. *US Army*

73

The Quick . . .

Joseph A. Pistone and Benjamin C. Shaub of F/502 round a bend in the maze of hedgerows near St. Marie du Mont. Minutes earlier, the duo had surprised a lone German sentry, who was guarding this corner. It was early morning on D+2, and the startled German awakened, stumbled to his feet, and raised his rifle. He tripped in his blanket and was shot by the troopers. Pistone then gave his camera to another member of their group, who snapped the photo as they again rounded the bend, re-enacting the scenario.

Shaub, who won the Silver Star for his one-man attack on a German artillery battery, died in Holland, September 1944. Pistone, who took many of the photos in this book, survived all the campaigns of the 101st in WWII.

This photo has appeared in at least two postwar books, with erroneous information, stating that Shaub was killed shortly after the picture was taken. These works also misspelled Pistone's name as Pastore, and Shaub's name as Schaub. *Pistone*

Three of us ran into an enemy patrol of 28 men. We each had M-1 rifles, the best damn rifle in the world! We emptied clip after clip at them, killing 10 and capturing 18—8 of whom were severely wounded. They were mostly kids of around 17 (one of them could not have been over 15). We then took them to our makeshift POW enclosure in an old monastery.

Moseley reportedly stayed in action with his regiment until 8 June, barking out orders from his wheelbarrow. Gen. Anthony McAuliffe saw him along the N-13 and ordered Moseley's evacuation; Lt. Col. Mike Michaelis was now in command.

. . . and the Dead

Joe Pistone examines the dead sentry's steel helmet. Pistone cannot pinpoint the location where this took place. He had landed in the area above Culloville, where he saw Col. Robert Sink of the 506th on D-day. He had worked his way north toward his objective at St. Martin de Varreville, where he met familiar faces. The F/502 men were probably heading south again when this incident happened. *Pistone*

Chapter 13

Pouppeville

On D-day night, Gen. Maxwell Taylor landed near Holdy and assembled a group of men. The first trooper he met in the darkness was S/Sgt. Ed Haun (KIA at Bastogne) of G/501, who had lost his helmet on the jump. The general hugged the sergeant because he was so glad to see him. Taylor's group was totally confused about its location until dawn revealed the domed church steeple of St. Marie du Mont.

Taylor merged his HQ group with Lt. Col. Julian Ewell's 3/501 men, mostly of G/501. Capt. Vernon Kraeger was there. He was mad as hell because two planes carrying men of his company had been shot down, and only three of the thirty-six men had survived. These three—Tetrault, Sgt. Word, and Art Morin—became the nucleus of the "Death Squad," which was later rebuilt and inflicted heavy casualties on the Germans.

One of the unique stories of Pouppeville actually took place on D-day night as the planes were flying over. Walter Turk of G/501 heard someone say, "One minute to the DZ," and doesn't remember what happened between then and 0600. He had jumped, but connector links apparently slammed him in the back of the helmet, dented his steel pot, and knocked him silly. Turk's buddies, David Mythaler and Fred Orlowsky, found him on the ground, disoriented and babbling incoherently. Fearing he would blunder into Germans, Turk's buddies tied a "jump" rope around him like a leash and led him around Normandy until dawn (they used the rope that each paratrooper carried to enable him to climb down in case he landed in a tall tree). Germans were all around and the men no doubt saved him from death or capture as they sought refuge in hedge ditches a number of times with a hand clamped over Turk's mouth.

Turk's first memory was at dawn as his buddies were asking, "Do you know where you are?" At this writing, he lives in Richland Center, Wisconsin.

Gen. Taylor's group was top heavy with staff people and officers, but he decided to move his force toward the nearest divisional objective—Exit 1 from Utah Beach at Pouppeville. Leading them across country south of St. Marie du Mont, he remarked, "Never in the history of warfare have so few been led by so many."

When the group hit the approach road to Exit 1, the men spotted a German platoon walking straight toward them, coming from Pouppeville.

The two enemy groups sighted each other and immediately took cover in roadside ditches east and west of the intersection. For several long minutes, neither side wanted to shoot. Then the angry Capt. Kraeger jumped onto the road and walked toward the enemy, firing his carbine from the hip. Shooting erupted from both sides and Kraeger was hit in the arm but refused to leave (he was later KIA in Holland). Maj. Legere, the operations officer for Max Taylor, was shot in the leg, and medic Edwin Hohl of 3/501 went onto the road to give

Lt. Col. Julian J. Ewell
Ewell graduated with the West Point class of 1939 and became CO of 3/501. Pouppeville was his battalion's first engagement of WWII. *Author's Collection*

75

Lt. Luther Knowlton
Knowlton, of G/501, met the first American tank to drive up causeway number 1 from Utah Beach on D-day afternoon. This photo was taken before Knowlton joined the 101st. At the time, he was a lieutenant in the 84th Division. *Grace Knowlton*

him first aid. A German bullet ended Hohl's life as he was working on Legere.

Cpl. Virgil Danforth, a G/501 man from Indianapolis, led the way into town, shooting a number of helmeted German heads as they bobbed up and down in the ditch. (Interesting to note: John Boitano of B/506 was supposed to go to Pouppeville on D-day but arrived a day late. It seemed like every dead German he saw there was shot in the head—probably victims of Danforth.) Danforth became one of the first twenty-five members of the 101st to win the DSC. Pvt. Meryl Tinklenberg, also of G/501, KO'd a German machine gun crew.

The group split in two directions to envelop the town; house to house fighting ensued. Curiously, prisoners taken in the town were from the 91st Division, with some Georgian volunteers and artillerymen present. Lt. Col. Ewell coordinated the tactics of moving through the town and a bullet dinged his helmet as he looked around a corner. In the same manner, Lt. Nathan Marks of G/501 was killed by a sharpshooting German as he looked around a building.

A G/501 trooper named Bell came face to face unexpectedly with a German in a doorway in town. Bell had his bayonet affixed to his M-1 and executed a textbook upward thrust, which caught the German under the chin, the blade coming out the back of his head. Bell reportedly swore off the bayonet after that incident.

While this battle was going on, Gen. Taylor sent Lt. Eugene Brierre around the town to make contact with the 4th Division, which was landing on the shore. Brierre met a lieutenant of the 4th, which may have been the first such contact at Exit 1.

A better-known meeting took place late in the afternoon when a tank came up the causeway and arrived near the east edge of Pouppeville. Lt. Luther Knowlton and a trooper from G/501 opened fire on it, not certain if friend or foe manned it. Orange smoke and flag signals were exchanged and the first official contact was established with the Ivy division.

Chapter 14

Bloody Holdy

Bloody indeed was the tiny hamlet (situated southwest of St. Marie du Mont) from the time of the first landings near 0100 on D-day. The stick dispersion maps tell the story of a heavy concentration of 101st jumpers landing in and just south of Holdy. It was the intended DZ for 3/501, HQ/501, and 1/506. But many DZ A sticks were misdropped here (mainly 502nd PIR troopers) instead of near their objectives (far north, near St. Martin de Varreville). The worst catastrophe resulted from the fact that intelligence had failed to pinpoint a German artillery battery, consisting of four 105mm cannons and their crews, situated in a field on the north edge of the hamlet. A stick from the 502nd PIR landed in tall trees on the edge of that field and were quickly slaughtered by the panicking artillerymen. An unconfirmed story was that the 2/502 troopers who were captured were slowly put to death by affixing thermite grenades to their legs and igniting them. (The troopers were armed with such equipment in order to melt the breeches of the guns at St. Martin de Varreville.) In any case, some who landed in the vicinity attested to hearing their agonized screams on D-day night. It was also near here that Donald Burgett of A/506 mentioned seeing a number of troopers lying shoulder to shoulder with their "manhood cut or shot completely away."

The guns and crews were captured in late morning by troopers of the 502nd PIR, reinforced by Capt. Lloyd Patch's troops of 1/506 sent north from Culloville. These men later moved on to join the fight at St. Marie du Mont.

One of Patch's men bore-sighted a captured 105 and put a round through the domed church steeple of St. Marie du Mont, firing clear from

Treating POWs
A scene in Holdy on D-day morning. George Lage (glasses, in center) and his medics treat wounded Germans captured at the 105mm cannon positions. A later counterattack on the town from the opposite direction was repulsed in the afternoon. *Lage via Koskimaki*

Guns of Holdy
In his travels on D-day, Al Krochka snapped a photo of a knocked out German gun position. The domed church steeple in the background verifies that this was one of the four guns at Holdy. This photo provides an idea of the distance of the bore-sighted round Patch's men fired that went through the steeple on the second try. *Krochka*

Holdy that afternoon. The object was to root out snipers or artillery spotters, but they did chase 1st Sgt. "Buck" Rogers of HQ/1 506, and others from the steeple in a hurry.

Lts. Raymond Hunter and Bernard McKearney of E/502 were left in charge of the artillery pieces when Patch's group moved on. Fearing the guns would be recaptured in a German counterattack, they began to destroy them one by one. A messenger came from Col. Robert Sink at Culloville to halt this, as the 377th PFAB was devoid of weapons, but only one of the guns was saved. McKearney was also involved in burying the dead from the artillery field, but was unable to verify the stories of thermite torture.

Capt. George Lage, surgeon for 2/502, established an aid station in Holdy and made trips between there and the division hospital at Hiesville all day. The evening crash of a Horsa glider south of town brought the day to a bloody climax.

Horsa Glider, June 1944
A view of the Horsa glider that hit tall trees growing from a hedge bordering a large field south of Holdy. The crash happened around 2130 on D-day. The towplane, unable to cut the glider loose, succeeded in making an emergency landing. Eight men from 82nd Airborne HQ died in the crash and many others were seriously injured. The domed steeple of the St. Marie du Mont church makes a good reference point. *US Army via Hood*

Horsa Crash
The most famous scene of the Horsa crash, just south of Holdy, was published in *The Longest Day*. The bodies of the eight fatalities have been lined up in front of the wreckage. Some had been thrown into the field across the road by the tremendous impact with trees. This detail was recalled by the locals, as well as the fact that the same field across the road was the site of a US field artillery battery a day or two later. From there, the battery fired on the town of Carentan. *US Army*

Chapter 15

Hiesville and Chateau Colombieres

The village of Hiesville lies some distance inland from Utah Beach in the DZ C area, and was the predesignated location for both the divisional CP and hospital. Later, it also became the site of the divisional POW compound and the first temporary German cemetery behind Utah Beach.

Teams of surgeons and operating equipment came in by glider at 0400. The doctors were set up and working on casualties on the morning of D-day.

Hiesville was also the rendezvous site for Pathfinders to report to with their signaling equipment after they had performed their missions. Joe Haller and Lt. Alfred "The Gremlin" Watson were

DZ D Pathfinders who made the six-hour trip north to drop off their Eureka equipment. En route they met, among others, Barney Momcilovic of HQ/1 501. Momcilovic recalls that as the group moved along hedgerows, the Germans kept flipping potato masher grenades over the top at random intervals, hoping to catch paratroopers in the explosions. They seemed to have an unlimited supply. Watson was wounded by a concussion grenade en route to Hiesville.

Bill McMahon of I/501 landed somewhat north of Hiesville and made his way there by dawn. In the afternoon, McMahon set off headed east to-

Airborne Transport
Sgt. Hopp of the 377th PFAB at the reins of typical improvised airborne transport in Normandy. Troops who assembled at Hiesville loaded their equipment and souvenirs on wagons, bikes, motorcycles, tanks, and cavalry horses. As

they later departed for the N-13 near la Croix Pan, they formed what *The Saturday Evening Post* called "the strangest military caravan of our times." ("Paratroopers of Purple Heart Lane," by Cecil Carnes and Bob Pick; 9 September 1944.) *Benecke*

German POWs
Lt. Joe Pangerl photographed this group of POWs in the courtyard across the road from the Chateau Colombieres several days after D-day. This courtyard is actually formed by three old stone buildings arranged in a *U* configuration. Most of the prisoners don't look too unhappy about being captured by the Americans. *Pangerl*

ward the beach fighting. He encountered a young and frightened German soldier, who was sheltering in a roadside ditch near Hiesville. McMahon talked gently and patiently to the German for about 15min, trying to persuade him to surrender. Finally, the German walked out and handed his rifle to McMahon.

"He was shaking like a dog shittin' razor blades," McMahon later said. As he marched his prisoner back toward the 101st's POW compound, some other sterling fighters grabbed the prisoner, pushed him into a field, and shot him. McMahon was upset but felt powerless to stop them.

The large Chateau Colombieres with castle-like turrets stood on the north edge of Hiesville

Digging Graves
Sgt. Davis, a non-jumping member of the 377th PFAB , guards German POWs at Hiesville as they dig graves for their fallen comrades. *Benecke*

and was used as the division hospital. It was the target of continual shelling, sniper fire, and bombing for the first four days. Supplemental hospital tents had to be set up outside to handle the overflow of patients. The hospital was bombed on the night of 9–10 June, when the Luftwaffe made one of its rare showings behind Utah Beach. Two large bombs landed near the hospital, with one detonating much later on a time delay fuse; there were a number of fatalities. Troops of the 501st PIR assembled at Vierville were also attacked by air that night. An MP battalion billeted in a field between St. Marie du Mont and St. Mere Eglise took a number of fatalities from butterfly bombs that night.

Lt. Al Hassenzahl of C/506 was hit in the chest by a rifle slug and laid in the courtyard in front of the Colombieres hospital awaiting treatment. Mortar shells were hitting the roof while he lay waiting and orange slate pieces kept flying off and raining down on the wounded. Hassenzahl kept hoping fragments wouldn't hit him in the eyes and blind him. When a Catholic chaplain knelt above him and began administering the last rites, Hassenzahl sat up and began cursing at the priest. Apparently, Hassenzahl was not ready to die.

In fact, so many shells hit Colombieres that the building had to be demolished and rebuilt after the war. Maj. Doug Davison, the 502nd's regimental surgeon, revisited the place in the 1950s and found the chateau had been replaced by a modern-looking brick house, which stands on the same spot to this day. He found that only the original massive stone fireplace had been retained and is a part of the newer house.

Across the small dirt road facing the chateau are three stone buildings, arranged to form a courtyard. This became the POW compound for the 101st, and prisoners were recruited from here to work in a nearby field, digging graves for Germans killed in the fighting.

At the opposite (south) end of town is the Lecaudey family farm, which was the site of the 101st Division CP. Gen. Taylor slept there the night of 6–7 June.

Col. Robert Sink's D-day Ride

Although it is not at Hiesville, Culloville lies down the road from the Lecaudey farm. Culloville is not a village but just a farm and courtyard formed by several buildings inside a walled area. Here, as predesignated in Field Order No. 1, Col. Robert F. Sink had established his regimental CP. The road in front of Culloville runs between Holdy and Vierville. A short distance south of Culloville and across the road, Maj. Louis Kent had established a regimental first aid station. One of the patients there was a nine-year-old French boy, who had been shot by a German sniper as he was helping paratroopers collect equipment bundles. The boy and his parents lived in Vierville.

Harold W. "Hank" Hannah, the S-3, wrote in his journal:

> The barnyard became a most dramatic setting . . . certainly it had not been the scene of so many diverse happenings. A sniper shot a youngster and Maj. Kent performed a major operation. Much weeping and pathos on the part of the relatives of the little French boy being operated on. [The boy eventually died.]

Sink had no radio contact with his 3/506 which was supposed to be at Brévands. At 1000 he commandeered a jeep from the 81st AAATB, which had come in by glider, and its driver, George D. Rhodes. Sink also selected Amory Roper and Salvadore Ceniceros of the 506th (both later KIA) to accompany Maj. Hannah and him on a personal reconnaissance toward Brévands. The jeep went south about a mile, hitting the D-913 in Vierville, then made a sharp right heading south. They eventually drove right through a sizable German unit, whose men were resting in ditches on both sides of the D-913. The Americans fired their weapons and sped on, seeing more and more Germans. Making a swift U-turn at the first Angoville turnoff, they sped back up the gauntlet the way they had come. The Germans were reluctant to shoot as they were too busy ducking lead. Also, they might have shot their own troops across the road. Hannah described the incident in his journal:

> The colonel decided to borrow a jeep and go to the 3rd Battalion jump area and see if we could

find out anything about them. A thousand yards past Vierville, we passed a German sentry guarding a picket line. Beyond him along the highway were several other Krauts, indicating that we were well past the mythical front line, which we had not commenced to think about as yet. I shot the sentry dead in his tracks with my .38 and Colonel Sink told the jeep driver to speed up. We drove for half-a-mile at 50mph—I emptied my pistol, and the two boys with us mowed down several (with TSMGs). As we approached a corner, we saw several Jerries in the road; we fired, they took cover. We turned around and came back through the "hostile boys" (as the colonel calls them) and shot up a few more before they could

Patheiger, Pangerl, and Leeds
After the fall of Carentan on 13 June, Lt. Joe Pangerl returned to Hiesville to take photos. This is a nice shot showing the front of the Chateau Colombieres with damage visible to the roof. (From left to right) Sgt. Fred Patheiger, Lt. Joe Pangerl, and Pvt. Leeds, all of HQ/502. Lt. Pangerl says the troopers were in such superb physical and mental condition that they were "astounded when they were wounded and saw their own blood." *Pangerl*

Ben "Chief" McIntosh, B/502
McIntosh was a Pawnee Indian from Oklahoma who said: "We went on sort of a rampage." McIntosh was a professional lightweight boxer who had fought in Madison Square Gardens. *Dunwoodie*

Hank Hannah, Then and Now
Maj. Harold W. "Hank" Hannah, of Texico, Illinois, in 1943 and a half-century later. Hannah was seriously wounded in Holland but still teaches law in Illinois today. He plans to be

in Normandy in 1994 for the 50th Anniversary D-day observances, at which time he will be 83 years old! *Author's Photo*

dive in their slit trenches along the road. A machine gun fired at us but missed. The Jerries use their MGs a lot but they are not always accurate. After we passed into friendly territory again, we met a 501 platoon and told it to clean the hostiles out. Colonel Sink recorded the name of the jeep

Thin Skin
Sgt. Benecke of the 377th PFAB points out the spot where a German anti-tank round hit this M-4 tank, off the D-913. *Benecke*

driver for a citation, and I had several offers for my .38!

On the morning of 7 June, combined tanks and paras drove down from Culloville through Vierville to Beaumont.

While at Beaumont, German die-hard defenders, firing from ditches along the road and the fields beyond, stalled 1/506. Lt. Col. Turner, commanding 1/506, got up into the turret of one of the tanks and was directing its fire when a German sniper shot him through the head, killing him.

In 1955, when Leo Conner was secretary of the 101st Airborne Association, he wrote a letter to Hank Hannah and mentioned Col. Turner's death at Beaumont. Conner wrote:

> I note that you arrived at Turner's CP on D plus 1 a short time after he was killed, and that you later took over his battalion. Turner was a personal friend of mine. I knew him in May 1942, when as a captain he commanded a tank battalion in the 8th Armored Division. I was at that time Executive of the 36th Armored Regiment and I did my damndest to talk him out of going Airborne.
>
> It was ironic that he should have been killed in a tank, as reported in *Rendezvous With Destiny*.

Chapter 16

Vierville

Although two gliders landed in the flooded fields east of Vierville, there was little activity in the town on D-day. An S-2 patrol from the 506th left Culloville on D-day, scouted in and beyond Vierville and reported that there were no German troops in the town. However, on 7 June at 0400, a task force of 1/506, supported by tanks, drove through Vierville from the north. They encountered some resistance, but pushed on to continue the fight near Beaumont.

The 2nd Battalion of the 506th came down the D-14 a couple hours later and encountered a veritable hornet's nest in Vierville. German paratroopers had circled around and taken up firing positions in the town. This held up the advance of 2/506 for some time. During the fighting, the battalion lost its brightest member, a Native American named Benjamin Stoney, who belonged to the S-2 section. Maj. Lewis Nixon had arranged for Stoney to be transferred into the intelligence section from E/506 back in the States when it was learned that he had an IQ of 147. Stoney charged across the D-14 to knock out a German machine gun nest and reportedly fell dead across the two-man crew after first killing them.

Tanks returned to the village to knock the German paras out and many of their number lay in the ankle-deep water east of the hamlet, killed

Guarding a Barricade
Steve Mihok and a buddy from HQ/2 506 man a foxhole at a typical barricade (gap opening) in a hedgerow. *Mihok*

F/501, Vierville, D+3
East edge of Vierville, 9 June 1944. Members of F/501 were recorded by Jack Schaffer, passing dead members of the 1st Battalion, German 6th Parachute Regiment. This meadow was flooded with ankle deep water at the time. *Schaffer*

501st Pathfinders, Vierville, D+4
Some of the 501st Pathfinders who survived included: (standing, left to right) O'Shaughnessy, Haux, Rofar, Robinson, Hunt, Larsen, Sarlas. (Below) Joe Bass, Ryan, Brazzle, Haller, Everly, and Lt. Faith. Capt. Brown and Rich Beaver were in the building. Others who survived were still wandering. *Alice Larsen*

by canister rounds. When Strayer's 2/506 moved on, the war was over for Vierville, and it became the assembly point for the 501st PIR to wash and regroup on 9 June. Jack Schaffer of F/501 manned a machine gun outpost on the east edge of town from which he could see a glider in the distance. Schaffer took a number of photos, showing dead Fallschirmjägers in the grassy area east of the village. In searching the bodies, Schaffer noticed the bolts were missing from each German's rifle. At the time, he took this to mean that the Germans had thrown them away and were coming in to surrender when they were gunned down. More likely, the 506th had removed the bolts before leaving the area so the guns couldn't be used by other Germans if they were re-captured.

Schaffer also recalls a deep hog wallow in the backyard of the first house at the east edge of the village. A German had jumped into the wallow feet first to escape small arms fire and was stuck in mud up to his neck. Someone had walked up and shot him through the forehead. Some of Jack's buddies went to great effort to haul the German's body up out of the mud, to see if he was wearing a pistol or any valuables. They found none.

Another gory sight in the town remembered by many was a dead German who lay in the center of the D-913. A tank had crushed his head on the blacktop road. The man's head was flat as a pancake and about 18in in diameter. All of his facial features were distorted but recognizable. His hair was still parted.

A humorous incident happened at Vierville on 9 June. Ernest A. Robinson HQ/3 501 Pathfinder had discovered a German cap and uniform in a house. As his buddies sat in the grass, celebrating their survival with some Calvados, Robinson peeked around the corner of a building wearing the German cap and outfit. "Iss dot you, Fritz?" he said, then ducked back around the corner. In a minute, he reappeared saying, "Iss dot you, Fritz?" The third time he peeked around the corner, he ducked quickly back as Tommy gun bullets beat the wall near his head.

"Hey you guys, it's me, Robbie!" he said. A German cap and tunic were tossed around the corner of the building as a token of surrender.

Chapter 17

Angoville au Plein

Lt. Col. Robert A. Ballard, CO of 2/501, was unique among the 101st's battalion commanders on D-day as he immediately recognized where he had landed. The large, wet fields southeast of Angoville were the DZ for his battalion, most of whom were able to assemble quickly in the hedgerows between Angoville and les Droueries. But the unit did not have an easy time because the men were isolated and surrounded by German troops for the first two days. Also, they suffered from a lack of doctor-surgeons, having only a handful of medics to treat the many grievously wounded troopers from local fighting. Medics Kenneth Moore and Robert Wright established an aid station in the town church, giving treatment to friend and foe alike. Both were later decorated with the Silver Star for treating over eighty patients here in the first two days of the invasion.

Ballard was supposed to move on St. Come du Mont on D-day morning, but his battalion became heavily engaged some distance short of their goal, at the approach to les Droueries and at Gillis' Corner.

Indeed, even en route to the assembly area there were casualties. S/Sgt. Leroy Pierce of F/501 was shot through the head by a sniper. T. V. Haddow received multiple shrapnel wounds, and the first two patrols sent toward St. Come du Mont by F/501 returned with casualties. Gutierrez was shot in the arm and came back with Sgt. Gainey.

Three men from 2nd Platoon fared no better. C. C. "Jumbo" Moore was the lone survivor when he, Huston, and Schinkoeth explored to the south. Huston crawled ahead on point, held up his hand to indicate he had spotted the enemy. Moore saw one of Huston's fingers disappear like magic as a bullet severed it. More rounds passed through Huston's body, one splashing water from his canteen into Moore's face. Huston was dead and Schinkoeth was wounded. Schinkoeth crawled to the rear for aid but never made it. A rifle grenade killed him en route. Moore spotted the German who fired at them in an apple orchard across the road and shot him, then pulled back.

Lt. Quincy M. Couger and Sgt. Leo Gillis of F/501 made one of the first successful forays a bit later in the morning (see the Gillis' Corner sidebar).

Gillis and Couger were dismayed that only a small percentage of the men assembled in the

continued on page 88

Angoville Church, 1990s
The church at Angoville has changed little since 1944. The 2/501 had a first aid station in this church on D-day and D+1. *Author's Photo*

Blood on the Pews, 1990s
Half a century later, the ancient pews in the church at Angoville still show stains from the wounded who laid in them on D-day.

Gillis' Corner

Sgt. Leo Gillis was born Francis Leo Gillis on 10 August 1923. He was born in Canada but raised in the Fenkell-Dexter area of Detroit, Michigan. Like his alter ego, Leo Francis Runge in HQ/501 (born 8 August 23), Gillis acquired US citizenship. Both men were outstanding combat soldiers born two days apart under the zodiacal sign of Leo and both had "Leo" in their name. Gillis was not a garrison soldier and disliked military discipline, having a problem with those in authority. But on his first day in combat, he suddenly became an important person in Ballard's assembly area. 1st Sgt. Parks, who had had little to say to Gillis in training and garrison life, suddenly found himself conferring with Gillis on the tactical situation. He found Gillis could draw diagrams showing the disposition of friendly and enemy troops, and he was at the forefront of the fighting.

Sgt. F. Leo Gillis, 3rd Platoon F/501 in a 1943 portrait. *Gillis*

Gillis, who was a crack shot with the M-1 Garand rifle ("I could shoot an apple off your head at 300 yards.") was moving forward along two parallel hedgerows that formed a line above les Droueries on D-day at dawn.

He saw Pvt. James Luce of Philadelphia running back toward him, holding his wrist with the other hand.

"Lt. Couger wants to see you," Luce gasped, obviously hurt.

"Well, where is he?" Gillis asked.

Luce released his wounded wrist to point, and his hand fell on the ground, dangling only by tendons. Artificial-looking pink blood gushed from the wound on his wrist. Other men came to Luce's aid and sat him under a tree as Gillis moved forward to find Couger.

Gillis was anxious to get into action. He describes himself as a competitor ("I like to play, and I like to win."). Despite the shock of seeing Luce's wound, he was confident and he double-timed forward. He could hear fast, ripping bursts of a German MG42 machine gun somewhere off to his left. Before Luce had arrived, Gillis had heard the gun and saw his buddy, Bob Gaitings, stand in the opening of a hedgerow at a wooden gate.

"Get the hell outta the way!" Gillis had shouted.

Gaitings had no sooner stepped aside than a long ripping burst of machine gun bullets tore the wooden gate apart, wood flying everywhere.

Gillis reached the end of the dirt, two-wheeled lane and saw that it formed a T with a small paved road. Just across that road was a stone trough. On the left was a tall hedgerow that paralleled the lane. Couger was lying below the hedge, near the end of it, but was in a position from which he couldn't see around the hedge's corner. Across the path, Gillis saw the suspenders and web gear abandoned by Luce after he was hit. Gillis flopped prone on the same spot where Luce had been. He looked to the right as Luce had done, seeing large farm buildings 150 yards away at les Droueries. He deduced that Luce had been facing that way when hit by a bullet from behind. A German had stood around the corner of Lt. Couger's hedge and fired but Couger couldn't see him from where he was. Gillis decided to face to the left instead, looking past Couger, down the road.

He could still hear the MG42, but due to the heavy foliage in the vicinity, thought the gun was about 200 yards to his left, near a visible road junction. A hay pile stood near the junction. As Gillis studied the hay pile, he couldn't believe it when three Germans jumped down from a hedgerow alongside the road, not 25ft past where Couger lay. Couger couldn't see them, but Gillis had a perfect view of the trio. They didn't bother to look in Gillis' direction. One was holding the MG42 machine gun and all three started running toward the distant road junction by the hay pile. Two jumped onto the road and one was running away through the ditch. It was an easy shot for Gillis.

He later recalled, "I shot the man on the right side of the road, then the man on the left side of the road. Then I shot the man in the ditch."

Re-enactment, half a century later. From this vantage point, lying on the spot where Pvt. James Luce was mortally wounded, but facing in the opposite direction, Gillis could see past Lt. Couger. In 1944, the earthen banks to the left of the road were heavily foliaged. In the early 1990s, the farmer trimmed them bare. Evidence of the Germans' hole is still visible atop the bank between the trees. When the three-man crew jumped down to change positions, they didn't know Gillis was behind them. He was able to shoot all three.

The Germans never knew what hit them. Lt. Couger said, "Did you get 'em?" but he said it in a skeptical tone of voice, because he didn't really believe Gillis was shooting at anybody.

"Yeah, I got 'em," Gillis replied.

He later said: "It wasn't a very good feeling and I wasn't too excited about it. Maybe I was a little bit ashamed. I'll never forget that little curl of smoke coming up from the bolt of my rifle. I told myself, 'Well, that's what I came over here for.'"

Lt. Couger stood up and walked around the hedge and looked down the road.

"Boy, you did! You *killed* 'em!"

"Yeah, I killed 'em."

One of the Germans was still alive and Couger went over and finished him off. They looked into the hedge where the Germans had jumped out, finding a pair of US binoculars with the name Huston on them, on a piece of tape.

James Luce died of shock on 8 June. Couger was killed later on D-day. We call the spot Gillis' Corner, because he avenged the deaths of Huston, Schinkoeth, and Luce there.

Schaffer's Masterpiece

This striking photo was Jack Schaffer's masterpiece of the Normandy campaign. Taken in the 2/501 assembly area in a hedgerow southeast of Angoville, the faces tell it all. Utter exhaustion and apprehension were heavy in the group.

Closest to the camera is Schaffer's buddy, Harry Tice. Next is Charles Carlsen of Service Company. Note the variations in size of the diamond-shaped unit stencils on the helmets. Small rocks visible on the ground are from a 500lb bomb crater nearby. *Schaffer*

2/501 area were taking an active part in the fighting on D-day. Gillis and 1st Sgt. Herschel Parks left the area at midday to search for Col. Howard Johnson's force, which they located at la Barquette. After they left, Couger became infuriated with some of his men and waved his WWI .45 revolver in their faces. Shortly thereafter, he was killed by a German at pointblank range.

In the afternoon of D-day, F/501 made a circling movement and at day's end were coming back at the same crossroads they had fought for in the morning, but from a different angle. They were still far from St. Come du Mont, and Lt. Col. Ballard received a radio message from Col. Howard Johnson telling him to move his battalion to la Barquette. Ballard was too heavily engaged to comply and there were repercussions later, as Johnson felt Ballard had let him down.

Battered casualties wended their way back to the church in Angoville all afternoon, and there was fighting right in the town, with the aid station changing hands. The Germans who stormed in saw that their own wounded were being treated and left the medics undisturbed. In the evening, two Germans who were scared and had hid in the steeple of the church all day, came down and surrendered to the medics.

There Was Death in the Air

Sgt. Leo Gillis, F/501, said:

Let me tell you about this-here . . . battle. On D-day, our guys saw some friends get shot-up, guys bleeding. . . . they're 4,000 miles from home and they start to wonder what the heck they're doing there. Then comes the realization that, just like snapping your fingers, you could be off of this earth. It was obvious that you could be killed very easily, and everyone was cognizant of this.

There was death . . . in the air . . . you could-not-divert yourself from that death. It was like a faucet being turned on that drained your ability to function. It affected some guys more than others. You functioned with what was left. Of course, I could feel the feelings too.

This feeling is impossible to imagine unless you're in the situation. Even then, you can't recapture the feeling yourself until you're in the situation again.

Everyone wanted to do the right thing, but some were not capable of doing it. They could not make themselves do it. Some guys would refuse to dig a foxhole, or throw their ammunition away. It's like in baseball. You might have some good friends but they're not players. You'd like for them to be players, but they're not and never will be. Combat separates people too. Some guys don't appreciate me saying this, but it's the truth.

On 7 June, three 8in shells from the cruiser USS *Quincy II* off the coast landed in F Company's area, killing and wounding a number of men. Lt. Leo Malek of F's 2nd Platoon survived, but Gerard Bosscher, the regimental dentist, spent the afternoon picking stones, grass, and shrapnel out of Malek's legs.

Chapter 18

Migration

The tight V formations flown by each serial of planes had deteriorated after passing over the western coast of the Cotentin Peninsula. Initially, cloud banks had caused this dispersion. Soon, enemy flak batteries had opened up and, in the words of A/502 trooper John J. Lee, the ack-ack parted the C-47's "similar to shooting a scatter gun into a flock of blackbirds."

Elements of the 502nd PIR and the 377th PFAB were to land on DZ A, to concentrate on the two northern exits from Utah Beach and to eradicate the German artillery positions near St. Martin de Varreville. Most of these planeloads were dropped too far north, in the St. Marcouf-Ravenoville area, or too far south, near DZ C, in the vicinity of St. Marie du Mont. Thus, throughout D-day and much of D+1, individuals and groups of varying size were making their way north or south, heading toward their assigned objectives. These cross-country migrations naturally resulted

in dozens of battles when German machine gun nests or dug-in units were encountered.

In Chapter 3, we saw how Lt. Col. Robert Cole's group moved from a confused beginning at St. Mere Eglise, back eastwards, eventually positioning itself near one of the beach exits. Also in that chapter, we saw how Lt. Col. Strayer's 2/506 group left the Foucarville area, moving south toward their objective.

The planes carrying HQ/501 are a good example of how widely dispersed the planes from one serial could be. The plane carrying Lt. Werner Meier, the IPOW (interrogator, POWs) officer, and Sgt. Amburgey of S-2, dropped its human cargo near Carquebut, far west of the DZ. Another plane of that serial, carrying Col. Johnson, dropped its jumpers near the Chateau le Bel Enault, near Addeville, the south edge of the airborne bridgehead. Yet another load, led by Lt. Foster Beamsley, had jumped close to the coast, east of St. Marie du Mont.

The last man out the door of that plane was Sgt. Bill Canfield of S-2. Canfield landed in the

Cpl. Donald Robinson, F/502
Eddie Sapinski snapped this photo at an unknown location in Normandy. Note the dead cow in rear with legs sticking up in the air. Dead horses and cows were a common sight during the campaign and French farmers were kept busy trying to bury them. *Sapinski*

"Ou Est l' Boche?"
This may be the first photo snapped in Normandy by 501st photographer Al Krochka. Lt. Beamsley (right) and another 501st trooper question a Frenchman for details of their location and on German troops in the area. This was most likely in the area north of Pouppeville. *Krochka*

Wrecked Glider, Vicinity of LZ E
Lt. James Haslam, who landed on DZ D with the 501st Pathfinders, took these photos two or three days after D-day, as he mistakenly wandered north toward Crisbec. The CG-4A Waco glider above came to rest after plowing through a hedgerow. Haslam's notation says that the jeep inside came forward, killing the pilot and co-pilot. "Never happened in training!" This glider was equipped with the protective "Griswold Nose." *Haslam*

Curious Cows
Norman cows inspect the remains of another CG-4A, probably south of St. Marie du Mont. This glider was equipped with the protective "Griswold Nose." *Haslam*

Motley Crew, D-Day
Albert A. Krochka snapped this wonderful shot on D-day afternoon, as his group paused in a hamlet near St. Marie du Mont. Two glider pilots in M-41 field jackets have joined the group, as well as a demolitionist from the 326th AEB. All others are from HQ/501. Those standing include Jack Robins, Paul Biron, Dick Maurer, John Kildare, Earle

Sheen. Kneeling next to the engineer are WOJG Frank Wolf, Lt. Foster Beamsley, and Sgt. Bill Canfield. Biron, when interviewed, thought that the glider pilots were killed later that day. Canfield was acclaimed a hero in *Life* magazine later in 1944 for his participation in the famous "Incredible Patrol" in Holland. *Krochka*

shallows of the English Channel at Utah Beach. Burdened by his heavy load of equipment, Canfield nearly drowned before struggling free. He had probably landed just south of the German strong point known as W-5, between exits 1 and 2. After surviving this hellish experience, Canfield joined a group under Lt. Beamsley, which moved inland from the coast. In the vicinity of St. Marie du Mont, the group turned south in search of consolidated 501st PIR forces. The nearest such group was Lt. Col. Robert Ballard's 2/501 group near Angoville, which was isolated and surrounded by German troops.

German Kettenkrad
In the bomb-shattered streets of Isigny, France, some 502nd troopers enjoy a captured German kettenkrad (tracked motorcycle). Isigny has been completely rebuilt since WWII. *Musura*

Chapter 19

Houesville

The group of houses designated as Houesville on the map lie just west of the N-13, north of St. Come du Mont. After moving west to la Croix Pan from Hiesville, the 502nd PIR troopers moved south and established a line near Houesville. On 8 June there were numerous German attacks on the area and a portion of the 502nd was surrounded there for a short time. Some 300 German troops were driven from the area by 9 June.

An incident happened on the morning of 9 June, which some accounts attribute to Houesville. Another account says it happened behind the Blosville church. The two towns are not far apart but the exact location of the incident has not been verified as of this writing.

Paul Dovholuk was first sergeant of HQ/502 and received a battlefield commission for his work in the Normandy campaign. He wrote:

502nd PIR Graves, D+4
This dramatic photo was taken by Red Larsen's camera at Houesville four days after D-day. The men pose over temporary graves dug by the Germans for 502nd troopers killed in the area on D-day. Larsen stands at far left, Bill Gibbons is next, Joe Bass stands with hand on hip, and Dick Beaver is at far right. Larsen, Bass, and Beaver had landed on DZ D with the Pathfinders. Bass was killed in Korea in September 1950. *Alice Larsen*

On the morning of 9 June, I proceeded near the edge of Houesville to look over portions of my company. An elderly Frenchman started talking to me in French and pointing to the back of the church. I couldn't understand him, but saw Wm. Bashlor and Robert McQueen of my company, coming our way. Coming down the road was a squad of men from I Company—I told them something was going on behind the church. Being a first sergeant, I took command and asked the I Company squad to place themselves in position so as to crossfire their machine guns near the church.

Bashlor and I went up into the church steeple and observed the grounds behind the church. Bashlor said, "There's nothing there," and went back down the stairs. I kept observing the grounds as he was leaving. I spotted a German moving around and fired my submachine gun in his direction. As I started firing, more Germans were moving around. I kept on firing and soon the I Company squad began firing their rifles and machine guns. I fired a couple of magazines of submachine gun ammo into the confused Germans. Next, I heard someone yell to stop firing. I did so and all was quiet.

I came down out of the steeple and lo and behold, the field adjoining the church was full of German soldiers. I immediately told the I Company machine gunners to move to the edge of the field and set up for a crossfire of the prisoners in the field. The riflemen stayed back from the prisoners in the field so they could shoot if necessary. I walked up to the German officer, who wouldn't put his hands on his head. He stated he was a German captain and took no orders from an enlisted man. He soon changed his mind because I pulled out my .45 automatic and stuck it up to his head and stated I'd "blow his damn head off." His hands went up fast. I also told him to relay to his men, that if any of them tried to escape or throw a hand grenade, my gunners would start shooting. Nothing happened.

The best part is that the German captain started getting talkative. He told me he lived and worked in Detroit, Michigan until 1938, when he went back to Germany and joined the army. This group of Germans had planned on hitting our regimental CP that night. We lined them up in a column of two's and sent for help to take them back to the beach. Quite a few were wounded—guess I got a few.

"It's Okay—I Wiped it Off"

On 8 June 1944, Capt. Cecil L. Simmons of H/502 won a Bronze Star for leading his men in repulsing German attacks on Houesville. As the light began to fade that evening, the Germans called it a day, except for a two-man patrol that, unknown to the Americans, had sneaked into a clump of trees and bushes near the H Company positions. The trees were situated in a low spot just in front of the American line.

Simmons watched as one of his lieutenants walked down into the bushes to get some privacy for a latrine call. Shortly thereafter, he heard a great commotion and thrashing in the bushes. Simmons surmised that an enemy scout had jumped his officer in an attempt to kill or capture him.

Big Cec carried a British Fairbairn Commando knife strapped to the outside of his long left forearm. He grasped the weapon in his right hand. Then, removing his Case M-3 trench knife from his ankle, he was on the run, grasping the second weapon in his left hand.

Simmons jumped down into the bushes, straining his eyes to see in the dim light. He saw his lieutenant locked in a struggle with a German soldier. As he moved to assist, Simmons caught a movement out of the corner of his eye. Another German was rushing him from the flank. Simmons pivoted, thrusting his M-3 deep into the midsection of his enemy. Then, coming downward with a powerful right-handed stab, he planted the British blade into the victim's face. Looking up, he could see that the lieutenant had finished his man also. As Simmons was about to remove his knives, he realized he had thrust the Commando knife into the eye socket of the German, and now could not dislodge it, as it was buried to the hilt. Planting one foot against the corpse's skull, Simmons pulled and pulled, but could not get the knife out. Finally, he gave up, removing his M-3 from the corpse's gut and wiping off the blade before replacing it in his scabbard.

As he walked away, Simmons glanced back at the dead man lying on his back, with the knife handle protruding from his face. He would later often wonder what the Graves Registration people thought when they came to bury this body.

The modern reader must bear in mind that these incidents happened long before the AIDS/HIV virus was

Capt. Cecil L. Simmons of H/502.

dreamed of. This was one of Simmons' favorite stories, and the ending goes like this:

The next day during a rest break, Simmons sat on the ground, broke out a K-Ration, and opened the small can of meat. Using his M-3 knife to serve as an eating utensil, he poked out little bites, eating them off the blade. His aide, noticing this, was aghast.

"Captain, I can't believe you're eating with that knife!"

"Why do you say that?"

"Just think about where it was yesterday."

"Oh, that," said Simmons, pondering for a moment. "Oh, it's okay, I wiped it off." With a shrug and a grin, Simmons continued his meal.

Chapter 20

St. Come du Mont

A number of activities took place near St. Come du Mont on D-day, although it didn't become the focus of 101st activities until 8 June. Pathfinders of the 501st PIR landed northeast, northwest, and southeast of the town.

Joe Beyrle of I/506 landed on the roof of the church, got free of his chute under fire, and got down to terra firma. He headed in the wrong direction for 2hr and realized it when he hit the railroad line that runs from Carentan to Cherbourg. Reversing himself, Beyrle got back into St. Come, planted explosives on a power generator, then headed south. Shunning the flooded area below Dead Man's Corner, he headed west across the N-13 once again. Crossing one of the hedgerows in the area near dawn, he slid down into the laps of a platoon of German paratroopers. Beyrle was captured and the Germans marveled over all his equipment. "We had a mutual admiration society," Beyrle says, "that probably helped me to survive."

Beyrle was taken to a large underground room, dug into a farm field just west of the N-13 and south of St. Come du Mont. The Germans had a CP there, and Beyrle was taken into the room and interrogated by an English-speaking intelligence officer. A blond lady sat nearby listening. She looked familiar to Beyrle, but he couldn't place her. Later, while marching south past Carentan, Beyrle remarked to a trooper walking beside him that he now knew where he had seen the blond before. She had been at a dance in England, several months before D-day, dancing with members of the 506th PIR. (See Chapter 29 for more about Joe Beyrle's POW experiences.)

Fred Berke of C/326 AEB doesn't know Joe Beyrle, but he was taken to the same underground CP after being captured. Berke was told to lie in the grass outside the large hole, but was never taken down inside for interrogation. At a 101st Airborne Division National Reunion in Washington, D.C., in 1990, Berke mentioned marching past Carentan as a POW, talking with an unknown trooper who was walking beside him. The trooper was telling him about a blond woman who sat in on his interrogation, and stated he had seen her in England before the invasion.

Berke also recalled seeing huge shells from the cruisers and battleships off the coast, tearing up the N-13 and the surrounding fields just east of the highway. He saw retreating cavalry and mule-drawn artillery troops, which looked like Ost volunteers, caught in the artillery. He saw mules, troops, and cannons blown high into the air, twisting around in flight.

Ahzez "Jim" Karim of the 81st Mortar Platoon, 2/501, had landed right in the middle of the N-13 on D-day night, in the town of St. Come itself. He barely escaped. Karim went on to lead a small group through enemy lines to Lt. Col. Robert A. Ballard's assembly area, knocking out a German machine gun nest en route. He was awarded the Silver Star.

On the night of the drop, Karim saw Cpl. Elmer Glasser of his stick land in a tree in the middle of town, where he was soon killed. When the division moved south a few days later, Karim was in the town for a while. He recalls seeing another trooper, hanging in his harness from a light or power pole. "Each time the wind blew, the trooper's body would rattle against a building. This had caused German troops to fire into the man every time they walked past. . . he was full of holes."

Jim's platoon leader, Lt. Bill Russo, had also landed near the town close to a German CP. Totally alone and unable to move far, he spent the first day in hiding. He eventually located Pvt. Daniel Martin, and they spotted a double concrete ramp, which they later learned was to be used to launch V-1 "Buzz Bombs." The bombs weren't there yet. Russo and companion rejoined the 501st PIR on 8 June when they saw the 401st Glider Infantry Battalion attack vigorously through their area. Back in England, intelligence officers questioned Russo about the insignia worn by Germans at the Buzz Bomb site. On the night of 15–16 June, the first of these robot bombs fell on England. A few weeks later, 101st Airborne troopers located another V-1 launch ramp south of Cherbourg.

Many troopers of 3/506 had landed in the St. Come area including Lt. Col. Robert Wolverton, the battalion CO, who lit in an apple tree in a small orchard just east of the town; he was killed in his harness. His executive officer, Maj. George Grant, met a similar fate.

Capt. Jim Harwick of H/506 landed about 100 yards from the church, got free of his chute, and took shelter in a hedgerow. He lost his weapon and all equipment from the opening shock of his parachute and had only his cricket and trench knife. He was able to move only 300 yards before daylight, then took shelter in a "triangle of shrubbery at a road fork." Harwick later wrote:

I no sooner hid than Germans began passing. Germans, more Germans, and equipment! They even stopped and ate so close I could have stolen their black bread. I sweated it out from 5 A.M. to 7:15 that night, when a couple of Germans, looking for a place to bed down pushed into the bushes, and there I was. He pointed a rifle at me and shouted "Raus!"

Harwick was searched and relieved of a short snorter dollar, 2,400 Francs, and a photo of his wife and daughter. "Mein frau and tochterlein," he protested, but to no avail. As the Germans walked him south, they repeatedly searched him for cigarettes. He saw German paratroopers moving forward and was eventually pushed into a field with some other prisoners. He recognized a few and spoke to them and "got my first idea of what had happened; it did not sound good."

Harwick still had an "escape kit pasted to the small of my back and a few toilet articles, which seemed awfully inadequate at the time."

He continued in his diary:

Just after midnight, they lined us up and started to march. As we got started, our artillery opened up along, on, and in the hedgerows by the road. The effect was terrible. Germans, horses, carts, trucks, all trying to leave at the same time. The crash of shells, yelling of men, roar of motors, diving for ditches, gave me a chance. I took off for the bushes and headed for the flooded area. I waded right up to the river then back to a little bush dike, and hid. For a little over two days I lay up to my hips in mud and water, sprinkling insect powder over me to keep the mosquitoes off. During this time, the battle ebbed and flowed by and near me, until I was so fed up I just didn't care. So at the end of the second day, I waded a ditch, ran past a German sniper, went into the river upstream, and eventually got to our lines. I picked up equipment abandoned along the road, outfitted myself, and rejoined the regiment. I found out then I was the only company CO left, and in command of 3rd Battalion. [Harwick's diary excerpts provided courtesy of Helen Briggs-Ramsey.]

As consolidated divisional elements fought their way south along the D-913 from the Beaumont-Angoville area, Don Burgett and a handful of A/506 men were the first to reach Dead Man's Corner at the intersection of the D-913 and the N-13. They had run through many fields and passed many hedgerows, thinking they were behind the main element, when actually they were in front.

Taking up positions just above the flooded

Who Blew Up the Steeple?
Sgt. Benecke of the 377th PFAB snapped this photo of the church steeple at St. Come du Mont in mid-1944, before returning to England. Although church steeples across Europe were routinely blasted off by both sides to prevent the enemy from using them for observation, this church has a slightly different story. Gus Liapes and other members of Lt. Winan's Ha-Ha platoon (bazooka section, HQ/1, 506th) were up in the steeple on or shortly after D-day. They opened fire on a German armored car that passed below. Liapes believes this caused the Germans to eliminate the steeple. There are probably other versions of who blew the steeple off, and why.

area east of the causeway, they soon realized that a large German force had been retreating parallel to them, on the opposite side of the hedgerow. The troopers, inspired by the boldness of Sherwood Trotter, began piling up the retreating Germans as they crossed the N-13. Trotter was running back and forth, chucking hand grenades clear across the N-13. More troops from D/506 also piled in to the area but things got too hot and the element pulled back, first to Dead Man's Corner, north of the intersection, then in darkness, withdrawing clear to Beaumont. This was after midnight, 7 June.

Before the 506th troopers withdrew in the night, a truck column of African American supply

Unsung Hero
Pvt. Ahzez "Jim" Karim, of HQ/2 501, landed on the main drag in St. Come du Mont. He won a Silver Star for knocking out a German machine gun nest. *Karim*

Captured Howitzer
This short-barreled 75mm German infantry howitzer was captured on the high ground between St. Come du Mont and Carentan. This model was also popular with German paratroops. *Benecke*

troops pulled up on the road, headed south. Lt. McMillan of D/506 halted them and informed them that they were at the vanguard of the Allied invasion. A few more yards would put them behind German lines. The surprised truckers gratefully turned their convoy around.

Later in the evening, a German platoon moved in behind the American troops at Dead Man's Corner and formed their line, facing north at the intersection of the D-913 and the St. Come du Mont turnoff. The bulk of 1/506 was advancing toward them with tank support, and firing erupted in the darkness.

Enemy rocket launchers fired at a US tank, hitting it several times, setting it afire, and wounding two of the crew. The burning tank withdrew several hundred yards, causing a break in the column. S/Sgt. Robert Mullins and Pvt. Edward J. Murray of HQ/1 506 immediately brought light machine gun fire to bear on the enemy force, causing them to miss additional shots at the tank, and finally driving them away. They left behind two rocket launchers, an MG34, and several of their dead.

In the darkness and confusion, elements of 1/506 began to fire at each other across the gap. The fire on the tank had been extinguished and its crew began firing their machine gun south on the D-913. Mullins and Murray, realizing what was happening, volunteered to cross the gap to contact the forward part of the battalion. Heavy fire from both directions made crawling necessary most of the way, but Murray informed a tank crew ahead that they were firing at one of their own tanks, which had withdrawn. The forward tank lit an orange recognition flare and fire from the rearward tank ceased. The battalion rejoined forces, but the advance was delayed until D+ 2 (8 June).

After midnight, the Germans re-established a line at the same intersection, again facing north, unaware of the A/506 and D/506 troops behind them at Dead Man's Corner. This force pulled back to Beaumont in the wee hours of the morning, walking right through the enemy line in the darkness. The Germans no doubt heard them, but must have thought it was their own troops advancing— there was no firing.

It was 0300 by the time A and D companies got to sleep near Beaumont, a factor that would influence the coming SNAFU Engagement in the morning.

Both S/Sgt. Mullins and Pvt. Murray were later KIA. Mullins was awarded the Silver Star for his actions on 7 June.

Maj. H. W. "Hank" Hannah, the S-3 of the 506th, had started the tanks moving on this advance and on a number of occasions, was to personally untangle logjams in advances. He wrote in his diary:

There is just one secret to functioning well when the going is tough—that is forgetting that you have any stake in life, and living only for the immediate situation.

The SNAFU Engagement

On 8 June, the division's objective was St. Come du Mont, the last town on the N-13 before the Carentan Causeway. Most of the participants from Lt. Col. Julian Ewell's 3/501 and Col. Robert Sink's 1/506 and 2/506 were so exhausted from the two previous days of fighting that they were sleep-walking. Few troopers who landed on D-day can now recall anything of 7–9 June; they were so tired at the time that they were running on nerves.

Signs of Struggle
This remarkable shot was taken by Eddie Sapinski of F/502, after his lost group rejoined the company. This was circa 11 June, at which time 2/502 was in reserve between Houesville and St. Come du Mont. It looks like a struggle took place here, probably resulting in a trooper's capture. The rubberized invasion gas mask bag in the lower right corner suggests this happened D-day night, when the trooper landed, as most men threw their gas mask away immediately after landing. We can also see bazooka round containers, a cartridge belt, canteen, and Griswold Bag (which also would have been discarded upon landing). The helmet shows markings for 1/506. Most of the 506th PIR sticks landed in a concentrated area near Holdy, but strays came down far north or south of there. The trooper in the foreground is Cpl. C. B. Williams F/502, from Texas. In the 1960s, Williams served as campaign manager for Lyndon B. Johnson. *Sapinski*

SNAFU Engagement POWs
A 101st paratrooper, armed with a folding stock carbine, escorts captured Germans of the 6th Parachute Regiment after the SNAFU Engagement. The German paras had orders to defend Carentan "to the last man."

Buzz Bomb Ramp
A concrete launching ramp for V-1 Buzz Bombs, captured below Cherbourg. Lt. Bill Russo of HQ/2 501 reports seeing a similar ramp in the outskirts of St. Come du Mont. *Nelson*

Dead Man's Corner, 1990s
The large house on the corner, which was used as a German aid station, has changed very little. This is the intersection of the D-913 with the Route Nationale 13 (N-13). The corner got its name when an American tank was knocked out right in front of the house, where it sat for days, with the dead commander sticking up from the turret. The troops began referring to it as "the corner where the dead man's in the tank." This was shortened to "Dead Man's Corner," and it is still known by that name in France today.

There are at least two versions of how the tank was knocked out. Don Burgett presented one in his book, *Currahee*, stating the tank was destroyed by German artillery on 7 June as it headed toward the D-913 to get more ammunition. Others claim the tank was knocked out by Panzerfaust fire from German paratroops sheltering in the ditch south of the intersection. *Author's Photo*

The fresh 401st Glider Battalion had come up to les Droueries from the beach and attacked briskly on Ewell's flank, but became engaged near Bse. Addeville and remained locked in battle there for most of the day.

Elements of D/506 returned to Dead Man's Corner, then made a right turn and stopped in the fields just east of the N-13 and just north of the corner where they spent a mostly inactive day. Elements of A/506 were spread out, some moving east along the road between the D-913 and St. Come du Mont, others moving south to Dead Man's Corner. En route, they passed the intersection of the D-913 and St. Come turnoff. In a field on the southwest corner of that junction were dozens of dead Germans, many still lying in their sleeping rolls with blood trickling down from their ears; they had been killed by the morning's artillery preparation.

1st Sgt. Charlie Hudson of A/506 recalls going into the large house at Dead Man's Corner and finding that the Germans had established an aid station inside. One of his men was shot dead upon entering the house. Shortly before this, the same trooper had commented to Hudson: "Sarge, I've never had so much fun in my life! You can shoot anybody you want around here and nobody cares."

Lt. Col. Julian Ewell, commanding 3/501, found the N-13 near Dead Man's Corner. Looking north, he could see German troops and horse-drawn wagons pulling out of St. Come du Mont, headed west. He decided to make a try for the Carentan Causeway, intending to block any German moves coming north. His unit fought all afternoon, blocking numerous German attacks. Later, he about-faced his troops to meet Germans attacking at the rear, coming south out of St. Come du Mont. In a brilliant series of moves and counterattacks, Ewell crossed the N-13, took some high ground, and routed the Germans.

At 1400, the second bridge on the Carentan Causeway exploded. S.L.A. Marshall claims the Germans blew up this bridge over the Douve River. However, Frank Carpenter of C/501 was at la Barquette with Lt. Farrell, the naval artillery liaison. He claims to have witnessed Farrell calling in fire from a cruiser sitting off the coast, which destroyed Bridge No. 2. The destruction of this bridge was, after all, one of the division's D-day objectives.

The term "SNAFU Engagement" was coined by S.L.A. Marshall and in no way reflects negatively on Ewell's battalion. It refers to the lack of co-ordination by the attacking units on the morning of the attack. Exhaustion and a breakdown in radio communications were largely to blame.

Also on this afternoon, Capt. Jere Gross, the CO of D/506, was killed by an artillery round on the hill two fields east of Dead Man's Corner.

The fall of St. Come du Mont set the stage for the advance along the causeway to Carentan. After crossing the N-13, A/506 encountered a horse-drawn supply wagon train still loaded with weapons and equipment that had been abandoned by the German 6th Parachute Regiment. A sizable German cash payroll was also discovered.

The area was littered with dead Germans and dead horses. Charlie Hudson saw a live horse still hitched to a dead horse, dragging it as it walked along. "It was kind of a pitiful sight," he later remarked.

"I'll Get the Sonofabitch Out!"
The only gun of the 105mm battery captured at Holdy to be saved from immediate destruction. An assortment of 101st troopers hauled it south to the high ground above the causeway and began firing it toward Carentan. Some 377th PFAB artillery gunners were in on this as well as members of Lt. Winans' 1/506 "Ha-Ha Squad" or "8-Ball Squad," which was an unofficial bazooka platoon where 1st Battalion mavericks were placed. Sgt. Ed Benecke, who took this photo, recalls that an empty casing eventually lodged in the breech and could not be dislodged. An engineer from the 326th AEB stated, "I'll get the sonofabitch out!" He tossed a live hand grenade down the muzzle, and sure enough, it blew the casing out. But shrapnel lodged in the bore. The next round fired exploded inside the barrel, blowing off half of the barrel and wounding eleven troopers. *Benecke*

Chapter 21

La Barquette

As Allied planners perceived it, the lock at la Barquette, over the Douve River, was of great strategic importance. Over a period of many months, the Germans had used the lock to flood the area behind the eastern Cotentin coast. In the case of a long siege behind Utah Beach, they could have continued to do so. As it turned out, however, the worst damage had already been done. Each time the tide came in from the Channel, the banks of the Douve would overflow because the Germans had closed the lock with huge wooden beams. (As of this writing, the beams were still in a barn beside the lock keeper's farmhouse.) Other written accounts have said that the Germans caused the flooding by opening the locks. Actually, they had closed them.

Col. Howard Johnson, CO of the 501st PIR, was to lead his regimental command group and his 1st Battalion in taking and holding this objective. They came over DZ D in the final serials of the 101st drop about 0135.

Johnson's stick, landing across the Chateau le Bel Enault west of Bse Addeville, became fragmented, and the colonel barely escaped with his life. Making his way across country, he assembled

Lock at la Barquette
The la Barquette lock over the Douve River, facing southwest toward the N-13 and Carentan. Half a century after D-day, the large wooden beams once used by the Germans to close the lock at la Barquette are still stored in the barn of the Parey family. Closing of the lock had caused the Douve River to overflow its banks at high tide from the Channel. This resulted in flooding the areas behind the Cotentin coast, an additional obstacle to invasion by air or sea. *Author's Photo*

a force and moved on the lock at first light. A brief rush chased away the few Germans posted nearby and the lock was in American hands. It was evident that the Germans had placed a low priority in defending la Barquette as a strategic objective. They knew well that they had already succeeded in flooding the lowlands as far north as Vierville; the floods even extended into the 82nd Airborne's area, west of the N-13. Now, the job of the 501st was to hold the objective until it came into the consolidated invasion bridgehead.

Throughout D-day, troops wandered into Col. Howard Johnson's perimeter. Many strays from the 506th PIR also arrived and were ordered to stay and help in strengthening the perimeter. The focus of defense shifted several times in the next few days. Initially, counterattacks were anticipated from the direction of Carentan or the N-13. These attacks never materialized, although efforts to reach Bridge No. 2 over the Douve at the N-13 were driven back. Destruction of that bridge was a D-day objective, but the bridge was not blown until D+2 (see Chapter 20).

A great debate rages as to whether Col. Howard Johnson made a personal visit to Addeville on D-day afternoon or if he only spoke to Maj. R. J. Allen (in command there) via radio. Evidently, for some time the colonel left the lock area with a small group of men to search for more of his men.

When his group returned to the area, they came under intense artillery fire from the high ground near Carentan.

This barrage came in where the road forks like the Y of a slingshot. Coming from Addeville, if one continues ahead, the road continues near the 3/506's objective at le Port then swings up to le Grand Vey and beyond. Turning a sharp right at the junction takes one first to the lock service approach road or, if continuing straight, to the N-13 above Carentan. Much of the surrounding terrain was either impassable marsh reeds or flooded pastures, devoid of cover, which were east of the road junction. This Y-shaped intersection became known as "Hell's Corners" to the men who fought there. On D+1, a battalion of German paratroopers wandered into the fork of the Y while retreating from the St. Marie du Mont area. As a result, one of the largest pitched battles of the 101st Airborne in Normandy was waged at Hell's Corners.

The first American to die at Hell's Corners was supply Sgt. Lawrence Ardrey, of the 501st PIR. A sniper shot him on D-day morning and, without skilled surgeons to help, he died. (A surgeon, Maj. Francis Carrel, 501st PIR, arrived later on D-day and did prodigious work at the lock on 6–7 June.) The only member of the 501st service company to die in Normandy was Norman Dick.

En route to the lock area, Dick Gilmore and Clyde Bruders, of the 501st's service battalion, drew fire from a sniper in a distant tree. He was hard to spot because he had wrapped himself in the camouflaged nylon of an American parachute. Each trooper fired two shots into the sniper's tree and saw him drop out head first. They continued on to la Barquette and six days later were able to return and examine the sniper's body. He was wearing an American wristwatch and had American cigarettes and K-rations in his pockets.

There was much movement on D-day, and Lt. Bill Sefton's S-2 patrol started from Angoville in the early morning, fought through the afternoon in Addeville, and wound up at la Barquette in the evening. Maj. R. J. Allen's force in Addeville pulled out just before dusk to join Col. Howard Johnson's group at the lock. Father Francis L. Sampson, the Catholic chaplain of the 501st, stayed behind in Addeville to protect the wounded. The entire aid station was captured by German paratroopers after Allen's group moved out, and Father Sam narrowly escaped death by firing squad. He was able to prevent the Germans from killing the wounded; his little aid station survived a heavy artillery shelling that night. They were liberated by friendly forces soon after.

Late on D-day, Sgt. Leo Gillis and 1st Sgt. Herschel Parks, of F/501, wandered into the Hell's Corners perimeter. They found Capt. Sammie N. Homan, their company CO, already there. Homan had already led a patrol toward Bridge No. 2 over the Carentan Causeway but was driven back by strong German forces. The F Company group dug in facing Bse Addeville (north flank). This would put them in a position from which they could not shoot at the German paras the following day. Jack Womer, a 506th demolition-saboteur of the Filthy 13, was dug in on the same flank with a group of 506th strays he had helped organize.

En route to his objective at Brévands, Womer never made it beyond la Barquette. While moving in darkness the night of the drop, he had seen a column of American paras freeze in the light of a flare, as taught in training. A German 20mm cannon had cut all of them down where they stood. The Germans had excellent observations of movement in the US perimeter, as Womer found out on D-day afternoon. At one point, he crawled out of a wheat field on his hands and knees, coming out onto a road. An 8cm German mortar shell

Souvenir Sleeve
Jack Womer was a demolitionist of the famous Filthy 13 from the 506th PIR. Prior to joining the parachute troops in England, he had served with the 29th Division's Rangers. The left arm of Womer's jump jacket was scorched by the near miss of a German 80mm mortar round near Hell's Corners. He kept the sleeve as a souvenir when he discarded the beat-up jacket at the end of the campaign. In this 1992 photo, Womer displays the sleeve—years of handling have diminished the powder burns, but the D-day elbow reinforcement is visible and the eagle patch is still in place. *Author's Photo*

landed right in front of him and the blast went up and just over him, only scorching the left sleeve of his jump jacket. Womer eased back into the wheat field. He later cut the burnt sleeve off his jacket.

On D+1, Womer climbed into the fork of a bare tree near his foxhole. He tried to spot a fat German soldier who had run across the road and was hiding among a group of cows. Suddenly, a flat trajectory artillery shell of 75mm or 88mm size streaked through the fork of the tree, missing Womer by inches. He came down in a hurry.

Lt. Farrell, a naval artillery liaison, had jumped into Normandy with the 501st PIR troopers. He was able to radio the Cruiser USS *Quincy II* in the Channel for 8in artillery support. Farrell brought the devastating fire down on targets near St. Come Du Mont and Carentan, and was able to reduce hostile artillery fire on the la Barquette area.

The First Night at the Lock

A number of German probes were made into the dark lock perimeter the night of 6–7 June, with one patrol walking right up to the Parey farmhouse from the south. They set off tripwire traps set out by 1/501 men and a number were shot, with some escaping. One of the wounded lay in the garden, screaming, not more than twenty yards from US foxholes. George Zeborowski of C Company crawled out with an M-3 knife and finished him off.

Harry Mole, of HQ/2 501, recalled another incident in the lock perimeter. He and his buddies could see a squad of lost Germans wandering indecisively in the bull rushes hundreds of yards away. As the light began to fade on the night of 6 June, the group was told not to fire at the Germans. They were last seen walking toward the US perimeter and might have been captured for information. Of what followed, Mole wrote:

> Something went wrong and there was sporadic firing and a 60mm mortar round was let go, then all was silent. A man doesn't sleep soundly in combat. He dozes often but doesn't really get a good sleep. At around midnight, I was startled awake by a loud, hideous moan, rather close by. It was one of those Germans and he lay wounded and dying in that field in front of us. This moaning kept up all night long, loud and often in the beginning, until towards daylight, you had to strain your hearing to pick it out.
>
> We were all new at this combat game and nobody wanted to go out and investigate, thinking, as we had been trained to believe that it was a trap, and the first guy to go out would surely get it. At daylight it was over. No sound. Everybody stood up to have a look out there but we could see nothing as the Germans were lying in deep pastures and couldn't be seen from our places. Someone said to me to go with him and some other guys. We were going out there to see what was up. I wish I hadn't been asked.
>
> When we got there, maybe 200 to 300 feet, we found about six of them. Pitiful shape. Twisted, broken. Horrible. The second man I came across was a pathetic mess. His head was blown to the size of a large watermelon. As I looked down in wonderment at his tremendous head, his eyes met mine. I was being looked at by the living dead. I felt sick, disgusted and told the others I was going back. A few rifle shots and their misery was over. Not that simple for me. I was not a rifleman; I never shot any Germans.

The Battle of Hell's Corners

On the morning of 7 June, elements of the 1st Battalion of the German 6th Parachute Regiment were moving south across country, retreating from their fight near St. Marie du Mont. The group still numbered nearly 500 strong and made its way cross country, guiding on the pointed steeple of the church in Carentan as its destination. Had the group reached Carentan, they could have reunited with their other two battalions for continued fight-

Hero of Hell's Corners
Pfc. Leo Runge was born in Austria, but was a Canadian citizen who joined the US Army and later became an American citizen. A member of the 501st's Regimental Demolitions Section, Leo could speak German and captured the German major commanding the 1st Battalion of the 6th German Parachute Regiment. After the war, Runge lived in Laureldale, Pennsylvania, where he operated a plumbing business. He received the Silver Star for his actions of 7 June 1944. Runge died in 1990. *Runge*

ing. When one stands in the road fork at Hell's Corners, you can look north and see the domed steeple in St. Marie du Mont. Without moving, you can do an about-face and see the steeple in Carentan.

The German battalion passed by Lt. Col. Ballard's force near Angoville but, despite some fire laid on their flanks, they kept heading with determination toward Carentan.

Two members of the 501st PIR had set off on a long-distance patrol that morning and happened to be east of Bse Addeville with a light machine gun when the German battalion approached across the open, grassy terrain. Lt. Fred Owens and Pfc. Leo F. Runge were in that position and opened fire on the German paras, shooting until their machine gun jammed. They then began falling back in the face of the massive group, giving them harassing fire from an M-1 rifle. They ran out of ammunition so Runge and Owens stripped cartridges out of the machine gun belt, feeding them into the chamber of the M-1 individually, to keep lead flying at the Germans. Owens later got some bad press in certain historical accounts because he allegedly fired into the Germans during a truce, but Runge was very impressed with the bravery of this officer. (It is also worth noting that Owens received the Silver Star for this action, although he died shortly thereafter in the Bastogne fighting.)

It has been previously written that when the American lock-perimeter force opened fire, the Germans were totally surprised. It is true that they had no idea of how many US troops were dug in there, but they had been receiving American fire all along their route of travel. The delays caused by Runge and Owen enabled Col. Howard Johnson to move a number of machine guns, riflemen, and mortars into position facing the German approach—right at the fork of the roads at Hell's Corners.

Orders were passed for all on the line to withhold fire until a signal gun opened up. The German battalion came on, struggling through ankle-deep water and weeds, concentrating on that distant Carentan church steeple.

When the group reached a point 350 yards from the road fork, the opening gun started firing and within a second all guns on the line were blazing away. It was impossible to tell how many Germans were hit by the initial fire as the whole group disappeared into the water and weeds in a matter of seconds. Leo Gillis and Jack Womer's group were dug in facing directly toward Bse Addeville and could not participate in the firing. But turning around to their right rear, they could watch. A stray bullet struck a soldier near Gillis, killing the man.

Gillis later said:

The Germans looked like a big black cloud crossing that area—you could see them coming.

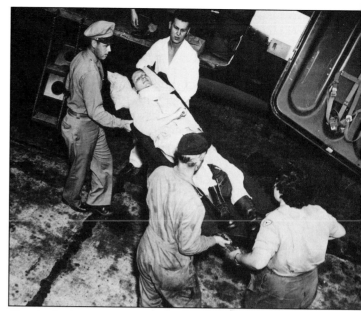

Shot in the Neck
Rich Reinhold, of the 501st's S-2, arrives back in the States with a brace on his neck. While out in the swampy area northeast of Hell's Corners looking for German wounded on 7 June 1944, Reinhold was shot by a wounded German paratrooper lying in the shallow water and weeds. "It was the dumbest thing he ever did," Reinhold said later. Several of Reinhold's buddies riddled the German with bullets a second after he fired. The German slug had entered just below Reinhold's chin, coming out the back of his neck, narrowly missing his spine. In the years after WWII, Reinhold made a full recovery, and his wound was not apparent to anyone who saw him. *Reinhold*

When firing started, it was like shooting 'em in a barrel. They were trapped and they made a stupid move to begin with. They never should've been crossing an open area like that. They were in a foot of water anyhow.

Jack Womer said:

The Germans are coming from the beach—and they're running. I'm not over there, but I can turn around and watch—and it's a nice scene. Here they comin'—Christ, they're mowing 'em down like *wheat*. The 501 now, they're really puttin' it to 'em! The wounded out there are wavin' to stay back. . . shooting their Goddamn *arm* off, shootin' *every* Goddamn thing.

The Germans pinned down in the swamp did return fire and succeeded in killing ten and wounding thirty-three Americans during the battle. Bart Tantalow, of Sefton's S-2 section, was among those killed.

The German battalion was taking heavy losses and some 10min after the shooting erupted, cries of "Kamerad!" could be heard coming from the swamp. Some Germans were throwing their rifles into the air, and some of those were reportedly shot by their own officers and non-coms for trying to surrender. Col. Howard Johnson was concerned that his troops might run out of ammo, despite the fact that they were winning.

Jack Womer said, "You can hear 'em: 'Cease fire!' Nobody wants to stop—they want to kill Krauts."

Two attempts were finally made to arrange the surrender of the surviving Germans. Readers of *Four Stars of Hell* (Declan McMullen Co., New York, 1947), *Rendezvous with Destiny,* and *Night Drop* will note a different cast of characters appears in the truce group in each account. We can be fairly certain that the last attempt, made by Pfc. Leo Runge, succeeded in bringing in the German battalion commander. The surviving German troops soon followed.

Because Runge—a Canadian national who had been born in Austria but became a US citizen while serving in the US Army—could speak German, he wanted to meet with the German commander. Attaching an orange panel to his rifle, Runge walked toward the Germans, waving it. When he got to their positions, Runge saw the German major rise and walk toward him. Runge stopped near a wounded Fallschirmjäger as the German commander walked toward him. The wounded man on the ground had been hit in the groin but asked Runge for a smoke. Lighting a cigarette, Runge bent down and handed it to him.

It developed that the arrogant German major could speak English.

"You're trapped," Runge told him. "Our forces from the beach are coming up right behind you, and we have you outnumbered." Actually the German force was twice the size of the lock force and Runge had no idea of how distant the beach landing forces were.

At that point, firing erupted from both sides. The wounded German on the ground grabbed Runge by the leg and pulled him down, shielding Runge from the firing with his own body. The major laid down beside them. Leo pointed his M-1 at the major's throat and said, "You're my prisoner!" He took the Luger pistol from the major's holster and when the shooting tapered off again, marched the German back into the American lines. The major was highly upset when he saw the small number of Americans manning the US line. He wanted to go back, get his battalion, and just walk over the lock force. But it was too late. The major was shoved into a horse stall at the Parey farm, and before long some 350 men of his battalion walked in in small groups to surrender. Some 150 more had been killed or wounded in the swamp.

According to German historian Paul Carrell, only twenty-five of the German paratroopers from the battalion escaped that day, making their way around to their CP on 9–10 June.

The 350 prisoners were lined up on the road that leads to Peneme and German artillery spotters in the distance saw them. Thinking that it was an American group, they began throwing mortar and artillery rounds on the road.

Jim Purifoy had been among those guarding the Germans and he dove into the roadside ditch to take cover from the enemy fire. Several German parachutists piled in atop Jim and nobody cared anything except to escape the fire. A number of Germans were killed by their own guns here and Capt. McReynolds, the 501st adjutant, was killed while attempting to keep order under the shelling.

Before the shells came in, the prisoners had been stripped of their equipment, including fancy parachutist gloves, smocks, and jump knives. A pile of photos on the ground grew to several feet in height.

Gillis said, "These guys were queer for pictures—every one of the had enough photos in his pockets to fill an album."

Womer said, "Then their own artillery came in on 'em—tore their ass up . . . we loved it!"

Chapter 22

The Wooden Bridges at Brévands

The two wooden bridges that crossed the Douve River at intervals of several hundred yards were situated in the hinterlands near the small town of Brévands. Only a few primitive roads circumvent the area. In June 1944, much of the surrounding area was also flooded by the backup from nearby la Barquette. At any time, the area is also laced with deep, flooded ditches and tall marsh reeds. It is nearly impossible to cross by foot unless one follows the two-wheeled cart paths or dirt roads that wind through the region. Any effort to send German reinforcements north from the N-13, between Carentan and Isigny, would logically be done via Catz, coming up through the Brévands area across the two bridges. What exactly the Germans had in the way of reserve armor, troops, and supplies was not certain, but the plan to seize the bridges had a simple objective.

Troopers of 3/506 were to capture both bridges (the southwest bridge was a footbridge, the northeast bridge was a vehicle bridge) and, if possible, were to gain a toehold on the opposite (southeast) bank.

In a perfect scenario, the rest of the division would be aware of the situation there, and the troops holding the bridges would be guided by higher headquarters, as well as by circumstances. If the Germans began crossing the bridges in force, sending reinforcements toward Utah Beach's defenses, the troopers were to blow them up. If they could be held in the event that German troops were unable to force a crossing, they could be used to shuttle US troops and vehicles across, as soon as the invasion front reached that area.

On D-day however, the scenario was far from perfect. With staggering DZ casualties (see Chapter 3), 3/506 sustained the highest rate of KIAs and POWs of any US Airborne battalion in the Normandy drop. Of the 723 personnel who jumped, less than 150 made it to the objective in the first two days.

As mentioned in Chapter 20, Lt. Col. Robert Wolverton, the battalion commander, and his executive officer, Maj. George Grant, were each killed upon landing. All the company skippers of 3rd Battalion were either killed or captured. It fell to one of the battalion staff officers, Capt. Charles Shettle, to lead the survivors in holding the bridges. Shettle landed far north of the objective, near Angoville,

A Mighty Warrior
S/Sgt. Fred Bahlau entered Normandy as H Company's supply sergeant. In addition to Bahlau's organizational and leadership skills, he proved to be a mighty warrior. He was one of the few men of the regiment to win two Silver Stars and also received a field commission. Here, he strikes a pose for the camera, facing away from the Douve River. Although the Germans across the Douve were the main concern, there was also fighting from the opposite direction, most notably the action which won Lt. Charles Santasiero his DSC. *Bahlau*

but knew where he was. He made a beeline straight for the objective, cutting down secondary roads on a 45 degree angle, picking up troops along the way. En route, he saw an officer and trooper of the 506th charge and destroy the crew of a German anti-aircraft gun; the pair was killed in the process.

Shettle's small group reached the objective before dawn. As day broke through, he realized his line would be the 20ft high earthen berm, which retained the Douve during high tide. Arriving troopers cut foxholes into the side of this sandy dike and quickly learned that looking over the top was hazardous. Such silhouetting would draw fire from the German side of the river. Also, to stray too far behind the dike was hazardous, as much of the ground on the German side of the Douve was considerably higher. This fact afforded the Germans with a view of movement behind the earthen berm. Pfc. James Martin of G Company found this out when he and others sheltered in a large depression about 150 yards northwest of the line. German mortars were laid on the position, which was visible from a hill across the Douve. Explosions bracketed the crater, killing and wounding a number of men. Jim Martin and the survivors moved up to the line at a dead run.

Lt. Turner Chambliss

In postwar correspondence to George Koskimaki, James Martin related a tragic story that happened just after daylight at Brévands. Martin's platoon leader was a very tall (6ft 4in) lieutenant named Turner M. Chambliss. Chambliss was an Army brat and also a graduate of the US Military Academy at West Point, a fact he mentioned often. Martin considered Chambliss to be "the most idealistic person I ever knew . . . very GI, strict, but fair."

It seemed evident that the other officers were envious of Chambliss, since they pumped the men for any lapses they might have used against him; there were none.

The tragic gag began back in England, when Martin had conceived the idea of asking "Are we Army or West Point?" since Chambliss was so "West Point" about everything. Martin had stenciled the words "West Point" on the chest of every man's jump jacket in the platoon.

The troops, who had expected an uproar, were disappointed at the next formation. Chambliss gave no reaction and didn't even let on that he had noticed. Thus did the entire 2nd Platoon of G Company jump into France with "West Point" emblazoned on their chests. The end of this story is best told in Martin's own words, as told in Koskimaki's book *D-day With the Screaming Eagles:*

[Lt. Chambliss] got to the bridge before most of us. During the fighting in the exposed area near

the bridge, he suddenly stood up and was shot twice through the mouth. I'm ashamed to tell you what happened next, but I must. As he lay dying, he asked if there was anyone there from the 2nd Platoon, and when told there were none, he told the H Company sergeant who was cradling his head that he would like to know why we put "West Point" on our jackets. He wondered if we were mocking his background. I cried tears of shock and frustration and shame as his body was carried past our position. I keep wondering how he could have failed to perceive the great pride and affection we felt for him.

Meanwhile, Capt. Shettle at the southwest footbridge could look approximately 500 yards to his left and see a German 88mm dual purpose gun on the hill adjacent to the town of Brévands. He called the available H Company men together and asked for volunteers to cross the bridge to estimate German strength on the opposite shore. First to volunteer was Pfc. Donald Zahn, who ran right across the top of the bridge, armed with a Tommy gun. Alone, Zahn worked to the left about 70 to 80 yards after crossing. He encountered no Germans, but visual checks of a wooded area indicated that German troops and gun emplacements were present. He proceeded along the river cautiously, until he could see the rear of the wooded area, finding it well fortified.

Zahn made his way back toward the bridge after a lone half-hour recon and met Sgt. George Montilio who was just coming across. They discussed the situation and were joined by approximately ten additional troopers led by Lt. Rudolph Bolte and Lt. Kenneth Christianson. Also in the group were Sgt. Harry Clawson (later KIA in Holland and a Silver Star winner) and Pfc. Hank DiCarlo.

While the group was discussing a plan for attacking the German positions, the enemy, aware of their presence, struck first. A P-38 pistol was fired through a nearby hedge, and the 9mm bullet struck DiCarlo in the back, exiting his right chest. Zahn sprayed the bush with his Thompson, killing the German, whose pistol was recovered.

More German troops charged the hedge, yelling as they came. The Americans began tossing grenades across the hedge. Mingled with the explosions, they could hear screams. Without further friendly casualties, the American group recrossed the Douve, working hand by hand along the lower bridge supports to avoid enemy fire. Training at the old obstacle course at Camp Toccoa paid off here. The wounded DiCarlo was also brought back to the friendly shore.

The reader of *Night Drop* by S. L .A. Marshall will find a different account of this action, including many facts the participants could not verify. Marshall cites two troopers who crossed the Douve first, hauling a light machine gun. He writes that both were killed. He was probably mistakenly referring to Zahn and Montilio, although neither was killed here. Zahn is positive that no one brought a machine gun across that day. Also, German casualties are given as thirteen killed and three machine gun nests destroyed. Zahn says, "If we killed three or four, we were lucky." When interviewed, Christianson also felt the figures were high and stated an accurate body count was impossible under the circumstances.

During the return trip across the bridge, the group could see that demolitionists in scalplocks and war paint, were already wiring the bridge for demolition.

Most of the available troops were from G/506 and H/506 because I/506 had been decimated by plane crashes and misdrops (see Chapter 3). Most of the G Company men were at the northeast bridge where they held with less than seventy troopers for the first three days.

On D-day afternoon, Lt. Charles "Sandy" Santasiero of I Company brought in a group of twenty-six men. Santasiero had landed way up near St. Marie du Mont. His arrival was perhaps the luckiest thing to happen to the Shettle Force.

Shettle's consolidated force was on the extreme southern flank of the Cotentin invasion. In addition to manpower shortages, it was plagued by an absence of radio equipment, making it impossible to communicate with the regiment, the division, or the fleet offshore. (Shettle made a personal call on Col. Howard Johnson at la Barquette and used his radio to report the status of 3/506 to the cruiser USS *Quincy II*. The information was not forwarded to 101st or 506th HQ, nor to the command Center in the UK.)

When a personal reconnaissance by Col. Robert Sink, as well as radio calls, failed to raise any information from Shettle's group, it was concluded that 3/506 had been destroyed. It was further concluded that the bridges were in German hands and that they must be destroyed by an air strike. Three P-51 fighters, loaded with bombs would depart England on D+1 to accomplish that mission.

Before noon on 7 June (D+1), the three P-51s flew in low, bombing the two bridges and strafing the foxholes northwest of the Douve with machine gun fire. Some friendly casualties were sustained. There would have been many more had it not been for the chaplain, T. S. McGee, who stood up waving an orange recognition panel, causing the planes to break off the attack. Donald Zahn found one paratrooper sitting upright in his foxhole, dead. A large piece of timber from one of the exploding bridges had impaled him.

A spectacular tragedy occurred at the north (highway) bridge, as one of the planes flew in so

H/506 Troopers
This photo was made with a German camera captured by S/Sgt. Fred Bahlau. (Left to right) Lt. Hegeness, Sgt. Bahlau, Sgt. Phil Parker, and Pfc. Gordon Yates, all of H/506. Parker and Yates are armed with Lugers. Note the extra pocket on the lieutenant's shoulder. Bahlau had rubbed foot powder on his jacket in England, to avoid having it gas impregnated (the foot powder gave the jacket the appearance of having been gas treated)

low that a wing tip struck the parapet of the bridge. Lt. Santasiero saw the aircraft burst into flames and come apart, scattering debris halfway to Utah Beach.

Lt. Richard Meason (pronounced May-son; nicknamed "Flash Gordon") the acting CO of H Company, led a patrol in search of communications equipment on the northwest (friendly) side of the Douve. The first German they spotted was about 100 yards away and running. Meason fired a reflex shot with his .45 pistol that miraculously hit the German, dropping him in his tracks.

This patrol eventually returned with twelve to fifteen prisoners some of whom, Capt. Shettle recalls, were Hungarian volunteers. Zahn recalls there was some talk of doing away with the prisoners, in accordance with the preflight verbal directives concerning "no prisoners for the first three days." However, arrangements were made to accommodate them and, in addition, a battalion aid station was established in the nearby Fortin farm.

The troopers near the north bridge had been pounded by direct fire from the 88mm gun on the hillside near Brévands, which worked up and down the embankment, trying to blow the Americans out of their foxholes. The German gunners succeeded in killing numerous cows behind the embankment. American dive bombers (not the

One-Man Army
On 8 June 1944, Lt. Charles "Sandy" Santasiero led elements of 3/506, in engaging several companies of retreating German troops. His valor write-up, originally recommending the Medal of Honor, was reduced to a DSC due to an old feud among the 506th officer corps. In twenty-five days of actual WWII combat, Santasiero was seriously wounded in action twice, and personally inflicted nearly 100 enemy casualties with small arms fire.

same planes that bombed the bridges) eventually took out the 88mm gun.

A One Man Army at Brévands

Lt. Charles Santasiero of Scranton, Pennsylvania, represented part of I Company at the north bridge. On D+2 (8 June), he won the DSC for the following action.

Santasiero was using binoculars to scan the area behind his Douve position, watching for the anticipated approach of friendly troops from the eastern Cotentin coast. Instead, he saw several German companies marching toward the bridge in retreat. They were unaware that US forces held the area. Santasiero alerted his troops, who remained concealed until the Germans approached to a distance of 75 yards. When he ordered the group to commence firing, they achieved total surprise. Most of the Germans in the forward companies were taken out, and the rear company scattered into a large field surrounded by hedgerows.

Santasiero decided to throw the enemy off balance before they could regroup to attack. Leaving Lt. Linton Barling (KIA-Holland) in charge of the bridge, Santasiero ran forward to the first hedgerow. In it, he found a perfect position that someone had previously dug. It was a slit trench, with a V cut into the hedge. Fifty yards ahead, Santasiero could see two German officers shouting to a group of men. Included in this group were six American paratroop prisoners, carrying stretchers. Santasiero opened fire on this group, dropping many of them. The POW stretcher bearers scattered in three directions, still dragging the now-empty stretchers behind them; Santasiero never saw them again.

A German MG42 crew opened fire on Santasiero's position, showering him with dirt and rocks. Then for some unknown reason the MG42 stopped firing.

In squad strength, the panic-stricken Germans began to run from left to right in front of Santasiero's position. He fired at the last in line, working his way up to the first. Then another squad would run past, and Santasiero reversed the procedure, traversing right to left. Santasiero took a heavy toll, firing until he ran out of targets. (Santasiero had been a weapons instructor at the Ft. Benning Infantry School. He told the author he used an M-1 rifle in this battle and used up a bandoleer of ammunition. Firing rapidly at less than 100 yards, most of his bullets found their targets.)

Three Germans with a white flag appeared. Santasiero walked out to meet them and began to render first aid. Soon the field was "alive with Germans and wounded, wanting to surrender." Santasiero pointed them back toward Capt. Shettle's position, then heard the word "Kamerad," coming from his right. It was the MG42 crew that had fired on him earlier. The gun, loaded with a full belt, was pointed at him. Luck was with Santasiero as the crew could have easily cut him down. Instead, they had remained concealed, watching the surrender, before giving up themselves. These prisoners were added to those being held near the southwest bridge and Santasiero gave the MG42 to the bridge force to increase their firepower.

In talking things over with Capt. Shettle, Santasiero learned that the 3rd Battalion was still out of radio contact with regiment and division. He and Lt. Barling set off across country, heading northwest, in an attempt to shoot their way through to headquarters. They took separate routes, and Santasiero reached Utah Beach. He flagged down a jeep driven by an officer of the 81st AAATB and got a ride to Hiesville, where he briefed a worried Gen. Anthony McAuliffe with news about 3/506. (McAuliffe is of later "Nuts" fame at Bastogne. At this time, he was the divisional artillery commander.) After listening to Santasiero's story, Mac took him by the arm and said, "Charlie, you have brought great news!" He showed the lieutenant the last entry he had made on the situation map, which read:

No word from 3rd Battalion, 506. Unable to contact by radio. Sent numerous patrols out but unable to get through due to enemy forces. We can assume that the 3rd Battalion has been annihilated.

Santasiero Leads the 327th GIR to Brévands

Lt. Santasiero talked with Lt. Col. Joseph H. Harper as he led Harper's regiment down the winding dirt roads to Brévands. (Harper replaced Col. George S. Wear as CO of the 327th. Wear was relieved early in the campaign for unsatisfactory performance.) Deep, water-filled ditches also crisscrossed the area. A short distance from the Brévands bridgehead, Santasiero spotted several German marines setting up an MG42 machine gun to ambush their column from the flank. He pointed out the Germans to Harper and said, "Give me your best BAR man. One good burst should get them all. . . ."

A young glider infantryman armed with a Browning Automatic Rifle was brought forward and followed Santasiero into the reeds beside the road. They flopped into some brush and Santasiero pointed out the targets.

As the lieutenant prepared to command the gunner to open fire, he glanced over at the gliderman and noticed that the lad had a death grip on the weapon, his knuckles turning white with the strain.

In a patient voice, Santasiero asked, "Son, have you killed anyone yet?"

"Well. . . no sir."

"Would you rather that I did it?"

"Okay," said the soldier as they traded weapons.

"When I fire, open up, then we'll rush them."

The tense youth nodded.

Santasiero opened fire and his aim was good. The enemy crewmen were all struck by bullets. A lieutenant, hit in the arm, stood up, clutching his

wound and wanting to surrender. Santasiero and the kid were running up full speed toward him. One of the German gunners, although wounded, was still trying to aim the machine gun. Santasiero came sailing in on top of him and the other wounded gunner. He grabbed the throat of one German, pushing his head into the water-filled ditch, drowning him. At the same time, Santasiero produced a razor sharp knife and slashed the throat of the other German. The Marine lieutenant still stood nearby, watching as he clutched his wounded shoulder. The young BAR man was also standing nearby, vomiting. The Marine lieutenant was taken prisoner and the 327th completed its trek to Brévands, where it relieved 3/506 in their bridgehead positions and assumed control of the prisoners.

When Lt. Santasiero reported in to Capt. Shettle, the front of his jumpsuit looked like a butcher's apron.

"My God, Sandy, where are you hit?" Shettle asked.

"That's not my blood," Santasiero replied.

Nineteen officers and 117 enlisted men, the survivors of Capt. Shettle's battalion, marched to Hiesville to regroup. During three days of fighting at the bridges, they had lost seven killed and twenty-one wounded. In the book, *Rendezvous With Destiny*, Rapport and Northwood credit the battalion with sixty to seventy German "casualties" as well as 258 prisoners. (Presumably sixty to seventy killed, as the wounded were counted with the prisoners. Of the 258 POWs, Santasiero claims 179 were captured in his fight on 8 June.)

At Hiesville, an additional four officers and 100 troopers who had been lost rejoined 3/506 On 9 June, Capt. Harwick of H Company, the only surviving company CO (who had escaped from captivity near St. Come du Mont), returned and assumed command of 3rd Battalion.

The 327th GIR Continues the Fight at Brévands

Soon after relieving the 506th, elements of 1/327th GIR began scouting the area for a means of crossing the Douve River. Engineers brought up rubber boats. Also, Lt. Carlton Werner, Pfc. Gordon Hatchel, Pfc. George Groh, and Pvt. William Webb located and salvaged a ferry from the far shore. (Lt. Werner was KIA-Normandy; Hatchel was KIA- Bastogne; Groh was WIA-Bastogne; and Webb was POW-Bastogne.) They brought the ferry across to the northwest bank and a patrol of A/327's 2nd Platoon crossed to the enemy shore. They were soon ambushed, losing one man killed and five wounded.

When the shot-up group returned to the Douve, they found the ferry wouldn't work, so they swam across. Two of the men began to drown, but were saved by Pvt. Arthur Mayer, a medic, who was shot in the arm and the leg during the rescue. Mayer became one of the first twenty-five men in the 101st to win the DSC.

After dark on the night of 9–10 June, C/327 crossed the Douve on rubber boats, followed by the rest of 1st Battalion. By morning, the entire regiment was across. The 1st Battalion, 401st GIR (which fought as the 3rd Battalion of the 327th-GIR) came across at low tide in the morning, wading in the then-shallow water.

German artillery had inflicted numerous casualties, but most of the Brévands defenders faded back. In the coming days, the 327th GIR helped liberate Carentan, coming in along the Bassin-a-Flot canal from the northeast. Other elements would make contact with the 175th Infantry, 29th Division at Auville-sur-le-Vey, which was the first known contact of troops who landed at Utah and Omaha beaches at 1400, 10 June 1944.

The 327th GIR would fight on through Catz, St. Pellerin, and Montmartin en Graignes, where they collided with elements of the German 17th SS division on 12–13 June.

The Continuing Ordeal of Hank DiCarlo

Meanwhile, Hank DiCarlo of H/506, was lying in the Theophile Fortin farm, where a provisional aid station had been established to treat members of his battalion. DiCarlo had been shot on D-day on the first Douve crossing but had somehow been left behind when elements of the 101st Airborne left the area. DiCarlo lay alone for what seemed like days, until a regular infantry outfit moved into the area and loaded him into an ambulance. Hank had received no real medical treatment since being wounded and his chest cavity was filled with blood. Breathing was difficult for him, and he was relieved at the prospect of evacuation.

However, due to the confusing road network in the area, the ambulance took a wrong turn and eventually wound up at the front line. Before he knew what was happening, DiCarlo was ordered out of the ambulance, handed a rifle, and told to join an attack which was about to jump off. He took the weapon and began charging across the field. Halfway across, he passed out, dropping unconscious to the ground. Finally, the battered eagle was moved to Utah Beach and sent to a hospital in England. The rugged DiCarlo would fight again at the epic battles in Holland and Bastogne, and was seriously wounded again.

A Note From the Author
Regarding 3/506 at Brévands

As official historian of the ETO, S.L.A. Marshall did superb work in documenting many of the major battles of the WWII 101st Airborne Division. Most notable are the accounts of Summers at XYZ, Lt. Col. Robert Cole's causeway battle and bayonet charge, and the battle at Best, Holland. In the case of these battles, Marshall's technique was to assemble a quorum of survivors and let each man tell what he saw or did, in the presence of the others, who would add, clarify, or interject. By this method, a picture of the whole battle would emerge as if by assembling pieces of a puzzle. Time and circumstances didn't always permit use of this technique, and it was notably not used when he assembled his accounts of 2/501 and 3/506 in Normandy. In the case of these units, Marshall relied on official after-action statistics and the testimony of battalion staff officers who may have embellished or distorted the truth to make better-sounding reports.

This author was acquainted with S.L.A. Marshall, via telephone conversations in the early 1970s, while Marshall still resided in Birmingham, Michigan. As Marshall stated in *Night Drop*, he had set his 1944 notes aside for fifteen years before resurrecting them to write the book. In the case of his notes on 1/502, and 3/502, his notes were and will remain forever unsurpassed in accuracy, as they were derived from the group testimony sessions described above. But he did admit that there might be inaccuracies in his reporting of the la Barquette battle, the Angoville-les Droueries fight, and the Brévands actions as he had not used the group talk method with the involved survivors of those actions.

In the case of the Brévands fighting, he relegated it to an odds-and-ends chapter entitled "Other Screaming Eagles" complete with the inaccuracies culled from reports and the testimony of commanders.

Rapport and Northwood as well as George Koskimaki came closer to the truth in their accounts, but certain nonexistent elements that crept into early accounts have been repeated in each new account. John Keegan in his *Six Armies In Normandy* (Penguin Books, Middlesex, England, 1982) describes Pfc. Donald Zahn firing a light machine gun while across the Douve. Surely Zahn himself would remember had he fired such a weapon while over there. Also, Zahn remembers patrolling with Lt. Richard Meason later in the day but didn't see him across the Douve. Thus, Meason's name has been omitted in the account of the crossing although he is credited with crossing in two other works. (Neither Kenneth Christianson nor Hank DiCarlo remember Meason crossing.)

Likewise, the inflated casualty statistics for enemy losses (thirteen killed, three machine gun nests destroyed) on the Douve crossing must have been guesstimated by someone at battalion HQ who thought it would sound good in the daily after

The Politics of Rank—How History Was Distorted for Propriety

Yet another example of distorted history follows in the saga of Zahn and Montilio. As previously described, Pfc. Donald Zahn was the first member of the 101st Airborne to cross the Douve at Brévands and was alone on the enemy shore for at least half an hour. Sgt. George Montilio was the second man across. It is no reflection on Montilio's courage, but the battalion adjutant, felt it was more appropriate to award the DSC to a sergeant than to a private. Thus, before leaving France, Montilio received the medal instead of Zahn. Montilio declared he wouldn't wear his medal until and unless Zahn received one also. Zahn recalls: "Montilio and I had a very good understanding about the D.S.C. He probably felt more disturbed about the initial outcome than I did. He was the second man across the bridge, and I have no qualms in sharing the medal with him."

Montilio never lived long enough to wear his medal. A trigger happy replacement killed him in a case of mistaken identity the night of 19 April 1945. Montilio was one of the last WWII battle fatalities of the 101st Airborne. A park in his hometown of Quincy, Massachusetts, is named in his honor.

In mid-1945, Donald Zahn, now a lieutenant in C Company, finally received his DSC for being the first man across the Douve footbridge on D-day. He credits his former CO, Maj. Jim Harwick with pushing the write-up through. To add insult to injury, as Gen. Maxwell Taylor awarded the medal, the pin broke.

action report.

These factors have been mentioned here not to discredit the brave deeds of 3/506, but to show how easily the truth can get distorted, the myths growing with each retelling. It is even more interesting to imagine cadets at West Point or Sandhurst critiquing such actions as the Douve incursion, armed with such misinformation. The main fault had arisen from not talking to the actual participants. Their testimony contradicts the official account with amazing frequency. (This afterword has also been included to justify why the author has dared to dispute the venerable accounts that have preceded this one, a fact which will surely raise some eyebrows.)

On the opposite side of the coin, almost nothing has been mentioned of the 8 June fight at the north bridge, an action of far greater consequence (in terms of casualties) than the bridge crossing. Lt. Charles Santasiero has never received credit in the written accounts for his leadership by example in that engagement.

Chapter 23

Catz

The small Norman village of Catz lies east of Carentan and southeast of the wooden bridges of Brévands. Catz is no smaller than most of the brutally contested villages to the northwest, but was spared from most of the fighting by a quirk of geography. The town is situated at the base of the peninsula and is somewhat outside the consolidated airborne bridgehead area.

After the 501st PIR had consolidated and moved south from Vierville, it crossed the Douve River near Brévands and followed the single, winding access road to Catz. The approach from this direction is difficult, with tall marsh grass and floods impeding travel unless one stays on the road. The only other approach to Catz is east along the N-13 from Carentan, then north on an auxiliary road.

"Screaming Meemie"
Sgt. Ed Benecke at Catz with 15cm Nebelwerfer 41 abandoned by retreating Germans. This six barreled "smoke thrower" was originally used by chemical warfare troops but became a terror weapon when loaded with high explosive rounds. The weapon was electrically fired and when reloaded could fire six rounds every 90 seconds. The "Screaming Meemie" shells made a lot of noise in flight and upon detonation but did more psychological than physical damage. *Benecke*

Catz was a passing point for advancing troops of the 327th GIR and the 501st PIR, which were forming up to encircle Carentan from the east. On 12 June, the 327th advanced along the Bassin-a-Flot, and the 501st attacked Hill 30 from St. Hilaire Petit Ville and linked up with the 506th PIR, which was coming from the west to complete the encirclement.

Sgt. Ed Benecke, again armed with his camera, passed through Catz with the advancing units. This demonstrates how fragmented units were even as late as 10–11 June. Benecke of A Battery, 377th PFAB , was at Catz, while other 377th men like Sgt. Art Parker were far west at the causeway north of Carentan, joining other scattered elements (including 326th AEB) in Lt. Col. Robert Cole's bayonet charge.

In the first week of the invasion, Catz had played only an incidental role. German troops contesting the Brévands bridgehead had shuttled through it and stray paratroopers had passed through or near it. In their hasty withdrawal, the Germans had abandoned some weapons and equipment in Catz, including a Nebelwerfer found by Sgt. Benecke.

A more poignant discovery was the grave of a lone trooper who had wandered into the village on D-day and was killed there. His helmet stencil indicates membership in the 506th PIR, although the battalion tic is not visible. The marker did not give the trooper's name, but the French people had buried him neatly and mounted his eagle patch on the cross. Like all the Americans killed on the peninsula, he was later re-interred in the US cemetery behind Omaha Beach or returned to the United States in 1947.

A stick dispersion map indicates that one planeload from HQ/1 506 dropped its men south and east of Brévands. Some of these men wandered into Col. Howard Johnson's lock position and fought the Battle of Hell's Corners. It is possible, even likely, that the dead trooper in Catz was one of the last of this stick to exit the plane. Or, we might surmise that he belonged to one of the 3/506 companies, and simply get lost in the confusing terrain. Supply Sgt. Fred Bahlau's H/506 stick landed just north of Carentan and the survivors drifted into the Brévands bridgehead after wandering the rugged hinterlands in darkness. Bahlau received a field commission after Normandy.

Chapter 24

Cole's Charge at the Carentan Causeway

On the afternoon of 10 June 1944, members of Lt. Col. Robert Cole's 3/502 began moving south along the Carentan Causeway (N-13), passing over the four rivers on the approach. Initially, their ultimate goal was to pass through Carentan and occupy a rise known as Hill 30 at the southeast edge of the city. This would set the stage for linking up with forces of the 29th Infantry Division, driving east from Isigny. (It developed that Hill 30 was far too ambitious of an objective and it wasn't taken until 12 June by 3/501 troopers.)

Lt. Ralph Gehauf of the 502nd PIR flew reconnaissance over the area in a Piper Cub. The ground troops crossed the Jordan River then the Douve, using an improvised crude bridge of ropes and planks over the Douve. The planks soon disappeared and the troops were hauling themselves through the waters of the Douve by hanging onto a rope only. While crossing, the troops were under intermittent mortar and artillery fire. Lt. John P. Painschab of the 502nd was shot dead during this approach and Lt. Raymond "Whispering" Smith, who could be heard from a long distance, suffered a mysterious wound to his posterior.

I/502 led the way, strung out along the elevated causeway. The lower ground on both sides was mostly flooded, but on islands of dry ground in the midst of the swamp, German snipers and machine gun nests had been set up. These banged away at the advancing troops, taking a toll, along with the mortar and artillery shells. By nightfall, the troops were exhausted. Many fell sound asleep and slid down into the water, not even waking up. The hard sides of the embankment were too hard to dig into, and officers moved up and down the line, waking the troops up to separate the living from the dead and keep them moving up. Pfc. Theodore Benkowski of G/502 was among the many men hit by German fire on the approach. He later counted himself among the fortunate because he wasn't killed. A German sniper shot one of his eyes out.

Some time after midnight, a German Stuka dive bomber came screaming north on the causeway from Carentan, firing its wing machine guns. A number of men were hit, and the bullets made sparks on the blacktop road as the plane came on. Halfway up the causeway, another German plane flew from east to west, perpendicular to the other plane's flight. This plane dropped some bombs that killed and wounded a number of men from I Company. The planes crossed paths so quickly that most of the survivors were only aware of the one that came up from Carentan. During this approach, fighting was done on the flanks in knocking out German positions that were firing on the causeway.

Medal of Honor
Lt. Col. Robert George Cole (West Point 1939) of San Antonio, Texas, commanded 3/502. He ordered and led the first bayonet charge of the Normandy invasion on 11 June 1944. Cole was awarded the Medal of Honor for this, but died before it was awarded. A sniper shot Cole in Holland in September 1944. *US Army*

German Bunker
The fields along the N-13 contained many German dugouts like this one, which was only partially completed. Members of the 502nd PIR inspect the bunker as a former tenant lies in front. *Dovholuk*

The 3rd Battalion came on, crossing le Groult (Bridge No. 3) then arriving at Bridge No. 4 at the Madeleine River. Here, the Germans had blocked the way by placing a large concrete and iron gate across the small bridge. Troops were forced to squeeze through one at a time, as bullets from zeroed-in machine guns clanged off the iron of the gate, making sparks in the darkness. G and H companies and part of HQ/3 followed I Company through the gap and troops began to shelter in ditches north of a cabbage patch. Art Parker and a number of strays from assorted units, including the 101st Recon Platoon and the 326th AEB, also arrived. All through the night, men fed through the gate gap at the rate of one per minute.

Beyond the last bridge was a large, open field. A farmhouse on the far side was a German CP. The hedgerow on the south edge of the field had been prepared with German troops and numerous dugouts in the field were manned by enemy troops. Near morning, H company came through the gap at an accelerated rate, numbering eighty-four men and officers. HQ/3 had 121, and there

were sixty left in G Company. Item Company had been reduced within 24hr from eighty men and five officers to twenty-one men and two officers. Lt. Col. Robert Cole ordered I Company to the rear, although Lt. Bob Burns stayed on until wounded.

Some troops made lemonade in their canteen cups and had a ration snack. Others even got a few minutes of sleep before daybreak. Lt. Gordon Deramus of HQ/3's 81mm mortar platoon spent the rest of the night just east of Bridge No. 4 with Sgt. G. F. Verley. At daybreak, it was evident that a large battle was about to take place. Verley remarked, "Heil Hitler, in case we lose."

At first light, Lt. Col. Cole was pacing back and forth south of the Madeleine bridge, giving commands in full view of the Germans. The only thing that saved him, besides God's providence, was the fact that the dug-in defenders had strict orders to hold their fire, lest they give their positions away. Pvt. Bernard Sterno of H Company remembers that his CO, Capt. Cecil Simmons, was whispering to his troops as he gave instructions to deploy them.

"Dammit Simmons," said Cole, "you don't need to talk so low! Those damned Heinies know you're here!"

Pvt. Albert Dieter of H Company advanced to the first hedgerow beyond the bridge and a fusillade of German bullets was fired at him. With one arm shredded by fire, he calmly walked back for first aid. Two men with Dieter had been killed and German fire continued, wounding and killing a number of others. Lt. Col. Cole conferred with Capt. St. Julien Rosemond of the 377th PFAB. Some artillery was in position back near St. Come du Mont and smoke shells were requested. Cole passed the word down the line: "Fix bayonets and prepare to charge the farmhouse upon the blast of a whistle." Many of the men never received the order.

The Charge

By all accounts, Cole's charge got off to a sporadic start. In the first place, many men hadn't clearly received the order, most didn't hear the whistle, and the enemy fire was murderous. Sgt. Elden Dobbyn, of H Company was among the first to rise.

"C'mon! C'mon!!" Dobbyn yelled, waving his arm.

Sterno joined him and more and more men began to get up and run toward the Germans. Another group off to the right was moving along spurred on by Lt. Col. Cole. Much of his group hit the ground when the first heavy fire came at them, but the colonel worked on each man, urging them on. He kept firing his .45 wildly in the general direction of the Germans, yelling, "Goddamn, I don't know what I'm shooting at, but I gotta keep on!"

Despite all the danger, some of the men who heard him couldn't help laughing.

The attackers snowballed, leaping a water-filled ditch which Cole fell into, led by Maj. John P. Stopka, the 3/502 executive officer.

Sterno and Dobbyn came upon a German crouched in a hole and fired on him at the same time. A cord led from the German's body to a P-38 pistol.

"I got that one!" Dobbyn yelled as he ran on.

Sterno wasn't sure if he or Dobbyn or both of them had shot the German, but he paused to get the P-38 pistol. As Sterno lifted the gun, something bumped his hand. An armor-piercing .30-06 round had passed clear through his trigger finger. Sterno was wearing a glove and saw blood coming out both sides of his index finger.

A medic gave Sterno first aid but the medic himself went down shortly thereafter. Sterno treated another wounded man, then firing the P-38 with his left hand, ran on to the farmhouse, now in American hands. Other troopers had carried the fight into an apple orchard behind the house. Lt. Col. Cole saw Sterno's bloody hand and ordered him to move back toward the bridge for more medical treatment. En route, he was hit on three separate occasions. This became known as "The Odyssey of Pvt. Sterno" as related in *Night Drop* and *Rendezvous With Destiny*. (These accounts slighted Sterno as being "runty" and "not the brightest." Neither description fits him. Sterno didn't lose his finger as reported, and the German weapon was a P-38, not a Schmeisser as reported.) With men dropping dead and wounded on all sides, Sterno survived to tell his story.

Back at a ditch near the road, Sterno encountered three wounded men. He sat near them, then heard three "whumps" of mortars being fired from the German lines. Sterno dove for cover, but still received multiple shrapnel wounds on the back, crotch, and legs. The other wounded men were killed by the blast.

One of them, a member of H Company, had a large handlebar mustache. Sterno recalled how Eisenhower had paused to ask the man at the airfield on 5 June, "What did you do before joining the army?"

"I was a waiter in a restaurant in Pennsylvania, sir."

"With that mustache, I thought you might have been a pirate," Eisenhower replied.

Now Sterno looked at the trooper sitting upright with the top of his head missing from the nose up.

Engineers had cleared the iron gate from the entrance to the bridge and Sterno could see Lt. Bob Pick of HQ/502 driving a weapons carrier under heavy fire over the bridge. Pick made numerous trips, bringing up ammunition and taking out

"The Odyssey of Pvt. Sterno"
Pvt. Bernard Sterno belonged to the 1st Platoon of H/502. Company H probably contributed more men to the bayonet charge than any other. Sterno was hit by bullets and shrapnel on four separate occasions on 10 June 1944, while participating in the bayonet charge and moving back for medical attention. He lived to tell about it, too. Sterno's experience has been described in *Night Drop* and *Rendezvous With Destiny* as "The Odyssey of Private Sterno."

the wounded. Sterno eventually walked back during an afternoon truce.

When the bayonet charge was about to begin, Capt. Cecil Simmons was knocked unconscious by a close explosion. While unconscious, he had an out-of-body experience, floating up over the battlefield and looking down on his own body and watching the battle. He saw one of his men ram the bayonet on the end of his rifle into a German, then lift him clear off the ground while impaled.

Simmons drifted back to consciousness about 15min later as one of his men was shaking him. Simmons and the man trotted across the field where heavy firing was still going on. Simmons reached the far hedgerow and came upon a German lying on his belly firing across the field. Simmons shot the German and the dying man made a

"Mad Major"

Maj. John Stopka, known as the "Mad Major" of D-day, led a mixed force isolated in a large chateau near Ravenoville Plage for several days, 6–8 June. He was at the forefront of Cole's Charge and was later awarded both the DSC and the Silver Star. Here, he displays a trophy of the Normandy fighting, a German MP40 machine pistol, usually referred to as a Schmeisser. Stopka was killed on 14 January 1945, north of Bastogne. In a tragic mix-up, he and other US troops were killed by a misdirected P-47 air strike. *National Archives*

Survivor's of Cole's Charge

Some of the key figures who survived the charge posed a few days later at Boutteville. (Left to right) Lt. Col. Cole, 1st Sgt. Hubert Odom of G/502, Sgt. O'Reilly (later captured at Bastogne), and twenty-six-year-old Maj. John P. Stopka, later KIA at Bastogne. S.L.A. Marshall conducted his post-battle interviews here. *National Archives*

face which Simmons later thought humorous, his tongue protruding out of his mouth as he died.

It was written that only two men who made the charge are known to have used bayonets—T/5 James O. Brune, the mail orderly of H/502, and Lt. Edward A. Provost. Brune was later killed, and Lt. Provost was evacuated with a serious face wound. Certainly, each individual who made the charge lived his own personal epic, and many didn't survive to tell about it.

H Company's 1st Sgt. Kenneth Sprecher had been the first to enter the farmhouse after shooting the lock off the door. He was awarded the DSC for his part in the charge. Cole and his command group moved in and occupied the house.

As the day wore on, much small arms, mortar, and artillery fire was exchanged. Lt. Homer Combs arrived from 1/502, which had begun cross-

ing Bridge No. 4. Most of them deployed to the south on both sides of the highway in and near the cabbage patch. Combs pushed west toward the railroad line with a small group of men where they fought a small war of their own for most of the afternoon. Combs was later KIA.

A truce was called in the afternoon to evacuate the wounded, and Maj. Douglas Davison, regimental surgeon of the 502nd, went down the N-13 waving a white flag. He carried a message to the German commander in Carentan, suggesting that he surrender his force. The German declined, but with less flair than Gen. Anthony McAuliffe displayed six months later when the ultimatum was reversed at Bastogne.

It was during the truce that Lt. Wally Swanson, now CO of A/502, was captured while snooping around German lines. Several German soldiers jumped out of a hedgerow, overpowered the big man, and bound him with ropes. He wasn't aware of the cease fire and had more or less blundered into captivity. When Maj. Davison returned from Carentan, the fighting resumed with a new ferocity. The Germans untied Lt. Swanson and gave him a shove back toward his lines (many German soldiers believed in following the rules of warfare). He went on to fight through the rest of the war with the 502nd.

The German troops laid down a terrific base of fire in the afternoon and advanced to one hedgerow from the US bridgehead. Sgt. Harrison Summers of B/502, who had won the DSC on D-day, was among those who helped hold back the Germans. Just when the situation looked hopeless for the paratroopers, an American artillery barrage from nearby St. Come du Mont fell on the front line, killing some friendly troops but crushing the last powerful German attempt to drive the 502nd PIR back across the Madeleine River.

During this day-long battle, the ditch along the east side of the causeway was a sight to behold. It was lined solid with the bodies of dead and wounded troopers. The surviving Americans passed ammunition forward from hand to hand for hours, like an old bucket brigade.

By late afternoon, the German force had been broken and with orders to "defend Carentan to the last man," the Germans pulled back. They would join forces with the 17th SS Panzer-Grenadier Division, which was starting to arrive, in counterattacks. But they would leave only a token force to defend Carentan itself. The might of the German 6th Parachute Regiment had been spent in trying to stop the 502nd PIR on the northern approaches to Carentan.

At this writing, a visitor to the N-13 above Carentan will discover that the town has expanded right up to the south edge of Bridge No. 4. The historic farm field where Cole's charge took place now has a warehouse built on it. The Ingouf farm, which was the objective on 11 June, still stands and is occupied by descendants of the family who lived there in 1944. A Peugeot car dealership now stands on the site of the old cabbage patch. In front is a small marker dedicated to the 101st Airborne. The marker states that at this cabbage patch American parachutists "swept" the Germans away from Carentan.

The Aftermath of Cole's Charge

Late on 10 June, 2/502 moved up along the causeway from their reserve positions to relieve the 3rd Battalion. Hans Sannes of D Company was among them. A half century later, he recalled seeing the water in one of the rivers still red with blood.

"Some things just stick in your mind," he said, "and that bloody water always stuck in my mind."

As the survivors of Cole's battalion, once about 700 strong, formed up in an orchard for a head count at 2000 hours, they now numbered 132. A last salvo of artillery shells burst among the apple trees, killing three more and wounding eight. The battalion marched north to go into reserve with 122 men. The survivors were given a recuperation period near Boutteville where ETO historian S.L.A. Marshall formed small groups and recorded testimony of their experiences. As each man spoke, the others added or corrected, until it was clear what had actually happened. Some fifteen years later, Marshall resurrected his notes from the attack and wrote *Night Drop*.

It is true that no great quantity of medals for

Medic Jack Rudd

Born 29 December 1921, T/4 Jack Rudd was "itching to go" to combat as a paratrooper. The medic from Gloversville, New York, was so determined to get overseas that he didn't even turn himself in for treatment when he was seriously injured on one of his qualifying jumps at Ft. Benning in 1943. Rudd had landed while oscillating and suffered severe pain in his lower back when sitting or if he looked downward while standing. It wasn't until several years after the war that a doctor informed him he had broken his tailbone. Rudd suffered in silence throughout his combat time, afraid only that the injury would prevent him from serving.

On D-day, Rudd had landed near Foucarville and was with his wounded company CO, Capt. Cleveland Fitzgerald.

On 10 June, immediately after Cole's charge, Rudd came up to the cabbage patch area with 1/502. During the hottest part of this action, Rudd ran into the open with only a Red Cross arm brassard to protect him and dragged or carried several wounded men back for treatment. He later found half a dozen nicks on his clothing and equipment where slugs had barely missed his flesh.

One badly wounded trooper evacuated by Rudd was nicknamed "Candy" in the company. Jack felt that the man would survive despite serious eye damage. Much as in the case of Lt. Bernard Bucior (see Chapter 8), Candy vanished before reaching England—perhaps through the same circumstances?

Medic Jack Rudd B/502 receives the DSC from Gen. Omar Bradley, CG of US 1st Army, near Cherbourg, July 1944.

Hill 30, Today
Just south of Carentan near la Billonnerie is a sizable rise some 30m above sea level. This Hill 30 was defended by Ost volunteers and is not to be confused with the Hill 30 near Chef du Pont where the 82nd Airborne fought. On 12 June, the 3/501 stormed up this Hill as its ranks were decimated by 20mm cannons, firing flat-trajectory. Pvt. James W. Bowie of Bowie, Colorado, was a member of HQ/3 501 and claimed to be a direct descendant of the Jim Bowie of Western legend. He was shot to death by an Ost volunteer near the crest of the hill. Few if any prisoners were taken. This photo taken half a century later shows how Hill 30 looked to the troops who charged up. Two DSCs were won in the fighting here. *Author's Photo*

valor were awarded in the 101st Airborne Division in WWII. Many of the men would have met the standards for the DSC as it was awarded in some other units. But exceptional feats were so commonplace in the 101st that many individuals who deserved at least the Silver Star received nothing.

It is also rumored that Gen. Max Taylor wanted only one Medal of Honor per campaign to be awarded within his division. Thus, S/Sgt. Harrison Summers, Lt. Richard Winters, Lt. Charles Santasiero, and others who perhaps deserved the Medal of Honor did not receive one. Lt. Col. Robert Cole became the first member of the 101st to receive that distinction and was to be the only member of the 101st to win the medal in Normandy. Cole would have received his medal around December 1944, but a sniper's bullet ended his life in Holland, 18 September 1944.

On 13 June 1944, Capt. Cecil Simmons of H/502 wrote his first letter from Normandy, saying:

Dearest Folks,
I've got the first rest since I landed in France and as I may get it in the next battle, I've got to hurry up and write while I can.
I think I've seen Hell face to face and have come through it O.K. for the present. I'll guarantee you that on last Sunday morning with my body prone in the mud of France, a dead man in front of me and some of my wounded behind me, I made some vows to God that if He would get me and mine out alive I certainly would keep. . .He did. . . and I intend to keep them too.

Dad. . . you have always admired a German Luger pistol and it might interest you to know that I fought a German Parachute Captain for his. When we were finished, he didn't need his anymore, so I have it now. Hope I can hang onto it. I think I've nearly caught up to my quota and got one for every one in the family. It seems for the present that our armies are victorious and for another hour of freedom I can look on a blue sky and green fields.

On 18 June, Simmons wrote:

You may be sure that the men I brought into combat are a good deal different than the men I am taking out with me. On one occasion my first sergeant and I had our bodies in a ditch and our heads buried in the mud for 5hr, with machine gun bullets ripping our shirts and piercing our first aid packets on our belts. When we got out and the battle had been won, one of the first things I said was, "Chaplain, I swear I'll go to church with you every Sunday, from now on."

Two men of Simmons' battalion wrote an epic poem about the battle of the Carentan Causeway and now it had a name: Purple Heart Lane.

Chapter 25

Carentan

A sizable city located at the bottom of the Cotentin Peninsula, Carentan had to be captured in order for the troops from Omaha and Utah beaches to link up. The 101st Airborne troops broke the main German resistance on 10–11 June in the causeway battles north of the town. Only a token rear-guard greeted the troops who entered the town on 12 June.

The entry of the town was expected to be more difficult and involved an envelopment from three sides, with the 327th GIR coming in from the northeast along the Basin a Flot canal. The 501st PIR was to come across the Vire Taut Canal from St. Hilaire Petit Ville on the east, storming Hill 30

and linking up with the 506th PIR south of the town. The 1st Battalion of the 506th had already reached la Billonnerie south of Carentan in the wee morning hours of 12 June.

The Carentan region is rich with history. Roman troops had used the peninsula as a staging area in their ancient raids on England. Napoleon's troops had built the canals that nearly surround the city, as he once hoped to make it an island, virtually surrounded by waterways.

Many troops of the 101st never got inside the town itself, merely bypassing it and taking up defensive positions to repel the counterattacks that were soon to come.

81st AAATB, Carentan, D+6
12 June 1944, on the N-13 on the south edge of town. A 57mm gun of the 81st AAATB heads west past the point where the N-13 turns north toward Cherbourg. This is not far from the railroad station on the south edge of town.

Crews of the 81st took up defensive positions south and west of the town and were instrumental in holding back attempts by tanks of the 17th SS to retake Carentan. *US Army*

Off Limits

Typically, soon after Carentan was taken, the city was placed off limits to the troops who fought to take it. *Devasto*

Carentan, D+6

A self-propelled 75mm gun mounted on a Czech chassis was abandoned in front of the Carentan church by retreating Germans. Perhaps they had run out of fuel, ammunition, or both. Before leaving, they had removed the track to render the vehicle immobile. It is believed that this is the same mobile artillery piece that fired straight up the causeway during 3/502's approach several days earlier. It may also be the same gun that scored a direct hit on D/506's CP (circa 8 June), killing Capt. Jere Gross and others. The hill where they died, near Dead Man's Corner, is plainly visible with binoculars from Carentan. *Pangerl*

Some troopers went into town to get haircuts at the local barbershop. The big event in town took place on 20 June when an awards ceremony was held in the town square in front of the WWI monument. German artillery fire interrupted the ceremony twice, killing a small French girl. In another incident, a time bomb left behind by the Germans exploded, demolishing a city block.

Recalling the award ceremony, Fred Bahlau wrote:

> Artillery fire broke up the presentation twice. Pictures and a movie were taken of the ceremony. A small girl was killed just after the presentation. She was one of the little girls presenting the flowers.
>
> During the ceremony, they didn't have a bouquet of flowers for me, so another girl ran into one of the buildings on the square and ran back out to present one to me. Of course, this was a big deal to the French and it was all photographed.

During the later part of June, the 501st and 506th were in position to defend Carentan from counterattacks launched from the south or west. During this time, companies were dug in in static positions, but sent out many patrols to keep informed of enemy strength and activities.

One such patrol went out in daylight from D/506. Art DiMarzio was along and Johnny Dielsi was walking point. They approached some farm

Silver Star at Carentan

Sgt. Bruno Schroeder was a graduate of Texas A&M and a member of the S-2 Section of HQ/506. He received the Silver Star for leading the regiment's night flanking movement around Carentan of 11–12 June. *Palys*

"Kidnap CP"
Officers of the 501st move into the former CP of the 506th in Carentan—note the "Kidnap CP" sign at left. Standing is Lt. Werner "Mike" Meier, the 501's IPOW officer. One of the officers has acquired a German paratrooper helmet, which is draped from his folding stock carbine on the wall. *Haslam*

buildings that at first looked quiet and unoccupied.

As the Americans checked the farm buildings, a platoon of Germans suddenly charged out of the nearby wooded area firing their weapons. The troopers immediately returned fire but were outnumbered about 8 to 1. Dielsi was struck by a number of bullets and dropped to the ground. As DiMarzio said: "He was flippin' around on the ground and we thought he was dead, and we left him there." The US patrol fell back to report on their contact with the enemy.

John Dielsi was in fact alive. The Germans bayoneted him and left him for dead. In a scenario more reminiscent of WWI trench warfare or a South Pacific battleground, the battered eagle began crawling in a long, agonized journey, and was eventually found by another company. He was given first aid and survived the war. Back in the States, Dielsi suffered nervous problems, especially during thunderstorms. He is still living in Pittsburgh.

Silver Star for "Iron Mike" Michaelis
Each colonel in command of the 101st's regiments was decorated with the Silver Star on 20 June. This was a day after the devastating rainstorm that played havoc with the Mulberry artificial harbors. Here, "Iron Mike" Michaelis of the 502nd PIR receives his medal. *Musura*

Silver Star Ceremony
Representatives of companies throughout the 101st Division stand at attention before the WWI Victory Monument in the main square of Carentan. This Silver Star ceremony was interrupted a few minutes earlier by German artillery fire. Note damage to buildings. (Standing left to right) Pvt. Walter Sanderson (D/502; KIA), Pvt. David Gifford (D/502; KIA), S/Sgt. Bruno Schroeder (HQ/506), S/Sgt. Harry Clawson (H/506; KIA), and S/Sgt. Fred Bahlau (H/506).

Battleship Barrage
A view of the railroad station at the south edge of Carentan. The tracks were hit by 16in shells from the battleship USS *Texas*. *US Army*

On to Paris
In the main square Carentan, members of the 327th GIR indicate where they'd like to go.

Who Sold Us Out?

On the foxhole line south of Carentan, Lt. F. E. Sheridan watched with concern as his troops guzzled liberated bottles of Calvados, cider, champagne, and wine. Suddenly, the exasperated troop leader shouted: "The next man who pops the cork on a bottle will be shot." Shortly before this episode, two of Sheridan's men, Lowell Whitesel and Eugene "Red" Flanagan, had walked to and from Carentan, returning with armloads of alcoholic beverages. Flanagan was a crusty, colorful character, a bit older than most of his buddies. A confirmed tobacco chewer, Flanagan was known for spitting from one side of his mouth, and talking out of the other side.

Like many others who had landed on DZ D on D-day, Flanagan wondered why the anti-aircraft fire had been so heavy and why the waiting Germans had seemed so ready to repulse the airborne landings. In retrospect, we know that the DZ D serials were the last 101st sticks to jump. Word of alert and alarm had long since arrived from Germans in the DZ A and DZ C areas to the north.

As Flanagan and Whitesel walked out of Carentan, they observed the famed war correspondent Ernie Pyle standing along the edge of the road holding a microphone. A nearby newsreel cameraman recorded the process as Pyle interviewed passing soldiers.

Spotting the battle weary troopers, Pyle called out to Flanagan: "Hey, paratrooper! Do you have anything to say to the folks back in the States?"

Red walked right up to the camera, spit a stream of brown juice, and said, "Yeah! Who the fuck sold us out?"

End of interview.

Flanagan never liked correspondents anyway.

Eugene "Red" Flanagan, bazookaman.

Captured German Paras
Two German paratroopers of the 6th Parachute Regiment captured on a recon patrol near Carentan by members of F/502. Joe Senger (left) and Laurence J. Welsh pose with the prisoners. Senger was killed in the liberation of Holland.
Pistone

Future Congressman
Lt. Jim Haslam took this photo outside Carentan using a German camera he found on a dead man in the ditch along the D-913 above Dead Man's Corner. On the French-made tankette of the 100th Panzer Battalion are Lt. Hugo S. Sims E/501 and Lt. Arthur Cady HQ/501. Sims later became the youngest member of the House of Representatives. He appears to be wearing a German RLB dagger. *Haslam*

Chapter 26

Counterattacks on Carentan

The best-known counterattack on Carentan happened on 13 June 1944, when armored elements of the 17th SS Panzer-Grenadier Division pushed up from Saintény and east from au Vers. But on 12 June, right after the fall of Hill 30, the 501st PIR swept around the south edge of Carentan and began moving down the old Roman highway toward la Billonnerie and beyond toward Eau Partie.

The 2/501 group led off, with F Company crossing fields east of the road and HQ/2 moving right along the road. They collided head-on with a battalion of the 38th SS Panzer-Grenadier Regiment at midday, and a fierce clash ensued.

F/501, with Capt. Sammie N. Homan back at the helm, had been reduced to three officers and about seventy men. They saw SS scouts and deployed to firing positions left and right of a hedge gap on the left (east side) of the highway. F/501's 3rd Platoon was strung out along a hedge on the left flank, with 2nd Platoon in the middle and 1st Platoon on the right.

Soon, dozens of SS grenadiers appeared marching in single file towards F/501's positions. A file of SS troopers came on toward the left flank with their hands raised, as if to surrender, but they still had weapons in their hands.

Another bunch was walking straight toward a gap in the hedge that separated the 3rd from the 2nd Platoon.

Set up in the gap with a light machine gun was Stanley "Pappy" Green who had already accounted for more than his share of enemy kills in the campaign. Green, in his early thirties, was one of the oldest members of F Company.

Crouched above Green holding his M-1 rifle was Leo Gillis (see Gillis' Corner in Chapter 17). Beside them was Walter Malten of Chicago who had been born in Essen, Germany, and spoke German fluently.

Gillis told Malten to yell at the Germans in their own language and tell them to drop their weapons and surrender. The SS troops never missed a step, despite the clear warning from Malten's booming voice.

"What's the idea telling them there's only *eight* of us here?" Gillis asked, chuckling. Malten frowned.

The Germans kept coming and Pappy Green looked up, saying, "Anytime you're ready, Gillis, an-y-time."

Gillis was impressed by Green's demeanor—he seemed totally without fear.

Gillis drew a bead on the lead man in the single file column and said, "Don't shoot yet—when I fire, then you start shooting."

Gillis squeezed his first shot off, from a range of less than 30 yards, putting the round squarely through the lead German's chest. The first three men in the file dropped and Green's machine gun opened up, slashing through many SS men before the determined survivors finally sought cover on the ground. Green's bullets sought them out, shearing through the sparse grass that concealed them and hitting more of them. The others who were foolish enough to get up and charge were quickly mowed down.

Shooting had erupted all along the line and as John Penta walked out to accept the apparent surrender of the SS troops on the left flank, they brought their weapons down suddenly and shot him dead.

The firing went on for perhaps 15min, with those who participated moving up and down and firing from different positions to keep from getting hit in the head. Sgt. Joe Bass caught a bullet in the head and was knocked unconscious but not killed. His buddies Schaffer and Tice dragged him back to battalion aid.

Eventually, the SS began waving white flags and Capt. Homan ordered his men to cease fire, thinking the Germans were ready to surrender. But this was another ruse and when Lt. Raymond Oehler of 2nd Platoon rose up to observe the surrender party, a German fired at him with an MP40 and a 9mm slug hit Oehler in the throat, severing his spine and killing him instantly.

The battle resumed, hot and heavy, with C. C. Moore and Chuck O'Neill manning a machine gun not far from Green's. They returned fire, shooting at any movement in the grass and received heavy counterfire that hit the tripod of their machine gun.

Members of HQ/2 arrived to help hold the line, but the SS grenadiers kept creeping up and built up a devastating base of fire that was clipping the leaves and branches off the top of the hedgerow. Capt. Homan asked his forward observer from the 907th to call for artillery support, but the man was

Pass the Ammunition
This item promoting War Bond sales was syndicated in camp newspapers across the country in 1943. Gillis and his buddy Merritts discussed the odds of such an occurrence, wondering if they'd ever get to make such a shot. Gillis duplicated the feat on 12 June 1944, near la Billonnerie, France.

Three SS Troopers, One Shot
This shot of Gillis was made on Mt. Currahee in early 1943. He holds his favorite weapon, the incomparable M-1 Garand 30-06 semi-automatic rifle. This weapon would shoot through 18in of pine boards at 300 yards, or three SS troopers at 30 yards. *Gillis*

too frightened to speak in the radio. Homan picked it up and ordered the barrage himself.

Allen Hurd of HQ/2 was with Gillis when a German slug wounded Hurd in the shoulder. A bullet hit the root of a tree near Gillis' arm, spraying his forearm and face with fragments and splinters. Around that time, SS troops were trying to turn the left flank. Gillis ran over to Capt. Homan and said, "There's just too damn many of 'em! We've got to pull back to the next hedgerow."

At that time, a general withdrawal began and F Company moved toward the path in the center of their position and ran back two hedgerows from there. Artillery began to fall on the field and aided in covering their withdrawal.

Before pulling back, Sgt. Clem Jahnigen of 3rd Platoon parted the hedge bushes to take a peek through. He was scared shitless, when he came face to face with an SS man who stood on the other side doing the same thing. A potato masher sailed over but the toss was long and the concussion of its explosion merely jolted Jahnigen forward into the hedge. Jahnigen ripped a grenade from the D-ring of his suspenders, bent the lever, ripped out the pin, and popped the grenade barely over the hedge. He heard the blast and a scream, then ran

to join the others in the retreat.

In the retreat, Pfc. Jimmy Lamar of 2nd Platoon was almost back to the safety of the next hedge when a slug caught him in the rear end. He went into a long flat dive, sliding face first through a hog wallow before reaching cover.

German mortar rounds followed the US retreat and Pvt. Al Lisk of 3rd Platoon was hit in the rear also. S/Sgt. Leon F. "Country" Evans of 2nd Platoon had a large portion of his skull blown off by a large mortar fragment. He lay dying on the path and offered up his wristwatch to "Jumbo" Moore before dying.

The company dug in on a new defense line. At that area more mortars came in, one killing Pfc. Leroy Prahm. Prahm had won a lot of money gambling before the invasion and had been mailing it home a little at a time because he wanted to go to college when the war ended.

The American artillery eventually forced the SS to pull way back. This was the closest they would ever get to Carentan on this flank. F/501 went forward to survey the damage and found about thirty dead SS troopers in front of Pappy Green's former position. Leo Gillis found a badly wounded SS man lying in the grass, mumbling in German. He raised his M-1 rifle butt to finish off the dying German, but Blanchard Carney grabbed his arm and pushed him aside. The German died on his own shortly thereafter.

Battle of Bloody Gulch

Elements of the 506th PIR collided head-on with the 17th SS on the afternoon of 12 June, and dug in near Douville. During the night of 12–13 June, Sgt. Louis Truax of D/506 heard SS troopers shouting insults and challenges at the 101st troopers. He even saw some SS standing on the roof of a farm building in the darkness. They were smoking in full view of the American line, hoping to draw fire so their comrades could pinpoint US positions.

The events of the following day were a shock to both sides. Part of Col. Robert Sink's regiment jumped-off early on 13 June in a westward attack, and found themselves passing tanks and infantry of the German 17th SS, headed east in an attack of their own.

Communications Sgt. Louis Burton, F/506's Company HQ, awoke to a shout of "Krauts!" followed by an explosion and shooting. His company had received air drops of candy and cigarettes, but were low on ammunition. They found themselves directly in the path of the German armored onslaught. When attempts to reach battalion HQ by radio failed, Burton was sent back to personally report on the situation to Lt. Col. Robert Strayer. F Company was forced to retreat, which exposed the flanks of the companies on either side of them—a fact that was strongly resented. Certain company-grade officers lodged bitter complaints, resulting in the relief of Capt. Thomas Mulvey as CO of F/506. This was a blow to Mulvey's men, who had served under him since Camp Toccoa. Most of the other companies who fought on 13 June didn't even see any German tanks. In mitigation, it might be stated that the other companies might have fared no better than F Company did, had the tanks hit their sector of the line.

F Company suffered many casualties that day, but one of their rifle grenadiers, Ostrander, made a one-in-a-million shot arcing a grenade that dropped right in the turret of a German tank and dragging the commander down inside before exploding. Despite brave fighting, F/506 was pushed back almost to Carentan before being relieved by the 2nd Armored Division.

West of Carentan is a terrain feature that resembles a dried riverbed or gully, with grass and bushes growing in it. This became the scene of much bloody fighting on 13 June. Members of the 506th PIR variously refer to it as "Bloody Gulch" or "Bloody Gully." This gully runs perpendicular to the railroad embankment west of Carentan and lies south of the embankment.

Lt. Charles Santasiero, who had distinguished himself a week earlier at Brévands, led I/506's attack westward past the gulch on 13 June. His companion for a while was a forward observer from a 155mm howitzer outfit who was to provide supporting fire. This man later went up onto higher ground and called the big shells in right in front of the US positions. Lt. Linton Barling helped Santasiero circle a German machine gun position but disappeared after his canteen was shot off. A trooper from another company told Santasiero, "I want to fight with you." Santasiero never got to know the kid's name. When the SS began swarming in, the kid was captured and spent the rest of the war as a POW.

Santasiero also encountered Lt. Eugene "Iggy" Knott at C/506's positions. Knott looked pale and apprehensive.

"What's the matter, Knott?" Santasiero asked.

"Oh—I'm scared," Knott said. Bullets were flying all around.

"Well Jeez, aren't we *all*?" Santasiero replied.

"Not that . . . If I get it, I hope it's quick."

Premonition of Death
Lt. Eugene "Iggy" Knott (at left, holding the mortar shell) was a tough, wiry man who had once commanded the 1st Battalion 81mm mortar platoon of the 506th. He had a premonition of death shortly before being killed at Bloody Gulch on 13 June 1944. *Don Straith*

Shortly thereafter, Lt. Knott was hit right through the neck and killed.

Santasiero recalled:

> While I'm going up to the gully, someone threw a grenade and knocked me down. I got up and stepped around a tree. The guy is behind the tree and I gave it to him in the stomach. I look up—as far as you could see—Germans coming. I opened up with the M-1, emptied a clip at all I could see. Then an MG42 burst went between my legs, but one round came up into my thigh.

Santasiero hit the ground and fired at another SS man, hitting him in the back. The man spun around and was hit by fire from a German machine gun—the one which had already wounded Santasiero. The wounded SS man was "screaming bloody murder."

Germans were coming up on both sides of the bank and Santasiero had his hands full. Santasiero spotted and shot the machine gunner who had shot him. Santasiero wounded another SS trooper who was almost right beside his hole. The

Carentan-Baupte Road, D+22
Two weeks after the turret was blown off this tank by an M-4 Sherman of the 2nd Armored Division, two 502nd PIR lieutenants stopped to pose for a photo in the chassis. They are Lt. Larry Hughes, and Lt. Joe Pangerl. *Pangerl*

155mm shells came in; "What a mess that was," said Santasiero. The nearby wounded German tried to crawl into Santasiero's hole to surrender to him. He wanted to escape the artillery fire. Santasiero beat the German away with his rifle.

After the artillery barrage, Santasiero was fortunate to be evacuated for treatment of his wounds, but before that, he says, "We stood there and got the situation under control."

S/Sgt. Jerry Beam of I/506 saw more chaotic fighting at the gulch. He was with Cpl. Bryan when an SS trooper jumped up, threw his helmet, rifle, and backpack down, yelled "Heil, Hitler!" and ran away. Beam saw Bryan fire seven shots with his rifle at the fleeing German, missing every shot.

"I *defy* him to try that again. . . j131
I'm going back to a Tommy gun!" Bryan said.

As Sgt. Beam changed positions, he saw one German firing an MP40 from the hedge and sprayed the German with his Tommy gun. He ran back, jumping over three dead troopers (American) whose machine gun had been hit by a mortar round—Beam saw that their gun was twisted as he jumped over them.

In the confusion of the fighting in this area, Len Goodgall of I/506 accidentally shot 1st Sgt. Gordon Bolles of H/506 with his Tommy gun, but most of the rounds were deflected by Bolles' equipment. Bolles returned to H/506 in England after Sgt. Fred Bahlau had already been promoted to first sergeant to replace him. So for a brief, awkward time, H Company had two first sergeants. Bahlau was moved up to HQ/3 506, which solved the duplication.

At a 506th PIR reunion some forty years after the war, someone pointed out Bahlau as the former first sergeant of H/506 to Len Goodgall.

Goodgall humbly approached Bahlau and asked, "Were you the first sergeant of H company?"

"Yes," answered Bahlau.

"I'm awfully sorry, I've felt bad about it all these years, but—I'm the man who shot you at Bloody Gully."

"Oh no, that wasn't me," Bahlau told him. "The man you shot is standing right over there."

Bahlau pointed out Gordon Bolles, and Goodgall was able to speak to him about the unfortunate incident. Bolles, who has since passed away, was reportedly most gracious about it.

God Takes a Hand

While moving up to rejoin his company on 13 June, Sgt. Lou Burton crossed numerous hedgerows. One in particular will always remain in his memory. As Burton was about to hurdle himself over the top, "someone" grabbed his combat harness from behind and jerked him violently backwards. Stunned, Lou landed on his back, just

Counterattacks on Carentan, D+7
This photo was taken along the D-971, just south of the D-223 intersection, facing north, toward Carentan. Road debris is from the failed attempt of the 17th SS Tank Battalion. The American anti-tank crew, armed with a 57mm cannon is from the 81st AAATB, whose A Battery was credited with knocking out three German tanks on 13 June 1944. This highway was also the boundary between the 501st and 506th PIRs.

Orphan of au Vers
Mike Milenczenko F/502 is charmed by an orphan of au Vers. *Pistone*

as a burst of German machine gun bullets shredded the leaves at the top of the hedge—right where he would have been. The mysterious part of the story is that when Burton looked around to thank the man who had saved him, there was no one there. Even more curious was the fact that he had been pulled back so strongly that there were red burns on his shoulders from the web suspenders scraping against them.

In the afternoon, vehicles of the 2nd Armored Division arrived and took the pressure off the 506th PIR. Sgt. Jerry Beam of I Company felt that the 2nd Armored "had more tanks and vehicles than we had men." Also, German forces attacking north on the highway from Saintény had been stopped cold, largely thanks to the 57mm guns of the 81st AAATB whose gunners would not retreat in the face of tanks.

In the afternoon, the Germans pulled back but continued tossing in occasional mortar and artillery rounds.

Sgt. Burton was talking to a group of his buddies when he saw Yochum, another F Company man, standing about 75 yards away. Yochum was waving and calling him to come over and talk. Burton left the group he had been standing with and walked over to see what Yochum wanted.

When Burton asked what he wanted, the puzzled Yochum answered, "I didn't have anything to say to you."

"Well then why the hell did you call me over here?"

"I didn't call you over here."

At that moment, a mortar shell exploded amidst the four troopers Burton had just walked away from. All were hard hit by shrapnel and concussion.

Reinforcements had been requested by 2/506, and Capt. Legs Johnson's F/502 was sent to help. The 2/502 launched a counter thrust without waiting for the promised support of the 2nd Armored. Capt. Johnson led F/502 in a rampage through numerous fields, until they suddenly found themselves outnumbered and almost surrounded by SS troops. He recalled:

When we jumped-off, F Company was jumping, hollering, shooting, and we got too far in advance. We did some crazy things in F Company, even put up some white flags to surrender. But the bastards would shoot them out of our hands; it was pretty hot action. Lt. Banker came in carrying Downey, another lieutenant, who had been shot in the ass. Banker was a big guy and had been a wrestler in college. He laid Downey on the ground.

A Half-Century Later
Site of the 13 June 1944 counterattack by SS Panzer-Grenadiers of the 17th SS Division and a Mark IV tank. The Germans were stopped here by troopers of the 81st AAATB. The D- 971 was designated 171 in 1944. *Author's Photo*

At this time, we were concerned about being captured or doing something to keep from getting our asses shot off. But we had two German prisoners reclining in the leaves, wearing forage caps and with their hands behind their heads. Banker, who was all hepped-up from the battle, saw them and shot hell out of them with his Tommy gun. Another guy hit him and grabbed his gun. I said, "Banker, we're about to be captured. If the Germans come in and see these two guys lying there all shot-up, wearing forage caps instead of helmets, they're going to know we shot them as prisoners."

At that time, the rumbling of tanks was heard and at a distance of 200 yards five tanks of the 2nd Armored could be seen, moving up. But the lead tank veered off to the south before reaching the besieged F Company. In approved fashion, Capt. Johnson ran toward them with Lt. Don Alexander, periodically hitting the ground, then dashing on. The two officers had trouble attracting the attention of the tank crews and finally resorted to firing their weapons at them. "What the hell are you guys *shooting* at us for?" the commander of the lead tank asked. The tanks then followed Johnson to relieve F/502 and the tanks remained for the rest of the day.

Johnson and some of his men clambered aboard the lead tank, which turned left after chasing the Germans away. They headed toward the Carentan-Baupte road on a sunken lane along a hedgerow. When less than 75 yards from the road, the American tank encountered a small German tank coming from the direction of Cantepie. The paratroopers jumped off and took cover as both

tanks stopped to duel. The turret gun of the American M-4 Sherman tank traversed a bit faster than the German main battery, enabling the US gunner to fire first. The 75mm round tore the turret clean off the German tank and sent its commander flying out. As the paratroopers rushed forward, Capt. Johnson saw the enemy commander lying with his intestines out. "He was still alive and his guts were wriggling—it was the first time I had ever seen anything like that."

The troopers tossed a couple of grenades into the opening atop the German tank chassis, and finished this encounter. The 17th SS Panzer-Grenadiers were on the run and eventually pulled back beyond au Vers. The 502nd PIR established a new line and with the 506th went into holding positions a mile outside of Carentan. While at au Vers, the 502nd was able to get some rest and recuperation and to mingle with the friendly French population. Children at the town orphanage became acquainted with the paratroopers.

Lt. Donald C. Alexander, a Rebel from Tennessee, was a bit older than most of the troopers and had a total disdain for the enemy. As he result, he didn't bother to crouch when running from place to place under enemy fire. He was fatally shot on 19 June and received a posthumous Silver Star for attracting the attention of the 2nd Armored tanks on 13 June 1944.

At la Billonnerie

At this area south of Hill 30, the 501st dug in for an extended holding period. Lt. William J. Russo commanded the 81mm mortar platoon of HQ/2 501. Lt. Russo's men were under frequent artillery fire and on one occasion some ancient coins were unearthed by the shelling along the old Roman road. Russo's men brought some of the curious, black, oval-shaped coins to him and asked, "What are they lieutenant?" Russo looked at a Bull's head design on the coins and realized that they were ancient gold coins of Roman origin. Not wanting his troops to abandon soldiering in favor of treasure hunting, Russo told them, "These are of no value men, get back to your positions."

One is often reminded of the great loss of property, homes, and lives that the French people endured during the battles for their liberation. In Normandy, these losses were especially hard to endure because the Norman people had suffered relatively little from the German occupation. Their simple life of dairy farming had gone on, and even in 1940 when France capitulated, the early war battles had not touched their region.

Maj. Harold W. Hannah, S-3 of the 506th, wrote in his journal:

The French are neither friendly nor unfriendly. They are quite noncommittal, as though they didn't know they had been liberated! There is a pre-ponderance of young and old and not many intermediate. They are shy and shocked—so many things have happened so suddenly before their eyes. . . . their homes shelled and bombed, their livestock killed, their homes used by soldiers, their yards and fields stinking with dead Germans and dead Americans. To me it is a sort of abstract and matter of fact reality—to them it must seem a terrible nightmare.

Lt. Russo will never forget a dramatic scene he witnessed while walking along a fenced field near la Billonnerie. In the field, a pregnant cow had been mortally stricken by artillery fire. A French farmer was pulling a stillborn calf from the dying cow. He looked at Russo, shook a bloody fist, and said in English: "Why did you come here?"

Beyond Hill 30 with the 501st PIR

To say that Russo was well liked would be an exaggeration. But his men respected and feared him, and one who meets him feels pity for the Germans who faced him.

As Russo put it years after the war: "A lot of sorry bastards who wore mouse gray regretted the day I joined the Army." Russo was a no-nonsense, all-business type of leader, very competent in all aspects of 81mm mortar gunning. He insisted on the same level of competence from his men.

Bill Russo had joined the CMTC (Citizen's Military Training Corps, founded originally by Calvin Coolidge). Russo had joined at 15 years of age, before the outbreak of WWII, and had received early training from WWI veterans of the 14th Machine Gun Battalion, who instilled a strong sense of professionalism. After being commissioned in September 1942, he served with the infantry before going airborne and joining the 501st. Russo had great respect for the 81mm mortar as a weapon. He knew he could walk HE (high explosive) rounds methodically through a village or city and destroy it more thoroughly than could an aerial bombing raid.

He later said: "If they had listened to me, it could have been done right. . . it could have been done so right." The powers in charge of the 501st had declared before D-day that each of the three battalion mortar platoons would get 120 rounds of

IPOW Team, D+14
Sgt. Fred Patheiger (driver) and Lt. Joseph Pangerl, German speaking interrogators of the 502nd's IPOW Team, paused at the west edge of au Vers. At this spot, the N-803 takes a sharp right turn from the Carentan-Baupte road. Two MPs ride "shotgun" on the back. A very tall crucifix stands here, the base of which is visible above the hood of the jeep near the left edge of the house. *Pangerl*

Master of the Mortar
Lt. William J. Russo HQ/2 501's 81mm mortar platoon, in a 1943 photo. Wherever he served, he took a heavy toll on the German Army. "Their cute tricks cost them a lot of men . . . that's a fact," he said. *Mole*

81mm ammo in equipment bundles. Russo was incensed: "Do you know how fast I can use that up? My guns can fire a round every second and half, and we can do it all day long." Russo wanted to make an ammo depot so his guns wouldn't run out of ammo the first day. If each trooper in the battalion had jumped carrying one round, he could have had his depot. "But they wouldn't listen to me."

By the time the 2nd Battalion faced the 17th SS in holding positions south of Carentan, Russo was getting 81mm ammo by the truckload. He built up his ammo depot at last. He had his four mortars laid on what he suspected was the CP of the 17th SS, about 800 to 900 yards beyond the front line.

He later said:

You can figure the enemy as you figure yourselves. How far behind the line will they have these men fed, if they're eating hot meals? How far are you going to get away from that position? Not too damn far, right? With the mortars, you can move a yard at a time . . . short, down, left, right. I could do 360 degrees in less than a minute. I had pieces of string from the bi-pod out to aiming stakes. I was pretty good with geometry. If I miss you, it will be the first time only, then I'll be right on you.

One afternoon, via binoculars, Russo saw a motorcycle dispatch rider turn at a distant intersection, then approach the suspected HQ of the 17th SS. The next day, the cyclist was careless enough to approach in the same way. 81mm shells from four of 2/501's mortars were on the way. They blew the motorcyclist sky high, just as he was pulling up to the German headquarters. Those who witnessed that incident are still talking about it.

Of this period when ammo was abundant, Russo said:

Maybe at noon, I'd say, "Give 'em twenty-six rounds!" Sit down for a while. "Give 'em another fifteen." All night long. Nooooo rest buddy. You don't feed anybody. . . . You don't move any thing. . . . Nooooo way. . . . To walk on any road in the area would be ab-so-lute suicide. There'll always be one gun popping away. I could make you wish you were never born. I mean that. I've seen woods and areas I've worked on. One time I caught those bastards inside a convent. The nuns weren't there. What a ball they had! HE light walking around the stone wall, 16 pound white phosphorus shells in the courtyard. You talk about a ball! That's what a mortar can do to you!

To deceive the enemy on his source of fire and thus avoid counterbattery fire, Russo used more tricks. The Germans would time the interval between launch report and explosion to estimate range. But Russo said:

I used "Charge Six." That's the most powerful charge there is. It'll launch a round three miles! And maybe I'm shooting at a target 300 yards away. Cheeeeoooh! It's gone for a week. You don't know where it is! Even if you hear them coming in on you. They're all up there . . . then down they come. You could get eighteen of them on you at once—a second and a half apart. The world blows up.

When word came that we were pulling out, I had ammo all over the place. They said, "You'll be required to carry your ammunition back with you." I said, "Yeah? That's what you think!" I bet those Krauts still think another war started. It was just search and traverse . . . with that Charge Six, I never had to worry about friendly troops. We were south of Carentan about 1,000 yards. Near la Billonnerie.

Before returning to England, Russo's men were stationed near Cherbourg. One rainy night, he made a surprise inspection tour of a farmhouse where they were sheltering and discovered some contraband hidden there. To this day, his men believe Russo himself planted it there as an excuse to get his platoon out in pouring rain for a half hour of close-order drill.

Lt. Russo jumped into Holland with D/501 and later went to C/501 as a platoon leader for the duration of the war.

Chapter 27

This Was the Enemy

When the 101st Airborne landed in France, they came in immediate contact with Germans of the 709th Infantry Division who were manning defenses at and behind Utah Beach. Included in Lt. General Karl Von Schlieben's order of battle was the 795th (Georgian) Horse Cavalry battalion of former-Soviet volunteers. Although their home base was in Turqueville, these Ost volunteers surfaced in the fighting at Pouppeville, near St. Come du Mont, at Hill 30, and as far west as la Fiere. Many miscellaneous nationalities served in the 649th Ost Battalion, also part of the

SS Panzer Troops
Elite, black-jacketed SS Panzer troops of the 2nd SS Panzer Division "Das Reich" and the 17th SS Panzer-Grenadier Division "Götz von Berlichingen" drove north from stations in France far south of the invasion front. These reserves were released by Hitler to help repulse the Allied landings, although many other elite SS units were held in the Calais area until Hitler's forces in Normandy were doomed.

This photo, captured later by Bill Canfield, 501 S-2 platoon, shows SS Panzer troops from Das Reich conferring with a regular army general in front of the bank in Parthenay. They were presumably on the move to Normandy at the time. Both Das Reich and Götz suffered staggering casualties in men and vehicles en route to Normandy, thanks to strafing attacks by American fighters. These "Jabos" (short for Jagd-Bombers or hunter-bombers) were feared by the Germans. The planes de-layed the arrival of these mighty German units at the invasion front and greatly reduced their striking power. The 2nd SS took up positions north of Périers and west of St. Lo. Götz went up against the 101st at Carentan.

Baron Von der Heydte, commander of the 6th Parachute Regiment was placed with his survivors under command of the 17th SS on 11 June. They were to counterattack Carentan and drive the invasion back into the sea. Gen. Werner Ostendorff, commander of the 17th SS, was overly confident that he could "get that little job cleaned up all right." Delaying the counterattack for an additional day, he told Von der Heydte that his paratroops would manage until then. "And surely those Yanks can't be tougher than the Russians," he said.

"Not tougher," Von der Heydte replied, "but considerably better equipped, with a veritable steamroller of tanks and guns." The clash of 13 June would tell the tale. *Canfield*

709th Division. Many of those had Asiatic features, which at first caused the troopers to speculate that they were Japanese advisors on Lend-Lease to the Germans to teach them about camouflage techniques. As mentioned elsewhere, some men of 3/506 had landed in the bivouac area of an Ost unit on D-day night, resulting in a no-holds barred slaughter by both sides.

Reports of the fighting efficiency of the Ost volunteers varies, but members of D/502 were tied up for hours on D-day, shooting it out with them near Turqueville. Hans Sannes recalls that the first dead German he saw was actually an Ost volunteer who looked about 6ft 6in tall stretched out on the ground. Others who fought in the area relate stories of wounded American troopers who were left behind in hopes of them being taken prisoner, only to have their throats cut by the Ost mercenaries.

The Georgians at Turqueville had taken some prisoners, as was discovered when they surrendered the village on 7 June. A Russian-speaking GI from the 4th Infantry Division persuaded them

Rommel at Utah Beach
In mid-1943, before Field Marshal Erwin Rommel's inspection tour and a year before D-day, German officers confer on Utah Beach. Although this coastal strong point would never equal the defenses at Omaha Beach, the Germans realized that this stretch of sand held great potential for an Allied landing. The nearby exits provided a means of moving vehicles across the salt marshes behind the coast. After considerable defenses were added, the Germans designated this sector as "Strong Point W-5." It was commanded by Lt. Arthur Jahnke, a Knight's Cross winner who had been transferred here from the Eastern Front to inspire the local garrison. Troops of the German 709th Infantry Division manned the sector, backed up by heavy artillery of the 1261st Artillery Regiment. The 10th Battery of that unit, equipped with 170mm guns, was situated some 10–11mi west of the beach, beyond St. Mere Eglise, its guns zeroed in on the water's edge. Lt. Joseph Pangerl, 502nd IPOW officer, obtained this photo from a German POW near St. Martin de Varreville. *Pangerl*

to give the town up, at which time twenty-three American parachutists were liberated.

The outlook for the Ost volunteers was hopeless—all who were not killed in battle were forcibly repatriated to the Soviet Union after V-E Day. There were suicides and mass rioting in the prison camps and all who returned to Russia were tortured and executed as traitors.

Two Russian-speaking interpreters had been attached to the 101st Airborne before Normandy, specifically for the purpose of interrogating these Ost volunteers. Lts. Imoliev and Judels were their names according to Joe Pangerl of the 502nd's IPOW Team No. 1. Imoliev was a large, impressive-looking man who had been involved in moviemaking in Hollywood before the war. Judels was quite the opposite in appearance.

One afternoon in the CP, the duo were examining some captured weapons at the table of a French farmhouse. The pistol that Judels held fired accidentally, striking Imoliev with a fatal wound to the head.

It is well known that Gen. von Schlieben, who commanded the 709th, retreated north to Cherbourg where he finally capitulated, although he refused to pass the surrender order on to his troops.

The German 91st Division had moved into the Cotentin area shortly before D-day, causing the reassignment of DZs within the 82nd and 101st Divisions. Many of their troops also engaged 101st troopers, and the 91st Division's commander, Gen. Wilhelm Falley, was ambushed and killed in his car by 82nd Airborne troopers of the 508th PIR. This happened at Picauville on D-day morning as Falley was speeding back to his CP from war games in Rennes.

The German 243rd Infantry Division had been stationed on the western portion of the peninsula to protect it from possible landings. A few days after D-day, their 922nd Grenadier Regiment was rushed east to help push back the Utah Beach landings. The 101st met them also, as verified by captured German documents.

Other German units included the 17th Machine Gun Battalion stationed near Brévands. (It was a member of this unit who put his boots on the wrong feet in the excitement of D-day night, as described by Cornelious Ryan in the book *The Longest Day* (Simon & Schuster, New York, New York, 1959), although he wasn't shot by a downed British flyer, as shown in the movie.) The 3/506 probably met these troops as well as German Marine units who had been stationed near le Grand-Vey.

To cover the causeway, the German Army's 191st Artillery Regiment had provided the twelve 105's and the 1261st Army Coastal Artillery Regiment manned the XYZ complex at St. Martin de Varreville.

SS Recon Trooper

SS Mann Eduard Kaermarck 17th SS Aufklärungs Abteilung (recon battalion); killed 12 June 1944, south of Carentan. Kaermarck was among the first members of the 17th SS Division to die in battle with the 101st Airborne. After passing Hill 30 on 12 June, John Urbank of G/501 saw Kaermarck leap out of a hedgerow south of Carentan and spray an American tank point-blank with an MP40 machine pistol. This suicidal attack was answered by fire from the tank's machine gun, which quickly ended Kaermarck's life.

Urbank witnessed this from across a field about 200 yards away. He crossed to search the SS man's body after the tank drove away. Urbank kept this photo and some insignia from the dead man and turned his Soldbuch over to an S-2 man. The interpreter read an insert in Kaermarck's paybook which indicated he was a "Volksdeutsche" (ethnic German volunteer) recruited from an eastern European nation, and that his conduct was to be scrutinized and his loyalty evaluated. This may explain his overzealous and fatal combat debut. *Urbank*

Right
German Grenadier

The first enemy soldiers encountered by the 101st in Normandy belonged to the 709th Infantry Division, like this grenadier killed near Houesville by Lt. Charles Matson of H/502. The German had a premonition of doom, writing in his diary before D-day: "We are going to be like birds going after the enemy and it will mean everyone will be in blood." He knew this would be his last battle. Note the chicken-wired helmet for attaching camouflage. *Matson*

SS Panzer-Grenadier

The pitiless visage of a grenadier of the 38th SS Panzer-Grenadier Regiment; this photo was found south of Carentan. *Urbank*

Fritz Bein, 1944
Fritz Bein of the 3rd Battalion, 6th Parachute Regiment, as he looked in 1944.

German Dog Tag
The identity disk of a German Fallschirmjäger. Parachutist tags had no letters, only numbers. Like all German ID disks, in event of a fatality one half remained with the body, the other half went home. *Author's Collection via Gordon Deramus*

In his combat journal, Maj. Harold W. Hannah of the 506th PIR wrote: "Our first enemy was the German 6th Parachute Regiment—most of the soldiers were young and they gave up easily—they were not tough fighters."

Art "Jumbo" DiMarzio disagreed with this in 1989 when he said, "The only soldier that could stand up next to the American paratrooper was the German paratrooper." There might be some Airborne boastfulness involved here, but consider the performance of Sgt. Alexander Uhlig's platoon of the German 6th Para a month later. Uhlig won the Knight's Cross of the Iron Cross when his forty men wiped out an entire battalion of the 90th Infantry Division near Périers (Seves Island), taking over 300 prisoners, including the battalion CO. French historian Henri Levaufre of Périers is currently preparing a book on this little-known battle.

Fritz Bein, 1989
Herr Bein on a visit to St. Mere Eglise for the forty-fifth anniversary of the invasion's front battles, 5 June 1989. *Author's Photo*

Chapter 28

The Far Flung

Nearly a thousand paratroopers of the 101st Airborne landed so far from their intended DZs that they could be considered beyond the consolidated bridgehead. The troop carrier pilots had scattered them from just south of Cherbourg to just north of St. Lo and as far east as Point du Hoc. The initial effect of this from the standpoint of grand strategy was positive, as it led the Germans to believe that the invading force was much larger than it actually was. For the unfortunate misdropped individuals, however, it became a nightmarish struggle to escape and survive. The epic of these lost men, without food and constantly stalked and outnumbered, is the essence of a paratrooper's war.

One little-known group from I/506 jumped from a crippled plane over Point du Hoc. The lieutenant of the stick (Lt. Floyd Johnston) landed topside on the cliffs and was wounded in the arm. Len Goodgall and Ray Crouch, two other jumpers, landed on the narrow rocky shore below the cliffs. The group had never been briefed about Point du Hoc or the significance of the cliffs and their gun emplacements. Goodgall and Crouch roamed up and down the beach all night, puzzled as to where they were and hearing bombs explode topside as planes flew over. Their plane had been losing altitude when they jumped and had crashed into the Channel with the rest of the men aboard.

At dawn, Goodgall and Crouch saw landing craft coming toward them and thought, "Great, they're sending a rescue party to get us." But it was in fact the 2nd Ranger Battalion coming to assault the positions atop the cliff. They landed and began firing their ropes and grappling hooks up to the top.

"If you wanta get outta here, Mac, come with us!" they said.

Goodgall and Crouch climbed the cliff with them and fought with the Rangers for several days. Both were cited by a Ranger officer for their excellent combat performance.

A B/506 stick was misdropped in the wasteland between Isigny and Carentan. This lost group was supposed to be at Pouppeville on D-day and obviously never reached its objective. Included in the group was a tough sergeant named Edgar Dodd who had been a member of the original Parachute Test Platoon back in 1940.

Sgt. Herb Clark was in this group and recalls that one of his buddies "Went Hairy Carey" when he found another buddy dead, hanging in a tree in his harness. The Germans had got there first and sprayed the trooper across the midsection so heavily with machine gun fire that the whole lower portion of his body (hips and legs) had dropped off, leaving only the head and torso suspended. The "Hairy Carey" trooper killed all prisoners subsequently taken by this group and was later transferred out of the 506th.

One group of Germans surrendered in a small hamlet and Clark talked to one of them. This prisoner was in his thirties and had a wife and kids. He spoke good English and stated that he used to live in the States.

"C'mon, you guys, you don't have to shoot me," he said.

The "Hairy Carey" trooper lined up all the prisoners, including the one Clark spoke to, and mowed them down.

This group eventually joined forces with a Ranger platoon led by a lieutenant. There was some friction between Sgt. Dodd and the Ranger lieutenant.

"Come to attention and salute me," the lieutenant said.

"Go to hell," Dodd told him, "You think I'm going to salute you in the field? You're crazy!"

Another stick led by Lt. Robert Saum of I/501 came down just north of St. Lo and worked north for a week, moving mostly at night. Despite some close calls, they reached Carentan without making contact with the German forces.

Sgt. Dennis McHugh of that group recalls their only casualty was a man who wanted to stay behind and surrender. He eventually stabbed himself in the leg with a trench knife and was taken prisoner by the Germans. In the battles of the subsequent weeks, the same man was recaptured and, once liberated, came back to the 501st PIR.

One plane of H/501 crashed two fields east of Dead Man's Corner (see Chapter 20). The plane had strayed to the south and was trying to correct its flight path but lost altitude as its men dropped out in the flooded area near Baupte. A group of the men, including their lieutenant, assembled and hid in the boondocks throughout D-day. On the morning of 7 June, the lieutenant called his men together and told them to shave ("It's an old army tradition to shave, even in the field").

At this point, Sgt. Norman N. Nelson stood up on a tree stump and addressed the group:

> Men, it appears to me that we're suffering from a lack of leadership here. We have more important things to worry about and we've got to do something soon. If you follow me and let me lead you, I'll get us out of here. If you want to shave, go over there with the lieutenant. Lieutenant, you're welcome to come along, but I'm in charge.

With that, Nelson, who had been in the regular Army since 1937, strode off and the men followed him. The lieutenant and Sgt. Joe Cardenas trailed along behind them. This group was found by Maquis (French resistance) leader Jean Kapitem, a salty man in his thirties with a scarred face. Kapitem had been waging war against the Germans since France was occupied in 1940. He led the group to his village at Saintény, on the Carentan-Périers road. The group hid in the outskirts as the Maquis supplied them with water, meat, and bread. Also in the area were misdropped men from 1/501.

Harry Plisevich and Leonard Morris of H/501 were also in Sgt. Nelson's group. While hiding at Saintény, everyone in the group was reported MIA. They saw endless columns of German vehicles and some tanks speeding up the highway. It was the 17th SS division coming up to the line in darkness. The enemy were too numerous and well equipped; attacking them would have been suicidal. Nelson's group eventually worked north by night, making contact with the 2nd Armored Division after the fall of Carentan.

Other sticks from 3/501 had landed near

Baupte, and Capt. Hotchkiss, the CO of I/501, was ambushed in a courtyard in the town and killed along with Pfc. Joe Gonzales, a member of his company.

After a brisk firefight outside the village of Baupte, more 3/501 troopers were killed and captured, including Cpl. Johnny Clapper (KIA) and Pfc. George King (POW). Capt. Albert W. Mitchell, S-2, and Sgt. Clarence E. Spangler did a splendid job, reportedly shooting forty Germans between them before they were wounded and captured. Capt. Mitchell had grown a magnificent handlebar mustache before the invasion, which extended from ear to ear. Col. Howard Johnson, who had "banned" mustaches in the 501st because they made the men look "old," had ordered him to shave it off. Mitchell, who waxed the mustache proudly each day, had refused.

H/501 medic Leo Westerholm was among the prisoners near Baupte, when Mitchell and Spangler were brought in. He wrote in his diary:

> 1st Sgt. Spangler and Capt. Mitchell came in all beat to pieces. The Jerry was mad as the dickens at them and we found out later why. The Jerries told us they had "murdered" an officer and two men. The captain and sergeant told us they didn't expect to see the end. They were taken to Cherbourg, interrogated, and shot. Their bodies full of lead were found later in a mud hole. That's war, I know, but I know both were married and the sergeant had two children.

Many troopers of the 377th PFAB had landed in the Valognes-Montebourg area and some were soon killed or captured. Felix "Doc" Adams, the 377th's surgeon, landed on the roof of a German CP east of Valognes and was knocked unconscious from the impact. He awoke to find himself a POW. Doc Adams did a lot of good work, giving aid to other prisoners and was soon liberated in the fighting near Cherbourg.

Elton Carr of HQ/377 landed up near Quinéville and was captured on D-day afternoon. He says 1st Sgt. Ralph E. Odom landed in the ankle-deep shallows of the Channel. As he stood unfastening his chute harness, Germans walked out to take him prisoner. After being captured, Carr was in an unknown village and saw an open-backed German truck drive through loaded with dead German soldiers. The 101st troopers in that area had taken a heavy toll, despite the many troopers killed and captured and despite the fact that many of these fierce fighters were artillerymen. When the 101st returned to England in July 1944, only 218 of the 450 troopers of the 377th PFAB who jumped on D-day were available to go back.

A group of B/501 men with strays from the 507th PIR became legendary at Graignes, France,

Somewhere in Normandy, Jack Breier of H/501 photographed these members of his group, including Cpl. Charles Starnes, S/Sgt. Clarence Tyrell (later KIA), T-4 John Posluszny, and two unidentified men. *Breier*

east of Carentan. Alternately hiding in the swamps and raiding the village, the group waged an isolated battle for a week. Capt. Loyal Bogart of B/501 had been wounded in the plane, but jumped anyway. He was eventually captured by the Germans who executed him along with two local priests. One trooper who was trapped in the town successfully hid from the Germans by concealing himself in the stone oven of the town baker. The oven is still there.

Yet another group under G-3 Raymond Millener landed far west of Carentan. These divisional HQ troops joined with men from HQ/501 and inflicted serious damage on Germans in the Picauville area. The list of far flung actions is extensive.

Adventures of Sgt. Arthur Parker
Sgt. Arthur Parker was one of the group of 377th PFAB troopers badly misdropped between Montebourg and Valognes (see Chapter 3).

My name is Arthur Parker and I was a sergeant in the 377th Parachute Field Artillery. I parachuted into Normandy on 6 June 1944 as a survey and instrument man. I was to map the targets we were to fire on and help the infantry when needed.

The history books show that the 377th PFAB got little credit for what we did as infantrymen. I for one was in the fight for the causeway above Carentan as were many men from other outfits, as their helmet markings indicated at that time. Many soldiers in the bayonet charge were not in the 502 PIR. We strays who couldn't find our own regiments or battalions just fought with any outfit we came across that had food and ammunition to give.

I know we can't change history, but somewhere, someone can insert facts that will make history a little more accurate. The following concerns my small role in the Normandy invasion. . . . I hope that all those lost and forgotten paratroopers that fought with other outfits at least get a mention.

I started down the flight path, knowing eleven men jumped behind me. After wandering, heard men talking, gave them the cricket, and located four men from the 377th PFAB, but none from my plane. We huddled around a map and one man said he had crossed a blacktop road off to the right. I suggested we go there, where we picked up six more men of the 101st but not the 377th. One of them suffered from a head wound and asked that if we have to leave him, to kill him first. I told him that he goes where we go, and nobody gets left unless he is dead. I took charge of this group because I was the oldest man there; I was the ripe old age of twenty-six.

Heading toward the sound of firing on the road, we challenged a group from the 82nd Airborne with a cricket. We received a voice reply, as they had no cricket. It was a captain from the 82nd and

three men. I think his name was Russell. We had another huddle and looked at his map, which was different from mine. We still didn't know where we were. It was starting to get light and I knew we had to get off the road soon or the Germans would be on us. The captain said that there was a big barn down the road where he came from and he wanted to go back there and hide out until daylight or until we found out what kind of troops were in the area. I told him we were going out in the fields and have a little cover and room to move around if we had to. I told him I was against going to the barn as this was one of the first places the Germans would look when they found all the empty parachutes in the fields. He said he could order us to go, but he was taking his men and we could go wherever we wanted, seeing as we were 101st.

The 101st men said they didn't like the barn idea and would rather be out in the open. We moved to the left of the road about two small fields over. Everyone was dead tired, but I insisted that one man would have to be on guard and another to lay on top of the hedgerow to watch the road. There was traffic on the road, and it was all German. Myself and another man crawled over to the next field and got a .50 caliber machine gun, complete with ammo, from an equipment bundle under an orange parachute. We were hoping the bundle was food and water as we were starting to hurt.

We brought the machine gun back and cut the orange chute in pieces and gave each man a piece to use as a friendly recognition signal. We changed bandages on the boy with the head wound and it didn't look good. We had no water left to wash his wound, and he wanted more morphine, but I couldn't ask the other men for theirs. One of the men volunteered to give half a shot of his morphine to ease his pain. My lookout on the hedgerow motioned for me to come up to him and pointed over the road where six German soldiers were marching Capt. Russell and his men down the road. I knew that the barn was not a good place to hide.

We saw three P-47 fighters open up on someone on the road and when they came back, I got the men out in the open and we started to wave our orange rags. The planes saw us as they flew over and tipped their wings, but they circled back and came back at us with every gun blazing. They churned up the field with those machine guns in the wings. Lucky for us they were bad shots as none of us were hit, but they did scare the shit out of us.

We began to move east, which was a big mistake; the planes must have radioed ahead to one of the cruisers off the coast. We heard big, heavy shells whistle toward us. When they hit, they would leave a crater about 50ft across. Four shells came in the first volley, but they were a little short. We ran to the nearest hedgerow to get behind it. As I crawled through the hedge, I fell in a foxhole with a German soldier in it. We were too close to use guns. I got my knife out of my boot and gave him a jab in the liver, and he went down without a sound. The next four shells came in right where we had been a few minutes ago, but on the other side of the hedgerow. There must have been a spotter plane that could see us and was calling fire down on us. We laid in the hedgerow for a while and no more shells came in.

We regrouped near the foxhole with the dead German and searched him for food. He did have a canteen of water, which we all shared, and a few pieces of hardtack with caraway seeds, which tasted very good to us. According to the dead soldier's pay book, he was only fourteen years old. He had cut shelves into the side of his foxhole and lined them with books. His rifle wasn't loaded.

Even though it was daylight, we figured we were spotted now; we collected our machine gun and moved on. We figured German patrols would be out looking for us, but headed southeast. We still didn't know where we were or where we were going. We crossed a field that had green oats growing in it. We tried eating these green oats; they were milky and bitter and had a hard green spike on them. They were very hard on the mouth, but everybody did eat a few handfuls.

We went through a hedgerow and found six paratroopers from the 101st Airborne who were as lost as we were. They said the way we were going, we would run into a lot of Germans, as they lost ten men in a fight they had that morning. They also led us to a small wooded area where we found four paratroopers tied to trees, with their penises cut off and left to bleed to death. Those Germans were mean bastards! We didn't know what division the dead men were from as the Krauts had cut off their shoulder patches and arm flags for souvenirs. (As most units of the 101st didn't wear the armflag in Normandy, the dead men probably belonged to the 82nd Airborne.)

We headed south, hoping to find friendly troops. We now numbered sixteen, and had a regular machine gun crew for our .50 caliber. Before that we were thinking about ditching the heavy bastard as we did not have enough men to carry the gun and ammo and two men to carry our wounded man, who was now going blind on us but could still walk with help. His head wound was now infected, and yellow pus was running down the side of his head. We asked him again if he wanted to be left by the side of the road where the Germans would find him and give him first aid. He said again that he would shoot himself if we left him. He said he knew he was slowing us down but would try to keep up. By now we were all giving him our morphine, hoping we wouldn't need it for ourselves if we got hit. Water was still our big problem, next to food.

We pushed hard all day and made five miles, which doesn't sound like much. But with the country we were going through, dodging German patrols and having a blind man with us, I thought we did great.

We found this little farmhouse and watched it for an hour with our machine gun set up to cover it. We saw no wires coming from the house so we knew that they had no phone to report us if they decided to. Four of us approached the house and knocked on the door. A real old man opened the door and stood there with his mouth open. For never in his life did he see four American soldiers with dirt streaked faces and dirty clothes, our beautiful jump boots worn and ragged, and four rifles stuck in his face. We showed him the American flag sleeve patch and he yelled for mama to come see the sight of the saddest looking bunch of American soldiers anywhere. They jumped around like kids, hugging us, and laughing and crying.

We asked if there were any Boche around; he pointed a full circle around his house. We then made motions like we were drinking, we wanted water. He thought we wanted wine or brandy and he brought out a bucket of Calvados. We indicated washing, and he understood and brought us a bucket of water. After we drank our fill, we took the water to the other men outside and everyone got their water. We brought the wounded man into the house and the French mama clucked over him like a mother hen. She washed and dressed his head wound, which made us sick to look at. There was a little spring house out back with a cement tub used to cool milk. We used the old hand pump to fill the tub and we all washed, soaked our feet, and put on clean socks.

We got our maps out and with help of the old man, located our position by St. Mere Eglise, which was on our maps, and indicated we were near Valognes, which was not on our maps. He pointed the direction to St. Mere Eglise and indicated he saw five troopers from the 82nd yesterday but they didn't stop. He drew two AA [the 82nd Airborne patch has an AA in the center, meaning "All-American"] on a piece of paper, and 5, and gave us two big round loaves of bread and a jar of apple jelly. We made him take a handful of invasion money and indicated he should hide it if the Germans came. We asked the wounded man if he wanted to stay with the Frenchman, and he said no.

We said good-bye to the old French couple, and headed south. We seemed to be between two paved roads, as we could hear traffic from both directions. After a few hours, we came to the railroad tracks, which we thought was miles from our position. We had to decide if we should cross the tracks or stay on the side we were on. Another sergeant and I crept up and saw there was a light coat of rust on the tracks, so no trains had used them for several days. We took turns covering each other as we crossed the tracks. We also pulled down the wires that ran along the tracks.

About a half hour later, we ran into trouble; mortar fire started to come in on us. We headed toward the embankment, but the fire followed us. The Germans had us under observation. We made the embankment and worked along the ditch by the tracks. The mortar fire let up for a minute, and we thought the Germans lost us. Working down the ditch, we found that we were getting squeezed by a river on our right and the railroad on the left. There was no chance of crossing the river in daylight, so we were forced to get on the other side of the tracks again. This time, the machine gun opened up on us, as each man tried to cross, but about ten of us made it across.

Mortars came down again and we were split into two groups. Our machine gun was with the small group on the other side of the tracks. MG fire was now raking the embankment, and I knew it would not be long before a patrol would follow up their fire and try to flank us. One of the men, Sgt. William Crowley, said that he would try to get our machine gun over to our side and to watch where the Germans were going to attack us from as he raced across the tracks. We spotted the machine gun that was firing at us and I shouted to Crowley to move back up the tracks a ways. I said when we fired at the enemy gun to try to get back across to us with our gun. After a few minutes, we opened fire on the enemy and drew their fire. Crowley and his group crossed the tracks, bringing the machine gun and the blind man.

We crawled south a few hundred yards down the ditch. One of the men spotted seven German soldiers heading across a field toward us. The German machine gun was still firing short bursts, but they were way behind us. The patrol was heading toward us. We split up, some going left and some going right, and quickly set up our machine gun on the edge of the ditch. We got it ready to fire.

I took a few men with me, and we crawled down the ditch. We had to stop on the right flank of the patrol or they would be in the same ditch with us. The German machine gun went silent, as they were getting close to our own men. The patrol wasn't sure where we were, as they kept firing their machine pistols in a sweeping fire in our direction. I told my men to put all their fire on the right flankers when our machine gun opened. Our machine gun started firing and we laid our fire on the flankers. The Germans hit the ground fast; I was surprised how seven men could hide in a few inches of grass. Two of them made a dash toward us, while the others gave them covering fire. Our machine gun just cut them down. The right flanker made a dash for our ditch, but he had a long run and before he even got close, the machine gun cut the legs out from under him. We now had to worry about the left flanker, as he was close to our ditch when he went down. We lobbed a few grenades in the direction where we thought he was. We still had three or four Germans lying out in front of us. Our machine gun raked the ground in front but we saw no movement and heard no outcry.

After what seemed like hours of waiting, two of the Germans jumped up and made a break back to their own lines. At least ten rifles and the machine gun stopped them dead in their tracks. We only had one or two Germans to worry about now. A Sgt. Swan said he would crawl out and see if he could find out if any Germans were alive out there. He crawled out and was gone about 15min. We heard a loud whisper "Don't shoot!" Sgt. Swan crawled back into the ditch. He said that all the Germans were dead, and he had a German pistol to prove it. A few of the men wanted to go out in the field and look for pistols and I reminded them that there was a German machine gun out there and one German that we didn't account for. We were all excited as we had met the enemy for the first time and beat him.

The missing German must have gotten back to his own lines or they knew their patrol was dead, as they opened up on us again. We fired a few bursts from our machine gun just to make them keep their heads down. We heard the cough of the mortars again as rounds began to walk across the fields toward us. Some of the rounds fell among their own dead. We made haste to get out of there and work our way south in the railroad ditch. We spotted a bridge that crossed the river (we found out later it was the Merderet River); we knew the Germans wouldn't let us get across that bridge. Heading east along the bank of the river, we began to receive direct fire from a tank or self-propelled gun. Two of our men were killed by the first round. We headed for the shelter of the riverbanks. As we crawled along the banks, the fire continued, but went over us. We came to another bridge. The river made a half circle and we were back to the railroad again.

Hearing all the firing, the Germans guarding the bridge were waiting for us to show up. As we dashed for the railroad ditch, the Germans opened fire with machine pistols and rifles. They did hit two of our men. We didn't know if they were killed or wounded and captured. We made the ditch, set up the machine gun, and fired at the bridge. The Germans didn't know we had a heavy machine gun; their firing stopped real quick.

We followed the tracks south until we met a paved road running at a sharp angle away from us. We got in a triangle-shaped field and found signs of a large firefight. Spent cartridges and bloody bandages were lying around, plus a lot of steel pots with 377th markings on them. These men were probably wounded and captured, no graves or bodies were around. We heard heavy firing off to our left and started in that direction, but picked up fire from the self-propelled gun again. So we reversed directions again.

We knew we would have to cross the paved road before dark. Sgt. Crowley and another man scouted around for a good place to cross. In awhile, they returned and said we could cross at the railroad tracks, as it was unguarded. We set up four men with the machine gun, covering the road and tracks. We all made it across without drawing any fire. The men were all tired and wet and wanted to stop and rest. I told them the self-propelled gun would get us if we stopped, as they knew this area and we didn't. Sgt. Swan and another man went to scout off to our left to see who was fighting there and what town we were near. We never saw them again.

We were now down to ten men, and one was blind. We took the machine gun apart, throwing the pieces in the ditch as we walked along. We were running out of ammo for it and it was getting heavier with every step we took.

Using the railroad ditches as good cover, we

moved the rest of the day and most of the night, with only a few short naps. We didn't understand why the Germans didn't come out in force against us, as they knew we were in the area. We later found out that the 82nd Airborne was off to our left, and they had the Germans tied up. Still heading southeast, we were having trouble staying on our course as the ground was getting swampy. We had to keep bearing to our left, where we could hear the sounds of heavy fighting.

We ran into a German patrol that was guarding the railroad and had a short firefight with them, and three of our men were killed there. We were real short of rifle ammo, no shortage of hand grenades. We had to get in the swamp to get away from the Germans, which made it slow traveling, but at least we had water to drink. Not very good, but it was wet.

We worked east along the edge of the swamp; that was the only direction open to us without going back the way we came. We heard light firing ahead and hit the ground. Two men went forward to see what the situation was. They returned in about half an hour and said they thought there was an American outpost ahead, but they were not sure. We all went forward on our bellies and watched for a while. We saw nothing but freshly dug foxholes. We clicked the old cricket a few times, no reply.

We saw a helmet and the barrel of a rifle come up from a foxhole. It wasn't a German coal bucket helmet. We hollered that we were Americans, and someone asked for the password. The only password we knew was a week old, but we shouted "Flash" and got a reply of thunder. The voice told us to stay down and crawl toward him. We got to about 50 feet and could talk without shouting. He asked which outfit we were from and I gave him our code name of Kite, which meant nothing to him. I asked him his outfit and he answered, "The Deuce." I asked, "You mean the 5-0-Deuce?" and said we were 377th. He said we should stay where we were for the time being as there were Germans close by.

He must have had to phone someone and said in a few minutes they would open up with their machine guns to cover us and to move to the right side of the hole. When the guns opened up, we crawled into the front lines of the 502nd PIR. These were the first Americans we saw in five days. A lieutenant took us back to a dugout they were using for a CP and questioned us, while we ate K-rations and smoked our first cigarette in a long time. A medic came and took our blind man away. The lieutenant told us he heard the 377th PFA was wiped out and had only one gun in action of the twelve we parachuted in with. I asked where Headquarters Battery was and as far as he knew, there was none, although some of our officers were with one of the regiments, south of St. Come du Mont. He pointed it out on our maps. We drew some ammo and I swapped my carbine for an M-1 rifle, and the four of us took off to try to find our battalion or some of our officers, so they could report us alive.

Here ends the ordeal of Art Parker and his group in getting back to American lines. Their experiences were somewhat typical of those who made it. Many misdropped troopers moved and hid alone for hours, days, or weeks until killed or captured. Ken Putterbaugh of B/501, wandered alone until 20 June before being captured. He had been dropped far southeast of Carentan.

As Parker mentions, food and water were a prime concern to the far flung and halizone pills were dropped into stagnant water taken from puddles, which killed some of the bacteria, but did nothing to improve the taste. John Kolesar, a 377th buddy of Parker's, relates that he even ate a raw chicken in his struggle to survive the long trip back to friendly lines.

It is interesting to note that 377th PFAB men were not eligible for the Combat Infantrymen's Badge (CIB) because their units were designated as "batteries," rather than companies. In some regular infantry divisions, there were artillery units known as Cannon Companies. The "company" designation made those men eligible for the CIB. Art Parker became an exception to the rule because of a special exploit in Holland in September 1944 wherein he knocked out two German tanks with a bazooka. He was awarded both a Silver Star and a CIB, which appears on his discharge. Around 1988, Parker received a letter from Washington, D.C., stating that he was no longer eligible to wear his CIB!

As we can see, members of the 377th PFAB did plenty of infantry style fighting and this was one of the great injustices of the military system in WWII. Members of the 326th AEB also did plenty of fighting in the infantry mode; they were also ineligible for the CIB because of their "engineer" designation.

To amplify the German atrocities (certain grisly details were removed in editing) reported by Parker, it can be said that another 377th PFAB man who landed in the same vicinity (Lamar Weeks, C Battery) entered a barn and discovered another war crime. Hanging from the rafter of the barn were two paratroopers and a French boy about ten years old. The Germans had apparently discovered the US soldiers hiding in the barn and executed the boy who lived there as punishment for aiding the Americans.

Of the handful of troopers who survived the trip back in Parker's group, one was later killed at Bastogne and two others have passed away since WWII. Art Parker is indeed a survivor. When Art reached the N-13, he headed south along the Carentan Causeway from Dead Man's Corner in search of his battalion. He remembers seeing a billboard advertising Singer Sewing Machines on the east side of the elevated causeway road and farther south, on the same side, a large yard full of cattle skeletons from a slaughterhouse-type operation. He made his way across the four bridges, along the hard sided elevated causeway embankment and had more close calls.

501st PIR Strays at
St. Georges du Bohon

Several planeloads of troopers from 1/501 were misdropped south of Carentan, north of Saintény, in the vicinity of St. Georges du Bohon.

Maj. Phil Gage of Atlanta, Georgia, was among the first casualties in the area on D-day night. He heard what he thought was a cricket signal and replied with his own. He received a blast of gunfire in response, which nearly severed his hand at the wrist. He was captured and the Germans finished amputating his hand while he was a prisoner. After playing hide and seek for half the night and into the day, the German parachutists, superior in number, began to close in. Bill Spivey, a Texan from A/501, lost an eye when a grenade exploded in his face.

A mixed group of troopers from HQ/1 and A/501 found themselves in a ditch, with their backs to a hedgerow, firing across a field at German paratroopers. Sgt. Alex Haag was firing his carbine across the field when suddenly a hard object thumped him on the back. It was a German eiergranate (egg grenade), with blue smoke sputtering out. A Fallschirmjäger had gotten behind the Americans and was moving along the rear of their hedge, tossing grenades over at intervals. Haag rolled away, but the concussion grenade exploded and knocked him unconscious. When Haag awoke some 15min later, he was surprised to discover the fight still going on. He retrieved his carbine and resumed firing.

Haag understood the German language but wished he didn't when he heard a German troop leader shout the command to close in and finish off the Americans. The US troops were outflanked and outnumbered, so Capt. William Paty, who was wounded, stood up to signal surrender of the group. All prisoners in the area were taken to the local church, which was about 300 yards from where most of them were captured. The Germans had observers in the church tower who had helped seal the fate of the Americans in the area.

Joe Taylor, a Native American trooper from A/501, was among the men captured and saw a number of wounded troopers lying in the aisles of the church. Maj. Phillip Gage was among the wounded and had not received any medical attention.

Taylor wrote: "The surviving troopers were ordered to bury our nine men killed in action. I knew only two of the nine and they were from A Company." He recalled that his group also buried Germans killed in the engagement in the grounds near the church. There were more dead Germans than Americans, and it seemed to Taylor that each German had been shot between the eyes or in the center of the forehead. For Joe, Alex Haag, George Brown, Allen Lyde, and others this was the start of a long ordeal as POWs. Maj. Gage, who was also wounded in the stomach, looked "like there was no way he could possibly survive." But he survived to become ranking officer at Stalag 221 at Rennes and was fortunate to be liberated there on 4 August 1944.

An interesting footnote to the action at St. Georges is that the church was later completely destroyed by shelling and bombing. It was rebuilt after the war in its original configuration. The church has an unusual shape to the spire, and contributed to the death of 1st Sgt. Wilburn Ammons of A/501. On the night of the jump, Sgt. Ammons' parachute caused him to oscillate into the side of the steeple, breaking his neck. He was among those buried in the church grounds by the POWs.

Before the division returned to England in July, word reached Lt. Sumpter Blackmon of A/501 that the bodies of some men in his company had been located by the ruins of the church at St. Georges, and he took a detail of men there to retrieve the bodies. They were interred in one of the US cemeteries at St. Mere Eglise, later to be re-interred at St. Laurent, above Omaha Beach.

Many years after the war, Lt. Thomas Johnson, a former surgeon of the 501st PIR who had been captured near St. Georges, returned to the small village and visited the local priest. He left with the priest a drawing showing the flight of US planes over the village on D-day and a few artifacts, including one of his dog tags. These items are now displayed in the Airborne Museum in St. Mere Eglise. The priest donated them to the museum around 1990.

Capt. Robert Phillips' Group

Several sticks from 1/501 landed far south of Carentan and assembled under the leadership of Capt. Robert Phillips, CO of C/501. Traveling mostly after dark, the group scored an impressive number of victories against enemy groups in their week-long trip back to friendly lines.

Some far-flung groups were constantly hounded and pursued by enemy troops. Others managed to avoid contact completely in their trip back. Phillips' group was perhaps the most brilliant of all, as they inflicted enemy casualties continuously while suffering only one of their own.

Phillips later wrote:

I can truthfully say I never considered surrendering. This did happen to others. Perhaps the circumstances were such that we never had to con-

1st Lt. Edwin B. Hutchison
Hutchison was killed outside Carentan just before Capt. Robert Phillips' group rejoined the 101st. Hutchison was a member of B/501 and Phillips called him "one of the most courageous and gutty men I have seen." *Hamilton*

sider such a proposition, but we did engage the enemy on numerous occasions at close quarters. We were stealthy, cautious, and bold at the proper times.

Phillips' group eventually joined up with other troopers led by Lt. Edwin Hutchison of B/501 and Lt. Chuck Bowser of C/501. They eventually comprised a group of eighteen men and three officers.

Lt. Bowser later wrote:

When I jumped, my chute opened just before my feet touched the ground. The plane seemed to be losing altitude when I jumped. I often wondered what happened to the other men in my stick. I knew them all, and knew them well, but don't recall seeing any of them on the ground.

Of the trip back, Phillips wrote:

At night a patrol of four or five would move to the nearest road where traffic was noticeable. The patrol would then ambush vehicles by means of Hawkins mines. Horses, ammunition carts, and

men would go sky high. We had over twenty boxes of machine gun ammunition and three or four machine guns. We were so loaded with ammunition and guns that walking was a real chore.

The group had continuous skirmishes with Germans and eventually left one machine gun and half of their ammunition in a barn, then fled across some fields. Phillips wrote:

I looked back and swarms of Germans were scouring the fields. In some fashion I can't recall, I later learned the Germans found our ammunition and burned the barn and farmhouse to the ground.

The group came under fire from two German motorcyclists who spotted them and opened fire with Schmeissers. Capt. Phillips killed one of them with a carbine after flanking him. A column of German vehicles then came up the road and the American group ambushed them. Phillips wrote:

We caught them in a crossfire from both sides of the road and they emptied fast. The Germans who weren't killed in the trucks were running down the road madly. One of our men jumped on the lead truck and, using the machine gun mounted over the cab, opened fire on the Krauts. The excitement was enervating and exhausting.

The group moved some distance and sheltered in a field surrounded by densely foliaged hedgerows. Phillips wrote:

One hour or so before dark, some Germans had moved into position around our thicket. They raked the area pretty continuously with machine gun fire, fired some mortar rounds, and made it seem like a big operation. The bullets were much too high to do us any harm, and we had the protection of the earthen base of the hedgerows. We just sat tight and silent. No fire was returned. The enemy fire ceased.

Writing about Lt. Edwin B. Hutchison, Phillips remarked:

Lt. Hutchison was one of the most courageous and gutty men I have ever seen. He liked to roam by himself at night, and I cautioned him several times. It developed he was the only man we were to lose.

By D+5, the group had reached the vicinity of Baupte, west of Carentan. A small, elderly Frenchman suddenly appeared through a hedgerow opening, bearing bread, milk, and a leg of pork. He stated he knew the group was in the area and apologized for the meager rations, but explained he was trying to help refugees who had fled from the heavier fighting to the north.

The group had spent many cold nights without

blankets, always posting sentinels, while the rest of the group slept. At a place where railroad tracks cross the Douve River, the group had its final battle before rejoining friendly forces. Phillips deployed his men and machine guns behind the railroad embankment as a group of 75 to 100 Germans approached. He wrote:

> They were retreating from Carentan. They appeared somewhat carefree, helmets off and sauntering along talking. We deployed along the tracks on both sides of a small utility type house. Frankly, our aim was to destroy them all. Starting with my hand signal, one machine gun opened fire, and each individual weapon fired simultaneously. If it weren't so deadly a business, it would have seemed funny to see that mob scatter like a bunch of wild men. I assumed our engagement lasted about 30 minutes. The Germans organized and started their attack. They advanced on our position; Lt. Hutchison kept exposing himself. I was in and behind a small house. I cautioned him several times to observe from behind cover. The last time I saw him he had stepped out the door of the house with a grenade in his hand. Just as he threw it, several Germans were as close as 20 to 25 yards. I saw him reel around. I was about 5 yards from him. He was hit in the stomach with what I later thought to be some sort of pistol grenade, because he was ripped wide open.

Capt. Phillips then ordered a lateral retreat, which soon left the Germans behind. Before pulling out, he paused to look at Hutchison: "He was done for!"

As the group made its final approach to Carentan on D+6, Phillips saw:

> German and American machine guns and ammunition and other abandoned equipment dumped all over the place . . . craters the size of homes, apparently from the naval gunfire offshore. As we entered the town, I saw a group of children who had been caught in the artillery. This was the most shocking scene of the entire week. I tried to guide our column away from it.

The Combat Diary of Pfc. Carl Beck

Pfc. Carl Beck was a machine gunner in 3rd Platoon, H/501. His specialty was the M-1919A4 light machine gun. The jumpmaster of Beck's plane was Lt. Felix Stanley of Waco, Texas. Their plane was hit by flak and losing altitude when the pilot turned the green light on over a flooded area near Baupte, France, west of Carentan. (So severe were the floods in this area that one farmer used a rowboat to paddle around his farm fields. It is believed that Beck's plane crashed after the paratroops bailed out.) Beck's day-by-day account gives us a harrowing look at the ordeals of yet two more of the far flung in their efforts to survive and rejoin their outfit.

6 June 1944. I went to sleep over the Channel and woke up over the French coast. All kinds of stuff coming up at us . . . beautiful 20mm tracers, red, green, blue, yellow . . . they make a sickening thud each time they hit the plane, and she rocks like a corpse. We went out the door at 0113 on the nose. . . . This is the first time I've been shot at on a jump. Those damn tracers reach out like fingers, then slip away as fast as they come. It's sure windy, and I can see the hedgerows, orchards, and houses slipping away below me like a map. Hit the ground in a ditch, with my rear end off the ground a couple inches and my feet almost straight up in the air. Took me about 30 minutes' struggle to get out of the chute. Paul Petty was on the other side of the hedgerow. . . . I told him to meet me at the end. Right after that, I heard a prolonged burst of MG fire. Petty didn't show up. Chalk one for Kraut.

I headed for a spot where I saw the equipment bundle light land . . . realized I'm unarmed, except for fragmentation grenades. After I fell in the ditches about a dozen times, I met Robert M. Johnson and we teamed up. We have only one rifle with ninety-six rounds, a long WWI type bayonet, and four fragmentation grenades to protect us.

Still a lot of stuff being thrown around in every direction, all small arms. We wandered around until about dawn and decided to hide and wait [for] developments. Slept off and on during the night. . . . About 0400 we heard the naval barrage beginning and the whole sky is lighted just like you see in the movies. We don't have a compass but we know the direction of the gun flashes is east to west.

About dawn, ate a K-ration and Kraut has spotted us moving in the hedgerows. Slugs are zipping all around with a horrible regularity. We crawled down the hedgerow about 50 feet on our

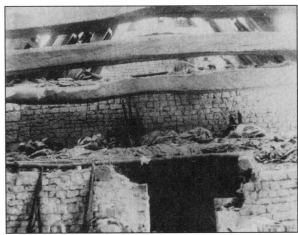

A Rare Luxury
Paratroopers somewhere in Normandy sleep in the tiers of a farmer's barn. This shelter from the elements was considered a rare luxury, even though the roof was blown off before they arrived. *Krochka*

The "Kawana Kid"
Pfc. Carl D. Beck, 3rd Platoon, H/501. Known as the "Kawana Kid," he hailed from Avondale, Missouri. Beck re-enlisted after WWII, serving with the 82nd Airborne at Ft. Bragg and in numerous other units before retiring in the 1960s. He then worked for the City of Atlanta, Georgia, as a public lighting engineer. Today, Beck lives in Atlanta in happy retirement. He has revisited Normandy and Baupte, France, several times. *Niles*

bellies, then crawled over, there we could stage and run. Found the equipment bundle but somebody had already been there. Picked up a Demo kit, don't know why. We went back to a corner of two hedgerows, crawled under some brush and went to sleep. The night was the same as last night, gun flashes and a distant roaring. God, we must be half way to Paris. Haven't seen a living soul but we know the Krauts are all around us.

7 June 1944. Got out of our "home," as we call it, and went snooping around. Found where Raul Seva dropped his paybook. There's a lot of GI equipment lying around, like a struggle, maybe. Found lots of Hawkins mines lying around, but every time we tried to mine the road, a vehicle came along. Finally gave it up as a lost cause. We found a better hiding place for a while, but I got to messing around with a booby trap igniter and it

goes off like a pistol and is promptly answered by a burst of MG fire. Boy! Those Krauts are sure on the ball. Those MGs are firing at about 800 yards but they sound like they're right on top of you. I never heard anything like it in my life.

We moved back to our old "home." Johnson gave me the rifle and ammo and I'm in the lead on all our excursions. We both read our New Testaments and prayed we'd get out okay. I hope the Big Boss isn't ready to scratch our names yet. I never knew how consoling the Bible could be, especially the 23rd Psalm. During our snooping, we found a signpost that said we were 3 kilometers from Baupte and 13 kilometers from Carentan. Boy! We're really lost. I have a hunch I know the directions, but I'm not sure.

8 June 1944. This morning Kraut woke us up with a long burst of MG fire about 0600. A big police dog came sniffing around but for some reason he didn't see us. I could have reached out and touched him. I had to hold my mouth shut so my heart wouldn't jump out. Oh, Lord! Was I scared. We decided it's about time we got out of here, so we take off north, we hope. We're going to try to swing around Baupte and make the coast. The idea was pretty vague, but we've got to do something. We're out of food and water, except for a D-ration apiece. I'm so thirsty and hungry, I can feel myself getting weaker all the time.

We moved north about a mile and a half then ran into a puddle of water that had green slime covering it. We scraped off the scum and filled our canteens, but couldn't wait the half hour for the halizone to take effect so we drank it anyway and ate our D-Bars. We rested awhile then swung west, dodged two Krauts and some trucks at a main road. We crossed the road after some delay, threw the Demo kit and bayonet away as we're getting weaker. We have to stop more often and we're praying at every stop . . . following a trail that a large group of men made over the countryside, but no sign of them. We ran into some Kraut positions on a hill which an 81mm mortar crew knocked them out of. Saw my first dead trooper today. He was Sgt. Albert Schill of Headquarters Company 3rd Battalion shot through the left eye. There was no weapon on him, so we still have only one rifle. . . .

Ran into two women pushing bicycles down the road . . . Johnson jumped out of the brush before I could stop him. The women were almost scared to death. All they could say was "Boche," and point. They took off. . . . A Frenchman came down on the road behind us and caught us. I covered him before he could squawk, but he seemed unruffled, and came toward us, making the V sign and saying, "Vive la France." He shook hands with us, fed us, and introduced us to his wife. He showed us where to leave the sunken road, and we hadn't walked a hundred yards 'til some Krauts went walking by on the road. They were laughing and playing the harmonica. I could have flipped a grenade and gotten them all.

It began to rain shortly after and we got soaked to the skin. We could hear a Kraut mortar plunking in the distance, so we knew we were headed in the right direction. By now I'm so tired I don't give a damn if we get caught or not. About 1600 we saw several Frenchmen and women digging an air raid shelter. They were sure scared. After a lot of bickering, the oldest one signaled for us to follow him. We walked through several hedgerows then he motioned for us to wait. He left us and it began pouring rain. He was gone about a half hour and came back; we were about to leave if he hadn't showed up. He took us to an old barn with part of the roof missing, and took us up into the loft. He gave us some hard boiled eggs, bread, pork, and wine. He left us and we pulled the ladder up into the loft after us. We crawled out of our jump suits and ate. We felt much better and went to sleep then, but I sure had some horrible nightmares.

9 June 1944. We woke up about 1100 today and finished the rest of the wine and food, which didn't help much. We got our equipment in shape, ready to scram at any time. I've lost so much weight that I can slip my ring off my finger without any trouble. The Frenchman came back about 1700 with a little chow and a paper written in English with French equivalents; we figure it was dropped to them by our planes.

10 June 1944. We're getting a little restless just laying around here. . . . About noon, a Kraut staff car rolled into the courtyard, fired a shot, then jabbered something in Kraut or French, fired another shot, then pulled out like a maniac. We just lay in the barn without hardly breathing, until they left. The Frenchman came back with more food and two pint bottles of Calvados and coffee. I got about half stewed because Johnson couldn't stand the stuff so I had it all to myself.

11 June 1944. Today (morning) a few shells started coming over; they're plenty big too. I'm sleeping like a rock and Johnson keeps waking me, telling me to quit snoring. The Frenchman didn't come back today. Johnson is in favor of going out and digging in. But I figure they're using these buildings as an aiming point for the artillery.

About dark, the tempo of the shells has increased 'til the shrapnel is bouncing off the walls like rain. Right after dark, the Kraut started fading back along this small road beside the house. They're under fire from 155s and 16in naval batteries. The Krauts sound like a mob of endless proportions going by. It's too dark to see them but it sounds as if they're all fouled up.

The shells are screaming down now, but I'm so tired I don't give a tinker's damn whether they hit here or not.

12 June 1944. This morning the shelling ceased entirely and about 1000 the Frenchman came back and signaled for us to follow him. We followed, but halfheartedly. We walked about a half a mile and stopped to drink a gallon of milk apiece and pass our cigarettes around to the civilians. Most of the women didn't smoke, but I guess they took one just to be polite. They sure had a helluva time.

1130. We rounded a bend and saw at the cross-roads one of the most beautiful sights I have ever beheld. There, taking a break, was a column of American infantrymen. They turned out to be 2nd Platoon, F Company, 508th Parachute Infantry Regiment, 82nd Airborne Division. We walked to the head of the column, spoke to the Battalion CO, Lt. Col. Shanley. We found they didn't have any rations because they left their musette bags behind when they forded the Douve River. They had tangled with four tanks the night before; they got two and ran off the others.

1205. We are all set to attack the town of Baupte with F Company on the left, jumping off 5 minutes after D Company on the right. E Company is in reserve. We jumped off according to schedule in one of the most beautifully conceived attacks you could ever read about.

1245. Knocked off a 20mm gun and crew, otherwise no resistance.

1305. Entered town and almost shot a priest who came out of a house we were searching.

1330. Met resistance from behind a railroad embankment almost 200 yards to flank. Approximately one company enemy infantry, with two 20mm guns in support.

1335. Krauts, about 40 of them, come over the embankment, making like they're going to surrender. But before they get too close, we see pistols and grenades in their hands, and yell for them to drop them, but they keep coming. The whole battalion opens fire at once, and Krauts pile up like jack straws. Don't know how many I got but it wasn't less than a dozen.

1340. Found an A-4 machine gun that the crew didn't know how to use, so I set it up. Those enemy can't get away without swimming because there's a dammed up lake behind them. We've got 'em where the hair's short now.

1345. Keeping up continuous fire . . . men are getting picked off all around, just me left on the gun.

1355. 20mm gun makes a break for it, pushing gun along R.R. track. Opened up long burst, saw tracers and armor piercing rounds hit men and gun breech. Got eight of the bastards on that burst and occasionally can see a helmet disappear behind the embankment. Must have got at least twenty Krauts in that position.

1400. Shooting's all over now and we take score. On our right flank, D and E companies with P-51 support get twenty tankettes (French), and 10 Mark IVs, all in a pack. We destroy a dump of gasoline, which burns all night. E Company in reserve, was committed to help D, which was having a hard time on our right.

1405. A tankette drove into view firing a 37 and a 31, coming hell bent down the street. It is hit with a 57mm AT, but keeps on charging down the street. Another guy and me are in a doorway when he comes by, so I heave a Gammon grenade, which goes over the tank and hits the side of the house across the street and blows it in.

The other fellow's Gammon hits the turret and stops the tank. One Kraut crawls out the turret and I shoot at him, but I can't get a bead cause a

Reunited, D+16

Of all the far flung photos, this is perhaps the classic. The troopers have rejoined the 101st Airborne on 22 June 1944, after seventeen days of evading Germans and working their way back. Here, they enjoy their first hot meal since 5 June 1944. The troopers have been identified as follows (left to right): Pvt. Lawrence J. Davis of the 377th PFAB (later died of wounds); 1st Sgt. Fred Fitzgerald; Sgt. Walter T. Murphy; and questioning them is Capt. John D. Harrell.

Harrell, a member of Division Artillery, wears the British made small mesh (1/4in) helmet net, which was common to 82nd Airborne troops in Normandy but was seldom seen in the 101st until the division returned to England from Normandy. The late arrivals were giving enemy troop dispositions, which they had observed on their long trip back. Part of their adventure involved wearing civilian clothing and posing as Frenchmen, according to Al Krochka, who made the photo.

This photo has been previously published but seldom with the subjects identified. The information first appeared in the 101st *Screaming Eagle* magazine, August 1957 edition. *Krochka*

slug knocked off my rear sight. He runs into a Gammon, and a guy cuts loose from behind a hedge with an M-1. When we go to search the bastard, he's dead, I swear he is, but when we turn to walk off, the son of a bitch raised up and moaned. I had my back turned and he scared me so bad, I turned and pumped 10 rounds in him before he could hit the ground. Now I know the S.O.B. is dead.

1430. Still flushing Krauts but not many. Saw one when a Gammon hit behind him and blew open his bowels and his shoe was about 10ft away, with his foot in it.

Spent quiet night under Kraut overcoats and blankets, gasoline dump still burning. Not such a hot MLR. Going to change MG in the morning.

13 June 1944. Moved the MLR today and have a Kraut 20mm gun on my left covering the road. I have nine boxes of machine gun ammo in a good Kraut position. Went looking over the town today and it's beat up pretty bad. One of the boys went hog wild today and shot five prisoners. Everybody is well fed on Kraut rations and French Calvados and champagne. Set up a new defense in an area to the west; we're not expected to stay here long. The French men and women are looting the Kraut food and clothing dumps. Picked up a Schmeisser machine pistol with ammo today. Tried it on outpost and she works okay. A Frenchman brought me about three-fourths quart of Calvados and some roast duck and I filled my gut.

14 June 1944. Pulled out today and rode until almost dark. We passed through the 505 area, don't know where we're going or why. Ran into Kraut about 2400 and had a little skirmish. Moved the MG about three times 'til we found a position to suit us. Patrols started going out tonight to Cretteville, recons only.

15 June 1944. Same positions not much new. A couple of the boys came back from the hospital, sporting their Purple Hearts. One got it in the back and the other got it in the leg. Not bad, but bad enough. That makes our squad five men, counting Johnson and me. Today, the lieutenant wanted me to be squad leader and Johnson assistant, but the colonel gave him orders to get us back to our unit. They still don't want us to go, and we don't want to go, but after all, a colonel is a colonel.

Patrols reported several dead Krauts in an armored car that were stringing wire. We must have got them last night. Today two tanks moved out in front of the positions and cleaned out Krauts in front of us. They clattered around for about an hour, then came back.

16 June 1944. Platoon on a combat patrol to Cretteville today. The way those 88s are singing over makes me discouraged. Orders to go to Hill 67 and try to knock out any resistance there. If there's no resistance we are to swing south and skirt the edge of a swamp.

1300. Jumped off with mortars and machine guns; the 88s are heckling us but still no casualties.

1330. Came across some Frenchmen and they gave us some cider and it sure hit the spot on such a hot day.

1445. Kraut giving us hell from the Cretteville hill, no resistance from Hill 67, so we swing south again.

1615. While crossing open hill on our return north, Kraut spots us and gives us heavy 88 fire. Johnson was carrying the machine gun and I swear he jumped an 8ft hedge without touching it with 35 pounds of MG cradled in his arm. It's not funny, but I still had to laugh. I could have knocked off his eyes with a stick.

1700. Pulled into area with no casualties, why, I don't know. I guess God is still with us. Still intermittent shelling going on. They don't have our positions so they are only heckling us and putting the fear of God in us. Found out tonight that the shells going over are knocking out the bridge at St. Saveur le Vicomte. Those poor engineers are working their balls off. I feel for them, but I can't reach them. Had to throw away my Schmeisser after that patrol; it's just too damn heavy, especially after toting an MG all the time.

17 June 1944. Got our walking papers today, bright and early. The colonel wrote us up a slip, saying we'd been with them all this time. I swiped a Schmeisser from his motorcycle before I left. Got

to division about 1200, hungry and dry. Those boys eat like kings there, so we weren't hurting long. The POW cage is here [division HQ was still at Hiesville], right alongside a battalion of 240s. One of them has "Widow Maker" stenciled on the barrel. It's good, but not as good as "Jivin' Joan" [Beck's personal M-1919A4 light machine gun].

18 June 1944. Got a Kraut Volkswagen down to 501 Regiment, and it was raining. We were forced to take a flask of Cognac on the way and it was quite dry by the time we got there (both the flask and the weather).

Found Klondike rear but not forward. After messing around 'til afternoon, they finally got us down to Blue, and then it took an hour to find the company. The boys were just about to move up and relieve Kidnap on the line, so we had a hand shaking fest. [Kidnap was the radio call sign for the 506th. Each regiment had a call sign beginning with K; i.e., 501-Klondike, 502-Kickoff, 327-Keepsake, 101 division was Kangaroo.] Johnson and I coming back make the total officer and E.M. company strength (H/501) thirty-nine. Most of the boys are missing in action. Aubin, Donst, Bray, and Capt. McKaig have been evacuated for wounds, also several others. Spitz, Gray, Pegg, Petty, Petzolt, and plenty others are KIA.

We returned to the 1st squad, 3rd Platoon, and "Jivin' Joan." Duffy and almost everybody else were missing from 24 hours to 9 days. The family is not half complete, but I guess we're lucky to be here. Pumphrey, Duffy, and I are on the gun together. The boys have had a pretty rough time around Carentan. Not much to do here except pull guard, two on and four off.

19 June 1944. Not much cooking today, intermittent shelling, mostly air bursts. They seem to be getting zeroed in but that's about all. No casualties.

20 June 1944. There's not much cooking these days, so I'll close this diary until we tangle with Kraut. We moved on the 28th with a regiment of 155s backing us up. The company is covering about 400 yards of front with thirty-nine men. It's not too rough though. The 79th Division relieved us there and we moved to Cherbourg and left the continent about July 12.

Chapter 29

Eagles in Captivity

Largely thanks to the misdrops that put many of the Screaming Eagles miles into enemy territory and well outside the consolidated assembly areas, some 665 members of the 101st Airborne Division were listed as MIA at the end of the Normandy campaign.

There was no disgrace in being captured under these circumstances and many troopers wandered for weeks with almost no ammo, food, or water and were eventually caught.

Some captured Eagles were liberated by friendly troops in minutes, hours, or days after being captured (their stories alone would fill a book). Others who were sent to Rennes, France, with serious injuries were liberated as early as 4 August 1944.

For Joe Taylor of A/501 and many other POWs, the Normandy invasion was soon followed

"Hungry Hill"
US Airborne prisoners look up at Allied planes flying over St. Lo in the "Starvation Hill" or "Hungry Hill" area. Here, their diet consisted mainly of "Whispering Grass" soup made from turnip greens. When the POWs arrived in the area, the city was intact; when they left, the city was in rubble from air raids. Second from left is Capt. John T. McKnight, erstwhile CO of I/506. He survived and was liberated in 1945. *via Winters and ECPA-France*

by an eight-month ordeal in German captivity. Taylor, who is still bone thin, has stomach problems to this day as a result of his time in the POW camps. "I just knew I would starve to death," he recalls. During moves from camp to camp, meals and Red Cross parcels were few and far between. Taylor resorted to eating grass, tree bark, and charcoal from fires just to stay alive.

After being incarcerated at St. Lo, the original groups of POWs from Normandy were marched through the city of Paris where German civilians from the embassy put on quite a show, jeering, spitting, and hitting the prisoners as they walked the gauntlet. These were dark days for the prisoners and many in the crowd were actually French civilians who didn't like Americans at the moment. German loudspeakers broadcast to the onlookers that these American "Terror Bandits" were actually convicts of the worst sort, who had been released from prisons in America to wage dirty warfare against the heroic German forces.

George Rosie and his buddy Jim Bradley had belonged to HQ/3 506 and were unfortunate to be in one of the groups that was paraded through hostile civilians in Paris. George later recalled:

As we marched through one section, this one gal was running down the column, spitting in men's faces. As she came up to Jim "Mr. America" Bradley to spit in his face, he spit in *her* face! Jim was right in front of me. I thought, "Boy, are we gonna get hell now." But the guard just pushed her back into the crowd, and we moved on.

Reg Alexander at Prétot

One of the most grueling ordeals borne by any 101st POW was that of Reginald Alexander of H/501. On a 1st Platoon plane jumpmastered by Lt. Robert Curran (later killed at Hill 30), the plane was badly hit and crashed after the troopers bailed out. Like other planes of the serial, this one had drifted south after emerging from the cloud banks and being dispersed in flak. Alexander was struck above the eye by shrapnel before leaving the plane. When he jumped, his chute streamered and he hit the ground on this feet at almost full force, shattering both his legs.

Alexander's buddies, Don Metcalf and Bob Beachy, soon found him but were forced to leave him. They alerted French civilians in a nearby

150

Liberated by the Russians
This POW mug shot for ID purposes was taken of Joe Beyrle, I/506, while he was at Stalag XII-A, Limburg, Germany, as a POW, following the Normandy drop.

Joe Beyrle landed on the roof of the church in St. Come du Mont on D-day night and was taken POW during D-day. A German took his dog tags and uniform and tried to infiltrate through the lines. The German was killed, probably by another German, who mistook him for an American. The body was buried in a US cemetery and Beyrle's parents received a telegram that he was KIA. Beyrle's camp (he was transferred from XII-A) was liberated by Russian troops, and he fought for months with a Russian tank crew, equipped with a Lend-Lease M-4 Sherman tank. Thus, Beyrle has more combat time with the Russian army than he has with the US Army. He visited his own grave after being liberated and is still welcomed as an old comrade on his return visits to the Soviet Union. *Beyrle*

church at Prétot, and a priest and nun arrived to carry Alexander to shelter.

Alexander's mission had been to meet Brig. Gen. Don F. Pratt, the assistant division commander, at Hiesville. Alexander was carrying important invasion maps to give to the general. The French

Reg Alexander
This 1943 photo shows Reg Alexander H/501 wearing his regimental pocket patch proudly on his jump jacket. The insignia was usually worn on the left chest. *Alexander*

hid these maps and Alexander's uniform. (Pratt had been killed on the glider landing and Hiesville was many miles from where Alexander landed.)

Several days passed and the French decided to dress Alexander in civilian clothes and attempt to move him eastward toward American lines. He sat in the seat of a farm cart pulled by one horse, as two young Frenchmen led the cart down a road. German troops intercepted them, and Alexander revealed his identity. After much excitement, he was taken into German custody and the French youths were led away. It is unknown what became of them.

Alexander found himself in a chateau, where he lay on the floor in great pain. A German SS man, berserk from shell shock, was brought in and lay on the floor in the same room. When the SS man learned that Alexander was an American, he viciously assaulted Alexander, kicking him repeatedly in the head. Alexander began to yell, and an English-speaking German doctor intervened and ordered the SS man restrained with ropes.

Alexander eventually began the long trip back toward Germany via ambulances. During this

Propaganda
A publicity photo staged by the Germans for the international press photographers at St. Lo, shows American POWs eating more than they normally ever got. POWs writing to their families were always required to state that they were being well fed. Not so. *Winters/ECPA*

time, his column was strafed at least once by British Spitfires. Also, French civilians, angered by Allied bombing raids, would sometimes pound on the outside of Alexander's ambulance when it stopped in various towns.

Liberation
101st Airborne paratroopers who had been captured and wounded stand in front of Stalag 221 in Rennes, France, on the day of their liberation. Ludwig Wirtheimer and Charles Egger of G/506 pose with French friends. *US Army*

Alexander was kept in a cave near St. Lo for a time, then continued on, eventually being placed on a cot in a basement in a town with canals. Some 104 days after D-day, an American armored division liberated the town and Alexander was sent to a traction ward in England before being shipped home.

Liberation of Stalag 221, 4 August 1944
The Germans had established a special POW camp in the city of Rennes, the gateway to the Brittany Peninsula. The camp was a departure from the normal German POW camps for a number of reasons. First, it was not located inside Germany. Also, the camp was reserved for wounded prisoners only. Unlike most stalags, enlisted men and officers alike were housed here. (Officers were usually segregated in Oflags.) Some British and Canadian prisoners were kept here as well, and the ranking officer was Maj. Phillip Gage of 1/501 who had lost a hand when captured near St. George du Bohon on D-day. The stalag was situated in or near the famous Jean Macé School, and the lucky prisoners liberated there were able to rejoin their units or return home almost a year earlier than the prisoners who were taken to Germany.

Chapter 30

The Journey Back

After pulling out of the Carentan perimeter in late June, the 101st Airborne moved west then north up the Cotentin Peninsula, stopping briefly at St. Saveur le Vicomte, Pont le Abbé and Tollevast, below Cherbourg. An ammunition crisis had plagued VII Corps, due to the Channel storm, but this had little effect on the 101st, which did little shooting during its last two weeks in Normandy. Most of its time was spent in resting, getting cleaned up, and eating, as shown on the following pages. The 82nd Airborne would also return to England in July but was engaged in fighting on the peninsula for more days than the 101st.

St. Saveur le Vicomte
Sgt. Ed Benecke stands in front of a building in St. Saveur le Vicomte. The Germans painted the name of each town in bold white or black letters on a prominent house at each approach to town so their troops would immediately know their location—the French had a nasty habit of turning or removing road signs to confuse the Boche. *Benecke.*

Fresh Milk
On a more wholesome note, Hromchak and "Jake" get their canteen cups filled with fresh milk from a French farmer. *Pistone*

Calvados

The delighted troopers in Normandy discovered a form of homemade apple brandy popular in the Cotentin, known as Calvados. Having a fragrance and taste similar to cognac, Calvados was preferably sipped like a potent liqueur. Potent it was, and batches aged less than ten years could reportedly take the skin off one's throat if consumed too quickly. Even small amounts had a distinctly mind-altering power, and the taste made it much preferable to Benzine, hair tonic, or Buzz Bomb Juice, which the die-hard alcoholics had consumed in a pinch.

Pee Wee Martin of G/506 likes to relate how his bunch moved into a farm area and after a brief but intense period of scrounging, located the farmer's stash of alcoholic beverages that had been secreted in a hole inside his barn and covered over with other materials.

"The Germans have been here four years and didn't find my liquor!" said the distraught Frenchman as he helplessly watched the troopers guzzle his stash. "You Americans have been here less than a week and are using up everything!"

An officer reportedly mollified the farmer by writing him a promissory note that the debt would be repaid by the US government.

While in the St. Saveur area, Capt. Cecil Simmons of H/502 caused another minor uproar with a French farmer. Simmons had located a large kettle used by the farmer to brew Calvados. Simmons was trying to get the foul odor of the gas impregnation chemical out of his jump suit. He filled the kettle with water, tossed his jump-suit in, and began stirring it over a fire. The Frenchman ran out yelling, very excited.

Another Calvados story happened in St. Marie du Mont. Lt. Gordon Deramus of HQ/3 502 was standing in the street when a medic rode up on horseback, holding a long Calvados bottle.

"Want a *drink*, lieutenant?" the medic said.

"Sure," said Deramus, about to have his first taste of Calvados.

"Wow!, What was that?"

"I'm not sure, lieutenant, but as long as this stuff holds out, we're gonna whip hell out of 'em!"

Joe Pistone takes a long pull on a Calvados bottle while fending off John "Hollywood" Hromchak. Ed Jacobson (kneeling) ravages a 10-in-1 ration. *Pistone*

Right
Frank Tiedeman, F/502, photographed in his Normandy foxhole, enjoying a bottle of Calvados. *Tiedeman*

Washing Up
501st troops at a washing trough in Normandy. Al Krochka wrote in his album: "Finally came the day when we could wash clothes heavy with mud, sweat, and blood." *Krochka*

Filling Up
Al Krochka's buddies sampling the new 10-in-1 rations while awaiting that boat ride back to England. *Krochka*

Taking in the View
The fort atop the hill at Cherbourg afforded a panoramic view of the French coast. Officers of the 501st take in the view. *Krochka*

Cherbourg
The large wall sign that greeted those entering Cherbourg from the south is still there. The city had already been captured by regular infantry outfits before the 101st arrived. (Left to right) Bill Kowger, Lee Estep, and Stanley J. Rogers, all of A/377. *Benecke*

White Bread
Cherbourg, July 1944. A mess sergeant holds aloft the first loaf of white bread seen in the 502nd PIR in months.

(Clockwise from lower left) Capt. George Buker, S-2; Evans Thornton, S-1; Lt. Bob Pick, S-2; Capt. Henry Plitt; and Capt. Frank Lillyman, Pathfinders. *Buker*

Nothing a Good Battle Won't Cure
Gen. George S. Patton at an awards ceremony where twenty-five 101st Airborne troopers received the DSC. His nemesis Viscount Montgomery of the British Army was also present. *Krochka*

War Trophy
While aboard an LST bound for England, a group from the 502nd PIR displays a trophy captured in France. *Dovholuk*

Back to England, 10 July 1944
Members of the 501st PIR are ready to board an LST for the voyage back to England where they will train and prepare for their next mission. Many companies sailed back with less than seventy remaining men. *Krochka*

England Again
More troops, having just debarked their LST, march in to waiting buses. The location is probably Southampton; again, July 1944. *Musura*

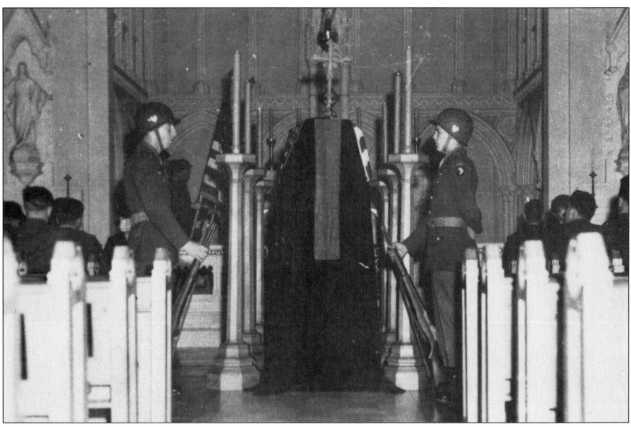

In Memorial to Those Who Fell
After returning to England, each regiment (here the 502nd PIR) held memorial services for their dead. And to the commanding officers went the unenviable chore of writing letters to the next of kin.

Rest in Peace
The dead from American Cemeteries No. 1 and No. 2 at St. Mere Eglise were re-interred at St. Laurent behind Omaha Beach several years after WWII. At that time, families had the option of having the deceased returned to the States for burial in a local cemetery. James Luce rests under a typical cross at St. Laurent, while Freddie Lenz has been returned to Dundee, Michigan. The seventeen-year-old who ran away from home to join the Army lies under a typical rectangular government marker. *Author's Photo*

501ST PARACHUTE INFANTRY REGIMENT
APO 472, C/O U. S. ARMY

21 July 1944

Mrs. Mary S. Lenz,
1460 Wells Road
Dundee, Michigan

Dear Mrs. Lenz:

It is with deep regret that I confirm the tragic news
of the loss of your son during the first stages of the invasion
of France. I realize that any words that I can say are small
and impotent during this period of grief, however I do hope
that you may find some small degree of solace in the fact that
Fred died a hero's death for a cause in which we all believed.

I was quite well acquainted with Fred, and knowing him
as I did it is my belief that he willingly made his sacrifice
for the ideals of life, liberty and the pursuit of happiness
which we all cherish and hold so dear. The loss of Fred and
others like him is a distinct blow to the regiment, felt keenly
by myself and his other comrades. Knowing how it hurts to miss
his face and personality in the regiment gives me some idea
of the suffering it must cause you at home.

The task for which your son gave his life is difficult
and as yet unfinished, however I promise that we of the regiment
shall carry on with increased vigor and inspiration for the
ideals in which Fred so freely believed.

Please accept my humble regrets and deepest sympathy, in
which all the members of the regiment join in this, your time of
great sorrow.

Most sincerely yours,

HOWARD R. JOHNSON
Colonel, 501st Prcht Inf
Commanding

Courtesy Max Lenz

Index

38th SS Panzer-Grenadlier Regiment, 135
74th Troop Carrier Squadron (TCS), 30
81st Airborne Anti-aircraft Anti-tank Battalion (AAAB), 90, 129
82nd Airborne Division, 52, 54, 66, 67, 71, 153
91st Air Landing Division, 66
321st Glide Field Artillery Battalion (GFAB), 9
326th Airborne Engineer Battalion (AEB), 9, 11, 16
327th Glider Infantry Regiment (GIR), 9, 16, 23, 109, 110, 112, 119, 122
377th Parachute Field Artillery Battalion (PFAB), 9, 11, 39, 44, 53, 54, 60, 80, 95, 112, 114, 139, 148
501st Parachute Infantry Regiment (PIR), 10, 11, 13, 22, 23, 27, 34, 35, 40, 44, 45, 46, 48, 50, 75, 76, 77, 80, 84, 85, 86, 94, 100, 101, 102, 103, 112, 119, 125, 132, 133, 137, 143, 146, 150, 151, 152, 156, 157
502nd PIR, 9, 11, 15, 19, 24, 26, 27, 28, 30, 32, 39, 44, 45, 48, 52, 54, 56, 57, 58, 59, 60, 64, 65, 68, 74, 77, 80, 81, 91, 92, 93, 113, 115, 116, 120, 121, 127, 128, 134, 135, 154, 157
506th PIR, 9, 10, 15, 16, 24, 35, 37, 40, 41, 42, 45, 46, 48, 49, 51, 52, 56, 65, 70, 74, 76, 77, 80, 81, 82, 83, 96, 97, 99, 100, 105, 107, 109, 110, 112, 119, 120, 127, 128, 129, 130, 134, 136
508th PIR, 51
709th Infantry Division, 133, 135
907th Glide Field Artillery Battalion (GFAB), 15

Alexander, Lt. Don, 130
Alexander, Reginald, 150, 151, 152
Ambrose, Allie, 71-72
Ambrose, Stephen, 70
Angoville au Plein, 8, 85-91, 103
Anness, Sgt. Frank, 14

Bahlau, Sgt. Fred, 105, 107, 112, 120, 122, 128
Ballard, Lt. Col. Robert A., 35, 85, 88, 91, 103
Battle of Bloody Gulch, 127
Beam, S/Sgt. Jerry, 38, 128, 129
Beck, Pfc. Carl, 145-149
Benecke, Sgt. Ed, 17, 33, 53, 61, 82, 112, 153
Benkowski, Pfc. Theodore, 113
Beszouska, Tom, 32, 33
Beyrle, Joe, 94, 151
Brévands, 105-111, 112
Brinninstool, Pvt. Donald, 52, 53
Brown, Capt. Frank L., 47
Bucior, Lt. Bernard, 58, 117
Burgett, Pfc. Don, 41, 52, 95
Burton, Sgt. Louis, 127, 128

Camien, Pvt. John, 63
Carberry, William, 68, 69
Cardenas, Sgt. Joel, 138
Carentan Causeway, 35, 94, 96, 97, 100, 102, 113, 119-124, 125-132, 144
Carrell, Maj. Francis, 36, 65, 101, 104
Cassidy, Lt. Col. Pat, 33, 56, 58, 59, 64
Chambliss, Lt. Turner M., 106-107
Chappuis, Lt. Col. Steve, 49
Christianson, Lt. Kenneth, 106
Clawson, Sgt. Harry, 106, 122
Cole's Charge, 113-118
Cole, Lt. Col. Robert, 20, 31, 48, 62, 110, 112, 113-115, 118
Couger, Lt. Quincy M., 85, 87-88
Culloville, 68, 80

Danforth, Cpl. Virgil, 76
Davidson, Capt. Richard L., 55, 62
Davison, Maj. Douglas, 80, 116
Dead Man's Corner, 45, 47, 94, 95, 98, 99, 124, 137
Deramus, Lt. Gordon, 59, 114
DiCarlo, Pfc. Hank, 106, 110

Dielsi, Johnny, 121
DiMarzio, Art "Jumbo," 41, 69, 120, 121. 136
Dirty 13, The, 38
Dobbyn, Sgt. Elden, 115
Douve River Bridge, 35
Dovholuk, 1st Sgt. Paul, 92

Escher, Sgt. Rudi, 65, 66
Evans, S/Sgt. Leon F. "Country," 126
Ewell, Lt. Col. Julian, 34, 75, 76, 97, 99

Filthy 13, The, 37, 101
Fitzgerald, Capt. Cleveland, 54, 117
Flanagan, Eugene "Red," 123
Foucarville, 54-55, 117
Frey, Louis, 15, 22

Gillis, Sgt. Leo, 40, 85, 86-88, 101, 104, 125, 126
Ginder, Maj. Allen W. "Pinky," 50
Grant, Maj. George, 94, 105

Haag, Sgt. Alex, 143
Haller, Joseph, 23, 27, 28, 79
Hannah, Maj. Harold W. "Hank," 49, 81, 82, 96, 130, 136
Harwick, Capt. Jim, 94-95
Haslam, Lt. James, 48, 90, 124
Hell's Corner, 36, 100, 101, 102, 103
Hiesville, 79-82
Higgins, Col. Gerald, 48
Holdy, 77-78
Homan, Capt. Sammie N., 101, 125, 126
Hromchak, John "Hollywood,", 154
Hutchison, 1st Lt. Edwin B., 144

Jackson, Schuyler "Sky," 34
Johnson, Capt. LeGrand "Legs, " 59, 61, 129, 130
Johnson, Col. Howard R. "Jumpy," 9, 10, 14, 20, 36, 40, 100, 101, 103, 104, 107, 112, 138
Juttras, Phil, 65

Kapitem, Jean, 138
Karim, Pvt. Ahzez "Jim," 94, 96
Knott, Lt. Eugene "Iggy," 127-128
Koskimaki, George, 46, 48, 57, 106
Krochka, Albert A., 23, 38, 40, 78, 91, 155

La Barquette lock, 35, 46, 100-104, 105, 107
La Billonnerie, 118, 119, 130
Lamar, Jimmy, 126
Larsen, Red, 29, 92
Le Grand Chemin, 68, 69-70
Lee, Gen. W. C., 9
Lenz, Freddiel, 158
Lillyman, Capt. Frank, 24, 26, 28, 29, 56, 60
Little, Sgt. Gordon, 47
Luce, Pvt. James, 86, 87, 158
Lyell, Pvt. John T., 54

Marshall, S.L.A., 26, 48, 56, 57, 58, 70, 99, 106, 110
Martin, James "Pee Wee," 11, 45, 106
Mauger, Paul, 45
McAuliffe, Gen. Anthony, 74, 109
McIntosh, Ben "Chief," 8, 81
McNiece, Jake , 37, 39
Meason, Lt. Richard, 110
Meier, Lt. Werner "Mike," 121
Michaelis, Lt. Col. Mike, 32, 55, 59, 74, 121
Mihok, Steve, 83
Milenczenko, Sgt. Mike, 68, 69
Millener, G-3 Raymond, 139
Montilio, Sgt. George, 106, 107, 111
Moore, C. C. "Jumbo," 85, 126
Morton, Lt. James G., 7, 42
Moseley, Col. George Van Horn, 9, 32, 59

Nelson, Sgt. Norman N., 138
Nickrent, S/Sgt. Roy, 64

O'Neill, Pfc. Charles, 50, 126

Painschab, Lt. John P., 113
Pangerl, Lt. Joseph, 59, 60, 62, 80, 81, 131, 134
Parker, Sgt. Artur, 139-142
Patheiger, Sgt. Fred, 60, 81, 131
Pathfinders, 22-29, 47, 56, 67, 84, 90, 94
Phillips, Capt. Robert, 143-145
Pistone, Joe, 68, 69, 72, 74, 154
Pouppeville, 8, 75-76
Pratt, Brig. Gen. Don F., 18, 30, 151
Purifoy, Jim, 104

Rudd, T/4 Jack, 117
Runge, Pfc. Leo F., 36, 102, 103, 104
Russo, Lt. William J., 7, 94, 98, 130, 131, 132
Ryan, Cornelious, 7, 134

Sampson, Father Francis L., 46, 101
Sanderson, Pvt. Walter, 122
Santasiero, Lt. Charles, 105, 107, 108, 111, 118, 127-128
Sapinski, Eddie, 33, 67, 97
Schaffer, Jack, 84, 88
Schroeder, Sgt. Bruno, 120, 122
Sefton, Lt. Bill, 45, 101
Shaub, Benjamin, 68, 69, 72, 74
Shettle, Capt. Charles, 105, 106, 109
Simmons, Capt. Cecil L., 17, 20, 21, 47, 93, 115, 118
Sink, Col. Robert, 24, 35, 68, 74, 80, 97, 127
Smit, Lt. Morton J., 57
Smith, Lt. Raymond "Whispering," 113
SNAFU Engagement, 97, 98
St. Come du Mont, 8, 35, 36, 88, 92, 94-99
St. Germaine de Varreville, 29, 56
St. Marcouf, 50-51
St. Marie du Mont, 31, 35, 47, 50, 68 , 71-74, 75, 77, 80, 100
St. Martin de Varreville, 28, 33, 50, 59, 61, 68, 134
St. Mere Eglise, 48, 65, 80, 143, 158
Stalag 221, 152
Sterno, Pvt. Bernard, 115
Stopka, Maj. John P., 20, 115, 116
Strayer, Lt. Col. Robert , 33, 56
Stroebel, Lt. Wallace, 34
Summers, S/Sgt. Harrison, 60, 61, 62, 63, 116, 118
Swanson, Lt. Wally, 56, 116

Tantalow, Bart, 103
Taylor, Gen. Maxwell, 16, 18, 34, 75, 76, 118
Taylor, Joe, 40, 143, 150
Tiedeman, Frank, 154
Tiller, S/Sgt. John F., 20
Tinklenberg, Pvt. Meryl, 76

Utah Beach, 76, 79, 91, 134

Vaughn, Maj. J. W., 48, 49
Vierville, 8, 83-84

Watson, Lt. Alfred "The Gremlin," 23, 79
Winans, Lt. Wayne "Bull," 95, 99
Winters, Lt. Richard, 48, 68, 69, 70, 118
Wolverton, Lt. Col. Robert, 94, 105
Womer, Jack, 18, 39, 101, 103, 104

XYZ complex, 33, 61

Zahn, Pfc. Donald, 106, 107, 111
Zebrosky, Cpl. Stanley, 49